The Emergence of
the Christian
Religion

The Emergence *of* *the* Christian Religion

ESSAYS ON EARLY CHRISTIANITY

Birger A. Pearson

TRINITY PRESS INTERNATIONAL
Harrisburg, Pennsylvania

To
GEORGE
and
NORMAN

Trinity Press International, P.O. Box 1321, Harrisburg, PA 17105

Trinity Press International is a division of the Morehouse Group

Library of Congress Cataloging-in-Publication Data

Pearson, Birger Albert.
    The emergence of the Christian religion : essays on early Christianity
/ Birger A. Pearson.
        p. cm.
    Includes bibliographical references and index.
    ISBN 1-56338-218-0 (alk. paper)
    1. Church history – Primitive and early church, ca. 30-600.
2. Christianity and other religions – Judaism. 3. Judaism –
Relations – Christianity. 4. Gnosticism. 5. Judaism – History – Post-
exilic period, 586 B.C.-210 A.D.   I. Title.
BR165.P37   1997
270.1 – dc21   97-38320
                                                                       CIP

Printed in the United States of America

97   98   99   00   01   02   10   9   8   7   6   5   4   3   2   1

Contents

Preface

I want to acknowledge here my indebtedness to those persons and institutions that have helped to make this book possible. First of all, to my Swedish colleagues in the universities of Uppsala and Lund I tender my sincere thanks for their hospitality and friendship. My sojourn in Uppsala in the spring of 1993 as a visiting professor provided the occasion for the material that appears in chapter 1. I am especially grateful to David Westerlund of the History of Religions department (then prefect) for making the necessary arrangements for my stay in Uppsala. To Samuel Rubenson, associate professor of patristics at Lund, I offer heartfelt thanks for the invitation to participate in the Nordic Patristics Conference in Lund in August 1993 and for arranging a travel subsidy, thus providing me with the opportunity to produce the material in chapter 9. Likewise, I am grateful for the invitation to lecture at the Indiana University Center on Philanthropy in Indianapolis in 1994, which resulted in the material in chapter 10. Special thanks go to my former student Jeffrey Kenney, now on the faculty at Indiana University at Indianapolis, for suggesting my visit, and to Anita Plotinsky, assistant director for research and academic programs, for her kindness in hosting me and making the necessary arrangements. Many thanks also go to Ivan Strenski, American editor of *Religion,* for encouraging me to produce the article that is the basis for chapter 2.

I wish to acknowledge here with thanks the permissions to use previously copyrighted material as follows: for chapter 2, Diagonal-Verlag GbR in Marburg; for chapter 2, the Academic Press in London; for chapter 3, the president and fellows of Harvard College in Cambridge; for chapter 4, the publishers of *Greek, Roman, and Byzantine Studies;* for chapter 6, the Foundation Compendia Rerum Iudaicarum ad Novum Testamentum in Amsterdam; for chapter 7, Hendrickson Publishers; for chapter 8, Yamamoto Shoten Publishing House in Tokyo; and for chapter 10, the Indiana University Center on Philanthropy. Chapter 5, "The *Apocalypse of Peter* (NHC VII,3) and Canonical 2 Peter," is reprinted in revised form from *Gnosticism & the Early Christian World*, © 1990 Polebridge Press, P.O. Box 6144, Santa Rosa, CA 95406; used with permission, all rights reserved.

The director of Trinity Press International, Harold Rast, has been a good friend for many years, and I am very grateful to him for many things, not least for publishing this book and for his encouragement in its preparation. Many thanks go to him, managing editor Laura Barrett, typesetter John Eagleson, and the rest of the staff.

The indexes for this book were prepared by Judy Elizabeth Gaughan, a doctoral candidate at the University of California, Berkeley. My thanks go to her for an excellent job. I am also indebted to the Academic Senate Committee on Research at UC Berkeley (where I have taught part-time since my retirement from UCSB in 1994) for subsidizing the preparation of the indexes.

My scholarly work over the years has not taken place in a vacuum, and I am quite certain that the contents of this book reflect the inspiration and insights derived from contact with respected colleagues. As for my colleagues and students in the Department of Religious Studies at the University of California at Santa Barbara, who have given me so much since I joined the faculty there in 1969, I cannot find words adequate to express my debt of gratitude.

Finally, I am pleased to dedicate this book to two close friends and fellow students of early Christianity, George W. E. Nickelsburg and Norman R. Petersen. Since graduate school days back in the 1960s, they have been my roommates and stimulating discussion partners at the annual meetings. Thanks, guys, *ad multos annos!*

BIRGER A. PEARSON
Emeritus, Department of Religious Studies
University of California
Santa Barbara, California

Abbreviations and Short Titles

AAR	American Academy of Religion
AB	Anchor Bible
ABD	*Anchor Bible Dictionary*
ACJD	Abhandlungen zum christlich-jüdischen Dialog
AGJU	Arbeiten zur Geschichte des antiken Judentums und des Urchristentums
Aland, *Gnosis*	B. Aland, ed. *GNOSIS: Festschrift für Hans Jonas.* Göttingen: Vandenhoeck & Ruprecht, 1978
ANF	Ante-Nicene Fathers
ANRW	*Aufstieg und Niedergang der römischen Welt*
APF	*Archiv für Papyrusforschung*
ASNU	Acta seminarii neotestamentici upsaliensis
ATR	*Anglican Theological Review*
BAGD	W. Bauer, W. F. Arndt, F. W. Gingrich, and F. W. Danker. *A Greek-English Lexicon of the New Testament.*

Barc, *Colloque International*
>B. Barc, ed. *Colloque International sur les textes de Nag Hammadi (Québec, 11–15 août 1978).* BCNH, "Études" 1. Québec: Université Laval, 1983

Bauer, *Orthodoxy and Heresy*
>W. Bauer. *Orthodoxy and Heresy in Earliest Christianity.* Translated and edited by R. A. Kraft et al. Philadelphia: Fortress Press, 1971

BCNH	Bibliothèque copte de Nag Hammadi
BEThL	Bibliotheca ephemeridum theologicarum lovaniensium
BEvTh	Beiträge zur evangelischen Theologie
BG	(Papyrus) Berolinensis Gnosticus (8502)
BHTh	Beiträge zur historischen Theologie

Bianchi, *Le origini*
>U. Bianchi. *Le origini dello gnosticismo: Colloquio di Messina 13–18 aprile 1966.* SHR 12. Leiden: E. J. Brill, 1970

BNTC	Black's New Testament Commentaries
BO	*Bibliotheca orientalis*

Böhlig, *Gnosis und Synkretismus*
>A. Böhlig. *Gnosis und Synkretismus: Gesammelte Aufsätze zur spätantiken Religionsgeschichte.* 2 vols. WUNT 47–48. Tübingen: Mohr-Siebeck, 1989

Böhlig, *Mysterion und Wahrheit*
>A. Böhlig. *Mysterion und Wahrheit: Gesammelte Beiträge zur spätantiken Religionsgeschichte.* Leiden: E. J. Brill, 1968

BTN	Bibliotheca theologica norvegica

BZNW   Beihefte zur *ZNW*
CBQ   *Catholic Biblical Quarterly*
CBQMS   Catholic Biblical Quarterly Monograph Series
CG   (Codex) Cairensis Gnosticus (= NHC)
CGL   Coptic Gnostic Library

Collins, *Apocalypse*
          J. J. Collins, ed. *Apocalypse: The Morphology of a Genre. Semeia* 14. Missoula: Scholars Press, 1979

CRINT   Compendia rerum iudaicarum ad Novum Testamentum
DSS   Dead Sea Scrolls
EKKNT   Evangelisch-katholischer Kommentar zum Neuen Testament
EPRO   Études préliminaires aux religions orientales dans l'empire Romain
EtB   Études bibliques
ExpT   *Expository Times*
FGH   *Die Fragmente der griechischen Historiker*

Foerster, *Gnosis*
          W. Foerster, ed. *Gnosis: A Selection of Gnostic Texts.* Translated and edited by R. McL. Wilson. 2 vols. Oxford: Clarendon, 1972, 1974

FRLANT   Forschungen zur Religion und Literatur des Alten und Neuen Testaments
GCS   Griechischen christlichen Schriftsteller
GRBS   *Greek, Roman, and Byzantine Studies*
Hatch-Redpath   E. Hatch and E. Redpath. *Concordance to the Septuagint*

Hellholm, *Apocalypticism*
          D. Hellholm, ed. *Apocalypticism in the Mediterranean World and the Near East: Proceedings of the International Colloquium on Apocalypticism, Uppsala, August 12–17, 1979.* Tübingen: J. C. B. Mohr, 1983

HKNT   Handkommentar zum Neuen Testament
HNT   Handbuch zum Neuen Testament
HTR   *Harvard Theological Review*
IB   Interpreter's Bible
ICC   International Critical Commentary
IDB   *Interpreter's Dictionary of the Bible*
IDBSup   Supplementary volume to *IDB*
JAC   Jahrbuch für Antike und Christentum
JAOS   *Journal of the American Oriental Society*
JBL   *Journal of Biblical Literature*
JEA   *Journal of Egyptian Archaeology*
JECS   *Journal of Early Christian Studies*
JES   *Journal of Ecumenical Studies*

Jonas, *Gnostic Religion*
          H. Jonas. *The Gnostic Religion: The Message of the Alien God and the Beginnings of Christianity.* 2d ed., Boston: Beacon Press, 1963

Jonas, *Philosophical Essays*
          H. Jonas. *Philosophical Essays: From Ancient Creed to Technological Man.* Englewood Cliffs, N.J.: Prentice-Hall, 1974

JR   *Journal of Religion*
JSOTSup   Journal for the Study of the Old Testament Supplement Series
JTS   *Journal of Theological Studies*
KEK   Kritisch-Exegetischer Kommentar über das Neue Testament
KNT   Kommentar zum Neuen Testament
Koester, *Introduction*
     H. Koester. *Introduction to the New Testament*. Vol. 2, *History and Literature of Early Christianity*. Philadelphia: Fortress Press; Berlin and New York: De Gruyter, 1982
Koschorke, *Polemik der Gnostiker*
     K. Koschorke. *Der Polemik der Gnostiker gegen das kirchliche Christentum: Unter besonderer Berücksichtigung der Nag-Hammadi Traktate "Apokalypse des Petrus" (NHC VII,3) und "Testimonium Veritatis" (NHC IX,3)*. NHS 12. Leiden: E. J. Brill, 1978
Krause, *Essays-Böhlig*
     M. Krause, ed. *Essays on the Nag Hammadi Texts in Honour of Alexander Böhlig*. NHS 3. Leiden: E. J. Brill, 1972
Krause, *Essays-Labib*
     M. Krause, ed. *Essays on the Nag Hammadi Texts in Honour of Pahor Labib*. NHS 6. Leiden: E. J. Brill, 1975
Krause, *Gnosis and Gnosticism*
     M. Krause, ed. *Gnosis and Gnosticism: Papers Read at the Seventh International Conference on Patristic Studies (Oxford, September 8th–13th, 1975)*. NHS 8. Leiden: E. J. Brill, 1977
Kümmel, *Introduction*
     W. G. Kümmel. *Introduction to the New Testament*. Translated by H. C. Kee. Nashville: Abingdon Press, 1975
Layton, *Codex II*
     B. Layton, ed. *Nag Hammadi Codex II,2–7 together with XIII,2*, Brit. Lib. Or. 4926 (1), and P. Oxy. 1, 654, 655*. 2 vols. NHS 20–21. Leiden: E. J. Brill, 1989
Layton, *Gnostic Scriptures*
     B. Layton. *The Gnostic Scriptures*. New York: Doubleday, 1987
Layton, "Prolegomena"
     B. Layton. "Prolegomena to the Study of Ancient Gnosticism." In *The Social World of the First Christians: Essays in Honor of Wayne Meeks*, edited by L. M. White and O. L. Yarbrough, 334–50. Minneapolis: Fortress Press, 1995
Layton, *Rediscovery*
     B. Layton, ed. *The Rediscovery of Gnosticism: Proceedings of the International Conference on Gnosticism at Yale, New Haven, Connecticut, March 28–31, 1978*. 2 vols. SHR 41. Leiden: E. J. Brill, 1980–81
LCC   Library of Christian Classics
LCL   Loeb Classical Library
LPGL   G. W. H. Lampe. *Patristic Greek Lexicon*
LSJ   H. G. Liddell, R. Scott, and H. S. Jones. *Greek-English Lexicon*
LXX   Septuagint
Ménard, *Textes de Nag Hammadi*
     J.-É. Ménard, ed. *Les textes de Nag Hammadi: Colloque du Centre d'histoire des religions*. NHS 7. Leiden: E. J. Brill, 1975

MNTC	Moffatt New Testament Commentary
MScRel	*Mélanges de science religieuse*
MT	Masoretic Text
Mus	*Muséon*
Nestle-Aland	E. Nestle and K. Aland, eds. *Novum Testamentum Graece*. 27th ed. 1993
NHC	Nag Hammadi Codex (= CG)
NHLE	J. M. Robinson and R. Smith, eds. *The Nag Hammadi Library in English*. 3d rev. ed. San Francisco: Harper & Row; Leiden: E. J. Brill, 1988
NHMS	Nag Hammadi and Manichaean Studies (= NHS)
NHS	Nag Hammadi Studies
NovT	*Novum Testamentum*
NovTSup	Novum Testamentum, Supplements
NRSV	New Revised Standard Version
NTApoc	W. Schneemelcher, *New Testament Apocrypha*. Rev. ed. 2 vols.
NTD	Das Neue Testament Deutsch
NTS	*New Testament Studies*
NTT	*Norsk Teologisk Tidsskrift*
NTTS	New Testament Tools and Studies
OrChrA	Orientalia Christiana Analecta
OTP	J. H. Charlesworth, ed. *The Old Testament Pseudepigrapha*. 2 vols.

Pearson, *Codex VII*
    B. A. Pearson, ed. *Nag Hammadi Codex VII*. CGL. NHMS 30. Leiden: E. J. Brill, 1996

Pearson, *Codices IX and X*
    B. A. Pearson, ed. *Nag Hammadi Codices IX and X*. CGL. NHS 15. Leiden: E. J. Brill, 1981

Pearson, *Future*
    B. A. Pearson, ed. *The Future of Early Christianity: Essays in Honor of Helmut Koester*. Minneapolis: Fortress Press, 1990

Pearson, *Gnosticism*
    B. A. Pearson. *Gnosticism, Judaism, and Egyptian Christianity*. SAC 5. Minneapolis: Fortress Press, 1990

Pearson, "Gnosticism a Religion"
    B. A. Pearson. "Is Gnosticism a Religion?" In *The Notion of "Religion" in Comparative Research: Selected Proceedings of the Sixteenth Congress of the International Association for the History of Religions, Rome 3rd–8th September 1990*, 105–14. Rome: "L'Erma" di Bretschneider, 1994

Pearson-Goehring, *Roots*
    B. A. Pearson and J. E. Goehring, eds. *The Roots of Egyptian Christianity*. SAC 1. Philadelphia: Fortress Press, 1990

Perkins, *Gnostic Dialogue*
    P. Perkins. *The Gnostic Dialogue: The Early Church and the Crisis of Gnosticism*. New York: Paulist Press, 1980

PG	J.-P. Migne. *Patrologia graeca*
PVTG	Pseudepigrapha Veteris Testamenti graece
RevScRel	*Revue de sciences religieuses*

RHPhR   *Revue d'histoire et de philosophie religieuses*

Ries, *Gnosticisme et monde hellénistique*

        J. Ries et al., eds. *Gnosticisme et monde hellénistique: Actes du Colloque de Louvain-la-Neuve (11–14 mars 1980).* Louvain-la-Neuve: Institut Orientaliste, 1982

Robinson-Koester, *Trajectories*

        J. M. Robinson and H. Koester. *Trajectories through Early Christianity.* Philadelphia: Fortress Press, 1971

RSPhTh   *Revue des sciences philosophiques et théologiques*

RStR   *Religious Studies Review*

RSV   Revised Standard Version

Rudolph, *Gnosis*

        K. Rudolph. *Gnosis: The Nature and History of Gnosticism.* San Francisco: Harper & Row, 1977

Rudolph, *Gnosis: Aufsätze*

        K. Rudolph. *Gnosis und spätantike Religionsgeschichte: Gesammelte Aufsätze.* NHMS 42. Leiden: E. J. Brill, 1996

SAC   Studies in Antiquity and Christianity

SANT   Studien zum Alten und Neuen Testament

SBL   Society of Biblical Literature

SBLASP   SBL Abstracts and Seminar Papers

SBLDS   SBL Dissertation Series

SBLSP   SBL Seminar Papers

SBLTT   SBL Texts and Translations

SBT   Studies in Biblical Theology

SC   Sources chrétiennes

Schenke, "Gnostic Sethianism"

        H.-M. Schenke. "The Phenomenon and Significance of Gnostic Sethianism." In Layton, *Rediscovery,* 2:588–616

Schenke, *Der Gott "Mensch"*

        H.-M. Schenke. *Der Gott "Mensch" in der Gnosis: Ein religionsgeschichtlicher Beitrag zur Diskussion über die paulinische Anschauung von der Kirche als Leib Christi.* Berlin: Evangelische Verlagsanstalt, 1962

Schenke, "Das sethianische System"

        H.-M. Schenke. "Das sethianische System nach Nag-Hammadi-Handschriften." In *Studia Coptica,* edited by P. Nagel, 165–72. Berlin: Akademie-Verlag, 1974

SHR   Studies in the History of Religions (Supplements to *Numen*)

SJLA   Studies in Judaism in Late Antiquity

SNTSMS   Society for New Testament Studies Monograph Series

SR   *Studies in Religion/Sciences religieuses*

Stone, *Jewish Writings*

        M. Stone, ed. *Jewish Writings of the Second Temple Period.* CRINT 2.2. Assen: Van Gorcum; Philadelphia: Fortress Press, 1984

Stroumsa, *Another Seed*

        G. A. G. Stroumsa. *Another Seed: Studies in Gnostic Mythology.* NHS 24. Leiden: E. J. Brill, 1984

StTh   *Studia theologica*

SUNT   Studien zur Umwelt des Neuen Testaments
SVF   J. von Arnim. *Stoicorum veterum fragmenta*
TDNT   G. Kittel and G. Friedrich, eds. *Theological Dictionary of the New Testament*
TextsS   Texts and Studies
ThF   *Theologische Forschung*
ThLZ   *Theologische Literaturzeitung*
ThR   *Theologische Rundschau*
TLG   *Thesaurus Linguae Graecae*
Tröger, *Altes Testament*
                K.-W. Tröger, ed. *Altes Testament-Frühjudentum-Gnosis: Neue Studien zu "Gnosis und Bibel."* Berlin: Evangelische Verlagsanstalt, 1980
Tröger, *Gnosis und NT*
                K.-W. Tröger, ed. *Gnosis und Neues Testament: Studien aus Religionswissenschaft und Theologie.* Berlin: Evangelische Verlagsanstalt, 1973
TU   Texte und Untersuchungen zur Geschichte der altchristlichen Literatur
UNT   Untersuchungen zum Neuen Testament
van den Broek, *Studies*
                R. van den Broek. *Studies in Gnosticism and Alexandrian Christianity.* NHMS 39. Leiden: E. J. Brill, 1996
van den Broek-Vermaseren, *Studies-Quispel*
                R. van den Broek and M. J. Vermaseren, eds. *Studies in Gnosticism and Hellenistic Religions Presented to Gilles Quispel.* EPRO 91. Leiden: E. J. Brill, 1981
VC   *Vigiliae christianae*
Waldstein-Wisse, *Apocryphon*
                M. Waldstein and F. Wisse, eds. *The Apocryphon of John: Synopsis of Nag Hammadi Codices II,1; III,1; and IV,1 with BG 8502,2.* NHMS 33. Leiden: E. J. Brill, 1995
WBC   Word Biblical Commentary
Wilson, *Nag Hammadi and Gnosis*
                R. McL. Wilson, ed. *Nag Hammadi and Gnosis: Papers Read at the First International Congress of Coptology (Cairo, December 1976).* NHS 14. Leiden: E. J. Brill, 1978
WMANT   Wissenschaftliche Monographien zum Alten und Neuen Testament
WUNT   Wissenschaftliche Untersuchungen zum Neuen Testament
ZÄS   *Zeitschrift für ägyptische Sprache und Altertumskunde*
ZNW   *Zeitschrift für die neutestamentliche Wissenschaft*
ZPE   *Zeitschrift für Papyrologie und Epigraphik*
ZRGG   *Zeitschrift für Religions- und Geistesgeschichte*
ZThK   *Zeitschrift für Theologie und Kirche*

N.B.: The abbreviations used for biblical books and other ancient sources are standard and presumably recognizable; thus, they are not given here. See the index to ancient sources for those cited.

Introduction

The essays in this book represent some of the results of more than three decades of my research in early Christianity, from the New Testament to the patristic period. Most of the essays are quite recent. All have a prehistory, in that all have appeared in some form elsewhere. They have been selected, edited, and organized for this book.

Chapter 1 deals with the problematic of Christian origins. Is Christianity a religion with a "founder" in the usual sense? If so, who was its founder? Jesus? Peter? Paul? Or is Christianity a "religion" at all? I take up these issues in that chapter and attempt to sort out some of the difficulties involved in locating in time and place the appearance of "Christianity" as a religion independent of its historical matrix, Second Temple Judaism, i.e., the emergence of Christianity as "one of the religions of the world." The essay was first prepared as a public lecture delivered in Uppsala, Sweden, in the spring of 1993, when I was a visiting professor in the Departments of Biblical Studies and History of Religions in the theological faculty of the University of Uppsala. An abbreviated version of that lecture appeared in a Festschrift for Kurt Rudolph.[1] It has been considerably revised for publication here.

The title of the first chapter has been used for the book as a whole, for reasons that I probably need to explain. Christianity as we know it is traceable back to the fourth century of the common era, which saw some momentous events that dramatically changed its shape. These events include, above all, the conversion of the Roman emperor Constantine, which led eventually to the establishment of Christianity as the religion of the empire, and the growth and increasing power of the Christian hierarchy, especially of its bishops. It is thus only in the fourth century that Christianity really "emerged" as the dominant religion of the Western world. All of the essays in this book provide windows into this histori-

---

1. "The Emergence of the Christian Religion," in *Gnosisforschung und Religionsgeschichte: Festschrift für Kurt Rudolph zum 65 Geburtstag,* ed. H. Preissler and H. Seiwert (Marburg: Diagonal-Verlag, 1994), 217–24.

cal process, some touching upon figures, movements, and events of
the "patristic" period up to the time of John Chrysostom (d. 407).
Readers who proceed to the very end of the book will also see that
I have another intention in giving the book the title that I did.

Chapters 2–4 contain work that I have done on the main parts
of the New Testament: Gospels, Pauline epistles, and catholic epistles. Chapter 2 has its origins in a seminar that I taught at the
Graduate Theological Union in Berkeley, California, in the fall of
1994. *The Five Gospels,* a "red-letter edition" of the Gospels produced by the highly publicized "Jesus Seminar," had appeared the
previous year; so I chose as the topic of my seminar "Examining
The Five Gospels."[2] The seminar was devoted to a detailed critical analysis of the translation and commentaries produced by the
Jesus Seminar, as presented in the book. My seminar provided material for lectures on the Jesus Seminar's work and current Jesus
scholarship that I presented at Indiana University in Bloomington
in November 1994, and at the University of California at Santa
Barbara and the University of California at Santa Cruz in May
1995. As a result of my lecture in Santa Barbara, I received from
the American editor of *Religion,* Ivan Strenski, a UC colleague, a
request that I write up my lecture as an article for the journal. I
readily consented to this and submitted the article to the journal
during the summer of 1995; it was published in the October issue.[3]
An expanded version of the article was published as an issue of the
Occasional Papers series produced by the Institute for Antiquity
and Christianity of The Claremont Graduate School, Claremont,
California.[4] This version has been slightly revised and updated for
publication here.

Most scholars, when looking back at things they did many years
earlier in their careers, find that their minds have changed on certain matters, or that earlier judgments need refinement. And very
few scholars would want to republish everything they wrote in
years past. I am certainly no exception to this observation; I would
not want to republish everything that I have written, and I have
had to rethink some of the judgments that I made in my past work.

2. R. W. Funk, R. W. Hoover, and the Jesus Seminar, *The Five Gospels: The
Search for the Authentic Words of Jesus* (New York: Macmillan, 1993). My seminar
took place on the campus of the Pacific School of Religion in Berkeley, where, nine
years before, Funk had convened the first session of the Jesus Seminar.

3. "The Gospel according to the Jesus Seminar," *Religion* 25 (1995): 317–38.

4. "The Gospel according to the Jesus Seminar," with an afterword by the director of the institute, J. M. Robinson, Occasional Papers 35, Institute for Antiquity
and Christianity, Claremont, Calif., April 1996 (44–48).

Some of this rethinking is reflected even in the essays published in this volume. Nevertheless, there is one article I wrote many years ago that has, in my present judgment, stood the test of time, and I would not now change anything of substance in it. That article is chapter 3 in this volume, where I argue that a certain passage in Paul's first letter to the Thessalonians, in the form in which that letter has come down to us, was not written by Paul at all and contains statements that the historical Paul could never have uttered. I marshal form-critical, exegetical, and historical arguments to show that 1 Thessalonians 2:13–16 is, in fact, an interpolation into the text of Paul's letter introduced by a later editor. My earliest statement of this position was presented at the annual meeting of the American Academy of Religion held in Boston, Massachusetts, in October 1969, with the title "1 Thessalonians 2.13–16: A Deutero-Pauline Interpolation." It was subsequently published as an article in the *Harvard Theological Review*.[5] I have only slightly revised the text for publication here, though I have updated the footnotes.

Chapter 4 has a very long prehistory, and in that sense it is the oldest section of the book. As a college student majoring in classical Greek and Latin back in the mid-1950s, I was doing some independent reading of the Greek New Testament and came at one point to 2 Peter 2:4, where I encountered the curious verb ταρταρώσας (<ταρταροῦν). Knowing something of the theogonic myths of Hesiod and other pagan Greek writers, I pondered the problem of how, or why, St. Peter would use a verb that seemed to reflect those pagan myths. (Of course, he didn't, since 2 Peter is a pseudepigraph.) Years later, as a graduate student at Harvard, I returned to that text and prepared a paper for a course taught by the late Amos Wilder. I subsequently presented that paper, entitled "ταρταρώσας at 2 Peter 2.4," at the annual meeting of the Society of Biblical Literature held in Berkeley, California, in December 1968. Upon my return to Duke University (where I was then an assistant professor), I gave my paper to a colleague in the Department of Classics, William Willis, who was then the editor of the journal *Greek, Roman, and Byzantine Studies*. He accepted the paper, with a new title that he suggested, and it was published in the journal.[6] It has been extensively reworked for publication here.

---

5. "1 Thessalonians 2.13–16: A Deutero-Pauline Interpolation," *HTR* 64 (1971): 79–94.
6. "A Reminiscence of Classical Myth at II Peter 2.4," *GRBS* 10 (1969): 71–80.

Second Peter contains vigorous polemic mounted against opponents who are usually considered to be "Gnostics" of some sort.
The apostle Peter turns out, however, to be the apostolic hero not
only of "orthodox" Christians but also of "heretical" ones, yes,
even "Gnostics." The Nag Hammadi corpus contains an *Apocalypse of Peter* produced by and for Gnostic Christians; and it turns
out, at least according to my argument in chapter 5 in this book,
that the Gnostic Christian who wrote the *Apocalypse* not only was
able to embrace the figure of Peter as a founder of his community, but also could freely utilize the putatively anti-Gnostic Second
Epistle in the composition of his work! This chapter was first presented as a paper read at the annual meeting of the Society of
Biblical Literature in Atlanta, Georgia, in November 1986. It was
subsequently revised and published in a Festschrift for James M.
Robinson.[7] It has been revised and updated for publication here.

Chapter 6 takes up the issue of the use of the Old Testament
by the Gnostics. It has been thought that the Gnostics rejected the
Old Testament, but that is certainly not the case. The manifold uses
made of the Bible by the Gnostics are described in this essay. The
essay has its origin in an invitation of the editor of a volume devoted to the Hebrew Bible (Mikra) in the series Compendia Rerum
Iudaicarum ad Novum Testamentum, to contribute an article to
the volume on the use of the Bible in Gnostic literature. I accepted
the invitation, wrote the article, and then presented a version of it
at the annual meeting of the Society of Biblical Literature held in
Chicago in November 1988. The article was published in the same
year.[8] It has been revised for publication here.

Chapter 7 has its origin in a working seminar on Gnosticism
and early Christianity held at Southwest Missouri State University
in Springfield, Missouri, in the spring of 1983. The essay addresses
the issue of the relationship between Gnosticism and Judaism and
between Gnosticism and early Christianity; I argue that some of the
sources now at our disposal can be defined as "Jewish Gnostic" literature. Two of the Nag Hammadi texts (the *Apocryphon of John*

7. "The Apocalypse of Peter and Canonical 2 Peter," in *Gnosticism and the
Early Christian World: In Honor of James M. Robinson,* ed. J. E. Goehring, C. W.
Hedrick, and J. T. Sanders, vol. 2 (Sonoma: Polebridge Press, 1990), 67–74.

8. "Use, Authority and Exegesis of Mikra in Gnostic Literature," in *Mikra:
Text, Translation, Reading and Interpretation of the Hebrew Bible in Ancient Ju-
daism and Early Christianity,* ed. M. J. Mulder, CRINT 2.1 (Assen: Van Gorcum;
Philadelphia: Fortress, 1988), 635–52. I have another article, "Jewish Sources in
Gnostic Literature," in the companion volume (Stone, *Jewish Writings,* CRINT II.2,
443–81).

and the *Apocalypse of Adam*) are given extensive analysis here. The essay was first published in 1986[9] and has been considerably revised for publication here.

Chapter 8 was first prepared in response to an invitation to contribute an article on Gnosticism for a volume on the fourth-century church historian and bishop Eusebius, to be published both in English and in Japanese. In the essay, I examine the use made by Eusebius of the sources available to him on "heresy" in general, and the Gnostics in particular. I conclude that, apart from the Manichees of his own day, Eusebius did not have much knowledge about the Gnostics and had certainly never read their literature. The essay was first published in 1992[10] and has been somewhat revised for publication here.

Chapter 9 is based on a paper written and presented in Swedish at the fourth Nordic Patristics Conference held in Lund, Sweden, in August 1993. The theme of that particular conference was orthodoxy and heresy in the early church, and its organizer, Samuel Rubenson, invited me to contribute a paper on unity and diversity in the church as a social phenomenon. In my essay, I take up the tension in early Christianity between the theological ideal of Christian unity and the actual reality of theological diversity, stressing the sociopolitical aspects of the problem. I devote part of this essay to a case study of early Christianity in Egypt. The essay was published in 1995[11] and has been translated and extensively revised for publication here.

Chapter 10 is based on a lecture that I presented at the Indiana University Center on Philanthropy in Indianapolis in November 1994, entitled "Ancient Roots of Western Philanthropy: Pagan, Jewish, and Christian." A revised version of this lecture was published in the Center's series "Essays on Philanthropy," no. 25 (1997). The version that appears here has been expanded and revised for publication in this book. In the essay, I analyze the use of

---

9. "The Problem of 'Jewish Gnostic' Literature," in *Nag Hammadi, Gnosticism, and Early Christianity*, ed. C. W. Hedrick and R. Hodgson (Peabody, Mass.: Hendrickson, 1986), 15–35.

10. "Eusebius and Gnosticism," in *Eusebius, Christianity, and Judaism*, ed. H. W. Attridge and G. Hata (Detroit: Wayne State University Press, 1992), 291–310; "Eusebiosu to Gunoushisu-kyo," in *Kirisutokyo no Seito to Ihan: Eusebiosu Kenkyu*, ed. G. Hata and H. W. Attridge (Tokyo: Lithon, 1992), 2:7–38.

11. "Enhet och mångfald i den tidiga kyrkan som ett socialt fenomen," in *Patristica Nordica* 4: *Föreläsningar hållna vid det fjärde Nordiska patristikermötet i Lund 17–20 augusti 1993*, ed. S. Rubenson, Religio 44 (Lund: Teologiska Institutionen, 1995), 93–104.

the term φιλανθρωπία in ancient Greek literature — pagan, Jewish, and Christian — as well as attitudes toward the poor in paganism, Judaism, and early Christianity. I also discuss the various philanthropic institutions that existed in the ancient world. I conclude the essay with some observations on the important role played by Christian philanthropy in the eventual success of the Christian religion in the Roman Empire.

In the epilogue, I present some personal reflections on scholarly method, mainly as reflected in, or extrapolated from, the essays in this book. I intend these remarks to be provocative, in the sense that I hope to provoke further discussion of the important issues involved in the study of early Christian history and literature, especially as this is done in secular contexts in our pluralistic world.

As is already noted, this book ranges over a considerable span of early Christian history, from the church's prehistory in the preaching of Jesus of Nazareth and its early history as reflected in the New Testament, to its triumph under Constantine and the problems attendant upon that triumph in its subsequent history, to the end of the fourth century. The book is not intended to be a history of early Christianity in the usual sense; instead, what is presented here are vignettes dealing with certain aspects of early Christian history and literature. Some of the ideas presented here are controversial, and I do not expect that my views will be met with universal acceptance. I do hope, however, that the essays will provide occasion for further study. It is also my fervent hope that the scholarship reflected here is presented in a way that will be intelligible not only to my scholarly colleagues but also to interested nonspecialists and students of religion.

Chapter 1

The Emergence of
the Christian Religion

"The Christian faith is not one of the religions of the world." These are the words of the late theologian Emil Brunner.[1] Brunner, of course, is not the only Christian theologian to make this claim. Numerous others, both systematic theologians and specialists in "missiology," have argued similarly.[2] Karl Barth flatly asserted, for example, that "religion is unbelief," and "unbelief... is sin."[3] This was a typical point of view of post–World War I "neoorthodox" theology, but, in fact, this idea is just a particularly extreme expression of the dominant position that the Christian religion has maintained in the Western world over the centuries. Even in the United States, where there is a constitutional separation of church and state and a prohibition against the "establishment" of any religion by the state, the predominant position of Christianity is very much in evidence, even in civil affairs. To be sure, the increasing religious "pluralism" in the United States, a result of the transplantation of non-Western religions by immigrants from all over the world, will eventually have the effect of reducing, but probably not eliminating, the dominant position of Christianity.

Some of the last bastions of the old view of the superiority of Christianity over other religions are to be found, oddly enough, in U.S. colleges and universities (i.e., in academic departments of religion). The presupposed superiority of Christianity and its claim to "uniqueness" has, in fact, been the guiding principle by which

---

1. "Der christliche Glaube... ist nicht 'eine der Religionen der Erde,'" quoted in W. C. Smith, *The Meaning and End of Religion* (New York: Macmillan, 1962; repr., Minneapolis: Fortress Press, 1991), 312.
2. See Smith's extensive note (ibid., 312 n. 39), wherein he cites A. C. Bouquet, H. Kraemer, W. Freytag, et al.
3. K. Barth, qtd. in ibid., 125.

academic studies in Christianity have been organized from the beginning up until now, not only in theological seminaries but also
in college programs. In such programs of study, Christianity is
not really treated as "one of the religions of the world." Rather,
"world religions" belong to a different sphere of study from that
of Christianity, with different approaches taken to the material.
That this is the case in theological faculties in European universities is understandable enough, given the status of Christianity in
the various European states. But even in the United States, with
its aforementioned constitutional separation of church and state,
this is the prevailing approach, not only in private colleges, universities, and seminaries, but even in some state universities where
"religious studies" constitutes part of the curriculum and often has
departmental status.[4]

But, leaving this digression, I want to return to the matter at
hand. In what follows, I shall take my stand firmly against the
theologian's claim and situate myself squarely in the camp of the
history of religions.[5] I shall proceed by unpacking the title of
this essay, moving backward from "religion" to "the Christian
religion" and, finally, to "the emergence of the Christian religion."

Religion

Wilfred Cantwell Smith, longtime director of the Center for the
Study of World Religions at Harvard, achieved considerable note
with his book *The Meaning and End of Religion,* published in
1962. Nowadays, in fact, this book is sometimes referred to as
"a modern classic of religious studies."[6] To Emil Brunner's claim
that "the Christian faith is not one of the religions of the world,"
Smith's response was, "Neither is the faith of any other people."

4. The Department of Religious Studies at the University of California at Santa
Barbara (where I taught for many years and am now emeritus) has striven to adopt
another approach, and there are now, admittedly, a few other examples as well.
With respect to the teaching of Christianity, see my article "On Treating Christianity as a Religion," in *The Santa Barbara Colloquy: Religion within the Limits of
Reason Alone,* ed. R. V. Norman and J. G. Larson, *Soundings* 71, nos. 2–3 (1988):
355–63.

5. An especially important model is provided in the work of K. Rudolph of
Marburg (who was professor of religious studies at UC Santa Barbara from 1984
to 1986). See esp. his "Early Christianity as a Religious-Historical Phenomenon,"
in Pearson, *Future,* 9–19.

6. J. Hick, quoted on the cover of the 1991 edition of Smith, *Meaning and End.*

Brunner and others are right with respect to Christian faith; their failure is "only to understand the faith of other men."[7]

It will be recalled that Smith's major thesis in his book is that the term "religion" is inadequate as a designation for peoples' relationship to the transcendent. After first treating extensively the origin and development of the Latin word *religio* and its cognates and counterparts, he argued that the noun "religion" should be dropped from scholarly discourse (the adjective *religious* was acceptable). He proposed that for the generic term "religion," one should substitute the word "faith"; for a specific "religion," one should say instead "tradition" or "cumulative tradition." "Religiousness" is acceptable, but "piety" is better. He also argued against the "objectifying" use of "-ism" words, such as "Buddhism," "Hinduism," and "Christianity." At the end of his book, Smith makes the following statements:

> I am bold enough to speculate whether these terms will not in fact have disappeared from serious writing and careful speech within twenty-five years.
>
> Such a disappearance could mean for the devout a truer faith in God and a truer love of their neighbor; and for scholars, a clearer understanding of the religious phenomena that they are studying.[8]

Now, several years after 1987, when the terminological change in scholarly discourse should have taken effect, according to Smith, we can see that Smith's proposals have obviously not been adopted, not in North America, certainly not in Europe, indeed, not anywhere.[9] On the contrary, the terms "religion" and "religions" are very much still in use, even if there is still disagreement over definitions and usage.[10] For example, Kurt Rudolph, whose approach I basically share, has expressed in his book *Historical Fundamentals and the Study of Religion* some wariness in the use of the singular "religion," especially by philosophers of religion in search

---

7. Smith, *Meaning and End,* 139.

8. Ibid., 195.

9. For some responses to Smith's *Meaning and End,* see E. J. Sharpe, *Comparative Religion: A History,* 2d ed. (London: G. Duckworth, 1986), 282–83.

10. See the article "Religion," by W. L. King, in *The Encyclopedia of Religion,* 12:282–93. See also K. Rudolph's important article "Inwieweit ist der Begriff 'Religion' Eurozentrisch?" in *The Notion of "Religion" in Comparative Research: Selected Proceedings of the Sixteenth Congress of the International Association for the History of Religions, Rome, 3rd–8th September 1990,* ed. U. Bianchi (Rome: "L'Erma" di Bretschneider, 1994), 131–39.

of some "essence" of religion.[11] He prefers the plural "religions": "The history of religions acquires knowledge of religion only through a historical study of religions."[12] But Rudolph perforce uses the singular "religion" throughout his own book (including its title!).

The utility of the use of the word "religion" in scholarly discourse has thus apparently been established, both in the sense of a discrete phenomenon of human experience and history (whether or not one speaks of an "essence" of religion), and in the sense of a historical complex of specific religious beliefs and practices (plural "religions"). One can speak of the cross-cultural phenomenon of "religion," and one can speak of "a religion" or "the [adjective: Buddhist, Jewish, etc.] religion."

My Santa Barbara colleague Ninian Smart has come up with an interesting way for scholarly discourse to sidestep the issue of the "essence" of religion and to avoid quibbling about definitions.[13] His suggestion is to identify the various aspects or "dimensions" of religion, or, specifically, of "a religion." He identifies seven of these: the practical and ritual dimension, the experiential and emotional dimension, the narrative or mythic dimension, the doctrinal and philosophical dimension, the ethical and legal dimension, the social and institutional dimension, and the material dimension.[14] Smart refers to these as "the seven dimensions of religion which help to characterize religions as they exist in the world."[15] I find this inductive approach quite helpful.

With these comments on "religion" in mind, I turn again to the

---

11. See K. Rudolph, *Historical Fundamentals and the Study of Religion* (New York: Macmillan, 1985), esp. 34 and 44–45. In his objections to the use of the term "religion" in connection with a quest for religion's "essence," Rudolph enters common ground with Smith, whose views are in other respects polar opposites to those of Rudolph. On the question of the "essence" of religion, see Smith, *Meaning and End*, 47.

12. Rudolph, *Historical Fundamentals*, 34.

13. Of the multitudes of definitions of "religion," one that I find useful is that of Å. Hultkrantz: "the conviction of the existence of a supernatural world, a conviction that comes especially to expression in beliefs of various sorts and that is concretely manifested in rites and observances, as well as epic depictions" (my translation). Such a definition has the advantage of covering even atheistic religions, such as Buddhism. See Hultkrantz, *Metodvägar inom den jämförande religionsforskningen* (Stockholm: Esselte Studium, 1973), 13.

14. N. Smart, *The World's Religions: Old Traditions and Modern Transformations* (Cambridge: Cambridge University Press, 1989), 10–21. See also Smart, *Dimensions of the Sacred: An Anatomy of the World's Beliefs* (Berkeley and Los Angeles: University of California Press, 1996).

15. Smart, *World's Religions*, 21.

theologian's dictum with which we began: "The Christian faith is not one of the religions of the world." To this I reply as forcefully as I can: The Christian faith is *indeed* one of the religions of the world. "Faith" is one of the constituents of that religion, and the exclusive claim that underlies Emil Brunner's statement is itself one of the data subject to inquiry in the study of that religion by scholars, especially scholars who claim to be "historians of religions."

The Christian Religion

We recall here, first, that my North American colleague W. C. Smith objected as vigorously to "-ism" language as he did to the use of the term "religion," arguing that such terms as "Buddhism," "Hinduism," "Taoism," and so on are essentially nineteenth-century Western inventions.[16] But here again I have to differ. The "-ism" words may be misused, to be sure, but they have their utility for scholarly discourse. "Christianity," in fact, is such an "-ism" word in its original Greek: *Christianismos.* The word is certainly useful as an umbrella term for a highly complex and richly variegated phenomenon. Indeed, so rich is the variegation of this religion, even in ancient times, that some scholars nowadays speak of "Christianities"[17] — in which case the usefulness of the word "Christianity" as an umbrella term is diminished. In any case, I look upon the designations "Christianity" and "the Christian religion" as virtually synonymous. Whichever term one uses, and in whatever context, one is referring to "one of the religions of the world," that is, one of the religions of the modern world and one of the religions of the ancient world as well.[18]

Here we do well to consider the very first recorded instances of the word *Christianismos* ("Christianity"). They occur in the letters of Bishop Ignatius of Antioch (d. ca. 110), in *Magnesians* 10.1, 3; *Philadelphians* 6.1; and *Romans* 3.3.

Magnesians 10.1–3 reads as follows (in William Schoedel's translation):

---

16. See Smith, *Meaning and End*, 60–71. Smith does acknowledge that *Ioudaismos* occurs as early as 2 Macc (first cent. B.C.E.), of course under the impact of "Greek thought," which is "pre-eminently reificationist-idealist" (72). He also mentions Ignatius's use of *Christianismos* (73), which I discuss here.

17. See J. Z. Smith, *Drudgery Divine: On the Comparison of Early Christianities and the Religions of Late Antiquity* (Chicago: University of Chicago Press, 1990).

18. Cf. Rudolph, "Early Christianity."

Let us not, then, be insensible to his [Christ's] goodness! For if he imitates us in our actions, we no longer exist! Therefore let us become his disciples and learn to live according to Christianity [κατὰ Χριστιανισμὸν ζῆν]. For one who is called by any name other than this, is not of God. Set aside, then, the evil leaven, old and sour, and turn to the new leaven, which is Jesus Christ. Be salted with him to keep anyone among you from being spoiled, since you will be convicted by your odor. It is ridiculous to profess Jesus Christ and to Judaize; for Christianity did not believe in Judaism, but Judaism in Christianity [ἀλλ᾽ Ἰουδαϊσμὸς εἰς Χριστιανισμόν], into which every tongue that has believed in God has been gathered together.[19]

Here Ignatius maintains that being disciples of Jesus Christ and being "of God" means living "according to Christianity" rather than "Judaism," which is the "old" and "evil" leaven.[20] The contrast here between "Christianity" and "Judaism" is very sharp, expressed mainly in terms of "new" versus "old" but also (implicitly) between good and true versus evil and false. Ignatius's statement about Judaism "believing in" Christianity picks up on observations made in his previous chapter, namely, about "those who lived in old ways" who came to "newness of hope," giving up the Sabbath and observing the "Lord's Day" (9.1). The reference is to the Jews of earlier times who adopted Christian beliefs and practices, most notably the original disciples of Jesus and their followers.

The first verse of *Philadelphians* 6 picks up the same theme:

But if anyone expounds Judaism to you, do not listen to him; for it is better to hear Christianity from a man who is circumcised than Judaism from a man uncircumcised [ἄμεινον γάρ ἐστιν παρὰ ἀνδρὸς περιτομὴν ἔχοντος Χριστιανισμὸν ἀκούειν, ἢ παρὰ ἀκροβύστου Ἰουδαϊσμόν]; both of them, if they do not speak of Jesus Christ, are to me tombstones and graves of the dead on which nothing but the names of men is written.[21]

Here Ignatius, when speaking of hearing Christianity from a circumcised man, tacitly acknowledges that those who first professed

---

19. W. R. Schoedel, *Ignatius of Antioch: A Commentary on the Letters of Ignatius of Antioch* (Philadelphia: Fortress Press, 1985), 126.
20. Here Ignatius alludes to statements made by the apostle Paul in 1 Cor 5:7–8 and Gal 5:9.
21. Schoedel, *Ignatius*, 200.

Jesus Christ were Jews. He absolutely rejects any kind of "Judaizing" on the part of a gentile in the interest of maintaining both the superiority of "Christianity" over "Judaism" and the boundaries separating the one from the other.

Ignatius's *Romans* 3.2–3 has a somewhat different emphasis:

> Only ask power for me both within and without so that not only may I speak, but also will, that not only may I be called a Christian but also be found one, for if I am found one, I can also be called one and prove faithful then when I do not appear to the world. Nothing that appears is good; for our God Jesus Christ rather appears by being in the Father. The deed is not a matter of persuasive rhetoric, but Christianity is characterized by greatness when it is hated by the world [ἀλλὰ μεγέθους ἐστὶν ὁ Χριστιανισμός, ὅταν μισῆται ὑπὸ κόσμου].[22]

Here Ignatius is speaking of his sought-for martyrdom (in the preceding context [2.1–2] he has asked the Romans not to try to intervene in his behalf) and allying himself with "Christianity," whose greatness is in being hated by the world. Ignatius's own martyrdom as a Christian is, in his view, an acting out of the primal martyrdom of Jesus Christ.

These passages from the letters of Ignatius can certainly be taken as evidence that, at least for the bishop who penned them, *Christianismos* is a distinct way of life centered on the life, death, and resurrection of Jesus Christ, separate from the Judaism from which it sprang. *Christianismos*, in Ignatius's usage, can be construed in history-of-religions terms as "a religion," or "the Christian religion," a distinct complex of religious beliefs and practices.

Having established that "Christianity" is a meaningful term in Ignatius's mind, and presumably in the minds of his audience, one could go further and inquire as to what in Ignatius's experience was included in this designation. Here one might usefully employ the strategy of Ninian Smart and inquire as to the "dimensions" of *Christianismos* in Ignatius's community as reflected in, or extrapolated from, his writings and those of his close associates (e.g., Polycarp).

I do not propose to carry out such an inquiry here. Suffice it to say that, for Ignatius and his co-religionists, *Christianismos* comprised a doctrinal dimension focused on a christocentric creed; a ritual dimension involving baptism and the Eucharist; a narrative-mythic

---

22. Ibid., 170.

dimension including biblical narratives and narratives circulating in the early church of Jesus' words and deeds, but especially featuring a "Christ myth" narrating the Savior's descent (incarnation), earthly life and death, and resurrection/ascension; an ethical dimension featuring patterns of Christian behavior; an experiential dimension reflecting Christian experience of the Spirit; a social/institutional dimension now centering largely on leadership exercised by the bishop and supported by the presbyters and deacons; and a material dimension of a rudimentary sort, which would involve, if nothing else, the ordering of space and furnishings for Christian worship.[23]

As to the most important of these, the ritual and mythic dimensions, the Jewish roots are quite clear. Both Christian baptism and the Christian Eucharist develop out of practices at home in eschatologically oriented sectarian Judaism, for which the Qumran sect of the Dead Sea Scrolls provides the best analogy. The Christ myth develops out of two subsidiary myths[24] or narrative patterns of Judaism: the descent of the feminine divine hypostasis "Wisdom" (Greek *Sophia*, Hebrew *Ḥokhmah*)[25] and the narrative pattern featuring the paradigmatic righteous man, who suffers and is vindicated by God.[26] In Judaism, "Wisdom" is eventually embodied in the Torah; in Christianity, she is embodied in Jesus Christ. In Judaism, the righteous sufferer is sometimes interpreted corporately, to refer to the people of Israel; in Christianity, he is embodied in Jesus Christ. Rather soon, in gentile Christianity, the Christ myth takes on features derived from the ancient Greco-Roman (Indo-European) "hero" pattern.[27]

Bishop Ignatius lays great stress on his claim that *Christianismos* is and must be distinct from *Ioudaismos;* yet, even he recognizes that the former is rooted, in some sense, in the latter (i.e., he realizes that the first Christians were Jews). This brings us to our next point, a discussion of how *Christianismos* emerged out of *Ioudaismos.*

---

23. We lack any evidence for Christian art and architecture for such an early period in Christian history.

24. The foundational myths of Judaism are the Exodus from Egypt, the giving of the Torah on Mount Sinai, and the promise of the land.

25. For the relevant texts, with discussion, see U. Wilckens, "σοφία, σοφός, σοφίζω," *TDNT*, 7:465–528, esp. 489–526.

26. See, for example, G. W. E. Nickelsburg, *Resurrection, Immortality, and Eternal Life in Intertestamental Judaism* (Cambridge: Harvard University Press, 1972), 48–111; see also Nickelsburg, "Passion Narratives," *ABD*, 5:172–77.

27. See G. J. Riley, *One Jesus, Many Christs* (San Francisco: HarperSanFrancisco, 1997).

The Emergence of the Christian Religion

I use the term "emergence" quite deliberately, for it would be historically illegitimate to refer to a single "origin" or "founding" of the Christian religion. Some religions have their historical founders (e.g., Zoroaster in the case of Parsiism, Siddhartha Gautama in the case of Buddhism, Mani in the case of Manichaeism, and Muhammad in the case of Islam). Even if in every case one must take into account the preceding religious-historical context and the traditions that fed into the new religion — Iranian polytheism in the case of Zoroaster; Upanishadic traditions in the case of Gautama; Christian, Jewish, Gnostic, and perhaps Zoroastrian and other oriental traditions in the case of Mani; and Jewish, Christian, Gnostic, and Arabian polytheistic traditions in the case of Muhammad — we can in each instance speak of the founding of a discrete new religion. This is absolutely not the case with Jesus of Nazareth: he was and remained a Jew, both in terms of ethnicity and in terms of religion.[28]

A case could be made for Peter as a "founder" of Christianity, in the sense that early Christian traditions make him the first witness to the resurrection (1 Cor 15:5) and the leader of the first organized community of believers in Jesus in Jerusalem (Acts 1–5; cf. Matt 16:18). But even if Peter can be regarded as, in some sense, the "founder" of a new community, this community was a Jewish one, and remained within the confines of the Jewish religion as one of the many varieties of Second Temple Judaism. That this new community regarded Jesus as the Messiah did not at all remove it from the parameters of Judaism. Even in our own day, the Lubavitcher sect of Hasidic Jews regarded their "Rebbe," Menachem Schneersohn, as the Messiah designate, and were eagerly expecting the old man to reveal himself as the Messiah. Some even now expect his reappearance. They are in other respects quite orthodox, and it would not occur to anyone that Schneersohn was the founder of a new religion. (Schneersohn died in 1994.)

Nor can Paul, "the apostle to the gentiles," be regarded as in any sense the founder of Christianity as a religion, as has so often been averred,[29] even if some of his teachings played a key role in the emergence of the Christian religion. Paul was and remained a

---

28. I stress this point in chapter 2 of this book.

29. A new variant on this old theme has recently been provided by H. D. Betz in an interesting article, "Christianity as Religion: Paul's Attempt at Definition in Romans," *JR* 71 (1991): 315–44.

Jew, and even his version of Christianity, radical as it was, should be regarded as a sectarian variety of Second Temple Judaism. Paul never uses the word "Christian" in his extant writings, and his notion of the role of gentile converts to Christ in the divine scheme of things is that they have been incorporated into the preexisting people of God as an olive branch is grafted onto a grown tree (Rom 11:17–24).

Thus, we see that there is considerable difficulty in tracing historically the process by which the Christian religion "emerged" out of its Jewish matrix; that is to say, how, when, and why Christianity became a distinct religion separate from Judaism. What is involved, nevertheless, is a process that unfolded in different ways and at different times with different groups of people.

We have earlier referred to Ignatius of Antioch and his conviction that *Christianismos* was separate from *Ioudaismos,* a conviction, by the way, that seems not to have been shared by all Christians in the communities known to him (a point to which we shall return). The starting point for our discussion of Ignatius was the earliest attested use of the term *Christianismos,* a noun based on the adjective *Christianos.* What of the adjective *Christianos?*

Here again, we find ourselves in Antioch on the Orontes River, where Ignatius would be bishop in the early second century. It is recorded in Acts 11:26 that "it was in Antioch that the disciples were first called 'Christians.'" The word *Christianos* is really a Latin (or Latinizing) word wherein "Christ" is construed as a proper name (perhaps in confusion with the name "Chrestos").[30] The term "Christian" was presumably applied to the "disciples" in Antioch by outsiders, and meant something like "partisans of Christ"[31] (cf. the Palestinian designation *Nazoraioi* [= *noṣrim*] in Acts 24:5). Exactly when this first occurred cannot be determined, but I assume it was quite early. The same source for this information (Acts 11:19–30)[32] also tells us that it was in Antioch that "the word" about "the Lord Jesus" was first extended to gentiles

---

30. The word *Christianos* occurs in the NT at Acts 11:26; 26:28; and 1 Pet 4:16. In Acts 26:28, King Agrippa says to Paul, "Are you so quickly persuading me to become a Christian?" But the story of the interchange between Paul and Agrippa tells us nothing about Paul's own usage. To be sure, it is not impossible that Paul would have accepted the designation *Christianos,* even though he was and remained a Jew. Still, the absence of this term in his rather extensive extant writings should be given its due weight.

31. See H. Conzelmann, *Acts of the Apostles: A Commentary on the Acts of the Apostles* (Philadelphia: Fortress Press, 1987), 88.

32. On the Antiochene source used by the author of Acts, see ibid., 87.

("Greeks"),[33] and that this took place *prior* to the arrival in Antioch of Paul (here called Saul), who would later, of course, be known as "the apostle to the gentiles." And who were the people in Antioch responsible for this innovation? They belonged to the "Hellenist" group of Christians represented initially by Stephen and the other Hellenist leaders in Jerusalem, a group banished from Jerusalem on the grounds of their rejection of Temple worship and their views concerning the Torah (Acts 6:1–8:4).

We can thus trace a "trajectory" that leads from a Greek-speaking group of Jewish believers in Jesus in Jerusalem (Acts 6–8) to a Greek-speaking group of Jewish and gentile believers in Antioch who are given the name "Christian" by outsiders (Acts 11); to a gentile mission led first from Antioch by Barnabas and Paul (Acts 13–14); to the independent activity of the apostle Paul, resulting in a network of churches influenced by Paul's teachings (Acts 15–28 plus the *Corpus Paulinum*); to Bishop Ignatius of Antioch, who embraces *Christianismos* as a religion distinct from Judaism and who also provides us with the first instance of the term "the catholic church" (*Smyrn.* 8.2). Ignatius thus represents a pivotal point for the future direction of this "catholic church" and the Christian religion in general.

But that is certainly not the whole story. Even in the case of the churches addressed by Ignatius, there were obviously people who did not share the bishop's views about a Christianity distinct from Judaism. Hence his vigorous arguments on that point and his passionate warnings against "Judaizing" (*Magn.* 10.3). The fact that Ignatius's views on the matter eventually won the day should not obscure the fact that other Christians of his time had other views. Ignatius's role, however, is instructive in the sense that it is precisely charismatic leaders like Ignatius who are able to effect the developments of the sort we are seeing here. Ignatius was not only a bishop; he was capable of inspired prophetic utterance (*Phld.* 7), and his authority was eventually sealed by his martyrdom.

Yet, "the emergence of the Christian religion" involves a more complicated process than is reflected in the aforementioned "trajectory." For, in fact, one can trace other trajectories that lead in other directions, some eventually melding into the catholic church and others eventually excluded therefrom.

---

33. The NRSV follows the 26th edition of Nestle-Aland in reading "Hellenists" here instead of "Greeks," a reading that must be categorically rejected on exegetical grounds because it clearly makes no sense at all in the context.

Consider the trajectory of the earliest community in Jerusalem founded by Peter. This is the community of Torah-observant "Hebrews" that remains in Jerusalem after the "scattering" of the Hellenists (Acts 8:1). Its leader becomes Jesus' brother James after Peter's departure from Jerusalem (Acts 12:1–17; 15; 21; Joseph., *Ant.* 20.200). This community's trajectory is broken, according to tradition, by its departure from Jerusalem during the Jewish War of 66–70,[34] and then becomes obscure, various groups spreading out in the Transjordan and Syria, but one group returning to Jerusalem and remaining active there until the Second Revolt of 132–135.[35] Of special interest here is that this group's trajectory leads to the "Ebionites," Jewish Christians first designated as such by Irenaeus. By Irenaeus's time, however, these Torah-faithful Jewish believers in Jesus (and despisers of Paul) had been branded "heretics" by the leaders of the emerging "catholic church." Although they persisted into the fourth century, and probably later,[36] they represent a historical dead end in the development of the Christian religion.

There are other trajectories as well, representing traditions and groups streaming from other apostolic figures, such as Peter, John, and Judas Thomas. The Petrine and Johannine traditions flow into that of the "catholic church," but that of Judas Thomas results in another dead end, unless the Mar Thoma Church of India be considered its heir.[37]

Nor should we omit from our discussion the importance of

---

34. This tradition is recorded first by Eusebius (*Hist. Eccl.* 3.5.3) and is variously assessed by scholars. For recent discussions, see, e.g., G. Lüdemann, *Opposition to Paul in Jewish Christianity* (Minneapolis: Fortress Press, 1989), 200–13; and R. A. Pritz, *Nazarene Jewish Christianity* (Jerusalem: Magnes Press; Leiden: E. J. Brill, 1988), 122–27. Lüdemann regards the tradition as unhistorical; Pritz defends its historicity.

35. According to Eusebius (*Hist. Eccl.* 4.5.2), all of the bishops of Jerusalem were Jews ("Hebrews") until the revolt of 132–135, after which the Jerusalem see was occupied by gentile Christians.

36. See S. Pines, "The Jewish Christians of the Early Centuries of Christianity according to a New Source," in *Proceedings of the Israel Academy of Sciences and Humanities,* vol. 2, no. 13 (Jerusalem: Israel Academy of Sciences and Humanities, 1966).

37. See P. J. Podipara, *The Thomas Christians* (Bombay: St. Paul Publications, 1970). On the shape of ancient Thomas Christianity, see, e.g., H. Koester, "*Gnomai Diaphoroi:* The Origin and Nature of Diversification in the History of Early Christianity," in Robinson-Koester, *Trajectories,* 114–57, esp. 126–43; Layton, *Gnostic Scriptures,* 357–409; and G. J. Riley, *Resurrection Reconsidered: Thomas and John in Controversy* (Minneapolis: Fortress Press, 1995).

external historical events, such as the Jewish revolt of 66–70, which led to the destruction of the Temple in 70 C.E.,[38] and the Bar Kokhba Revolt of 132–135, which led to the banishment of Jews from Jerusalem (renamed Aelia Capitolina) by the emperor Hadrian. One can hardly overestimate the importance of the destruction of the Temple for the development of rabbinic Judaism, on the one hand, and Christianity, on the other. What is involved here is a process by which two religions — rabbinic ("normative") Judaism and Christianity — emerge out of a single one, Second Temple Judaism. This process illustrates an important phenomenon in the history of religions: that of religious change and development.

Christianity's emergence as a religion separate from Judaism involves certain important changes in religious belief and practice as necessary ingredients. But it can equally well be said that rabbinic Judaism's emergence and persistence as a *Jewish* religion involves important changes in religious beliefs and practices as necessary ingredients. Many of the groups and sects that were a feature of Second Temple Judaism ceased to exist after the destruction of the Temple and the end of the Jewish War. The most obvious of these are the Sadducees and the Essenes. Even the Pharisees no longer persisted as a party of *perushim* ("separatists") in the aftermath of the war, for their interpretations of Jewish tradition eventually became the basis for the development of "normative" Judaism.

The British scholar James D. G. Dunn has recently published an important book dealing with these issues: *The Partings of the Ways between Christianity and Judaism and Their Significance for the Character of Christianity.*[39] In that book Dunn discusses, first, four aspects of what we would call the "doctrinal dimension" of Second Temple Judaism, what he calls "the four pillars of Second Temple Judaism": monotheism; the doctrine of election; the covenant, focused in the Torah; and the land, focused on the Temple. He then takes up the words and deeds of Jesus, as well as those of Paul and other early Christian writers, in relation to these four pillars, tracing the origins of divergences on these points between the

---

38. See, e.g., S. G. F. Brandon, *The Fall of Jerusalem and the Christian Church* (London: SPCK, 1957).

39. J. D. G. Dunn, *The Partings of the Ways between Christianity and Judaism and Their Significance for the Character of Christianity* (London: SCM Press; Philadelphia: Trinity Press International, 1991).

developing Christian sect of Judaism and the rest of first-century Judaism. He argues persuasively that the final parting of the ways between Judaism and Christianity is to be located historically between the two Jewish revolts of 66–70 and 132–135. What is involved on the Jewish side is a process of consolidation around Torah and a narrowing of communal boundaries that leads to the expulsion from synagogues of religious deviants, including Christians (*noṣrim*) and other "heretics" (*minim*).[40] On the Christian side, developments in belief and practice tend either to compromise or to drastically reinterpret the four pillars: the developing doctrine of the deity of Christ compromises monotheism; the development of the idea of Christians as the "true Israel" or a "third race" reinterprets the doctrine of election; the emphasis on the "new covenant" diminishes the significance of the Torah; and the interpretation of the destruction of the Temple as a sign of God's disowning of Israel[41] is a direct contradiction to the older view of the centrality of the Temple. But, as Dunn points out, there is also a parting of the ways among Christians: between a "mainstream" Christianity and other ("heretical") varieties of Christianity, especially Jewish Christianity (i.e., the aforementioned Ebionites).[42] These are the people who wished to retain their identity as Jews, both ethnically and religiously.

As to the development of what Ignatius referred to as "the catholic church," one can see here a process by which Christianity becomes more and more a religion of gentiles. In its expansion throughout the Mediterranean world, the Christian religion takes on the shape of other "diaspora" religions of the Greco-Roman period, religions in which native elements are either lost or reinterpreted — the Isis cult is a prime example — and Greek elements taken on. In other words, Christianity emerges as one of the "syncretistic" religions of the Roman Empire and thus takes its place as "one of the religions of the world."[43]

It would take us too far afield to analyze the reasons why the

---

40. The *minim* and *noṣrim* are the groups cursed in the famous *birkhath ha-minim,* inserted into the *Shemoneh Esreh* ("Eighteen Benedictions") of the Jewish liturgy toward the end of the first century C.E. For a still useful discussion, see W. D. Davies, *The Setting of the Sermon on the Mount* (Cambridge: Cambridge University Press, 1964), 275–79.

41. See chapter 3 of this book.

42. Dunn, *Partings of the Ways,* 239.

43. The term "syncretistic" is used here neutrally, with no derogatory connotation. On this point, see Rudolph, "Early Christianity," 18.

Christian religion succeeded in becoming an enduring world religion whereas the other main religions of the Hellenistic-Roman
period ceased to exist.[44] I would suggest on this point, however,
that those aspects of the Christian religion which most account
for its persistence are precisely those which it retains as a modified inheritance of its Jewish origins: the doctrine of one God,
Creator and Father; a consciousness of a universal peoplehood
wherein the doctrine of ethnic election is transmuted into a doctrine of a "universal" ("catholic") church, featuring "networks"[45]
binding together into a spiritual whole believers in various places;
the notion of a "new covenant" that is also able to include normative scriptures from the "old covenant," unified by the theme of
"promise" and "fulfillment"; and the doctrine of an embodiment
of the presence of God with his people, now, of course, centered
in the Savior Jesus Christ rather than in a national temple with
priesthood and sacrifices. This divine presence is mediated by the
developing sacramental system of the church, which also eventually
takes on more and more of a "priestly" coloration.

Concluding Observations

We began this essay with the claim sometimes made by Christian
theologians that "the Christian faith is not one of the religions
of the world." Historians of religions know, of course, that this
claim makes no sense either historically or phenomenologically. I
would like to suggest, finally, that it may now be time for Christian systematic theologians to take seriously the actual position of
the Christian religion as one of many religions of the world and to
abandon once and for all the exclusivist claims of the past.[46] It does

44. The sociologist R. Stark has treated this and related issues in an important
new book, *The Rise of Christianity: A Sociologist Reconsiders Religion* (Princeton:
Princeton University Press, 1996). Cf. my concluding remarks in chapter 10 of this
book.
45. "Network theory" is one of the more useful contributions of social theory
to an understanding of early Christianity and its expansion, and is a prominent
feature of Stark's *Rise of Christianity*. See also L. M. White, ed., *Social Networks in
the Early Christian Environment: Issues and Methods for Social History, Semeia* 56
(1992).
46. An important example of this is provided in the very last public words uttered
by P. Tillich on October 12, 1965 (he died ten days later), a lecture entitled "The
Significance of the History of Religions for the Systematic Theologian," published
in Tillich, *The Future of Religions*, ed. J. C. Brauer (New York: Harper & Row,
1966), 80–94.

not in any way diminish the Christian religion for its adherents to recognize the validity and value of other religions. Yes, this may have the effect of "relativizing" Christian faith. But it may finally be salutary for Christians to acknowledge that there is only one Absolute, and that Absolute can never be the exclusive property of any single religious tradition.[47]

47. F. Heiler put it very well in an important article of his ("The History of Religions as a Preparation for the Co-operation of Religions," in *The History of Religions: Essays in Methodology,* ed. M. Eliade and J. Kitagawa [Chicago: University of Chicago Press, 1959], 132–60): "Most Christian theologians fear nothing so much as 'relativism.' I have a way of answering such theologians that the greatest of all relativists is God himself, the Absolute, for he is fulness in itself and his fulness is revealed in the immeasurable diversity of nature and the spiritual life" (156).

_____ *Chapter 2* _____

The Gospel according to
the "Jesus Seminar"

*On Some Recent Trends
in Gospel Research*

The Jesus Seminar

In March of 1985, Robert Funk, a well-known New Testament scholar, presided over the first meeting of a group of scholars that he had convened, dubbed the "Jesus Seminar." Meeting on the campus of the Pacific School of Religion in Berkeley, California, the seminar embarked on an unprecedented group project — to examine the available sources, canonical and noncanonical, in quest of "the voice of Jesus," that is, "what he really said."[1] The procedure would be as follows: The group would meet biennially, focusing in each meeting on a particular set of sayings attributed to Jesus through discussion of previously circulated position papers, with a view to achieving a consensus on the authenticity or non-authenticity of each of the sayings. After discussion and debate, a vote would be taken, with each participant dropping a colored bead into a box. There would be four colors: *red,* indicating that Jesus undoubtedly said this, or something very close to it; *pink,* indicating that Jesus probably said something like this; *gray,* indicating that Jesus did not say this, though the idea(s) contained in it may reflect something of Jesus' own; and *black,* indicating that Jesus did not say anything like it, the saying in question reflecting

---

1. This first meeting of the Jesus Seminar is briefly discussed by one of the participants, M. J. Borg, in a recent book, *Jesus in Contemporary Scholarship* (Valley Forge, Pa.: Trinity Press International, 1994). The quotation is from Borg's excerpt of R. Funk's address to the assembled group (161).

a different or later tradition.[2] Each color would be assigned a rating (red = 3; pink = 2; gray = 1; black = 0), and the results would be tabulated to achieve a "weighted average" on a scale of 1.00 (.7501 and up = red; .5001 to .7500 = pink; .2501 to .5000 = gray; .0000 to .2500 = black). The tabulated votes would be reflected in the published results, in which sayings attributed to Jesus would be color-coded, in a kind of "red-letter edition" of the Gospels.

The Jesus Seminar proceeded in this fashion for six years, averaging around thirty participants per session. From time to time, its results would be reported to the press, resulting in newspaper and magazine articles intended for public consumption. The attendant publicity was designed to guarantee an awareness of and stimulate interest in the work of the Jesus Seminar among the general public, and to create a ready readership for the published results. Part of the project was also a new translation of the Gospels known as the "Scholars Version," prepared by a group within the seminar. This translation, and the work of the Jesus Seminar as a whole, includes the noncanonical *Gospel of Thomas,* preserved in a Coptic version as part of the Nag Hammadi codices discovered in Upper Egypt in 1945.[3] The results of all this work appeared in 1993 as *The Five Gospels: The Search for the Authentic Words of Jesus,* by Robert W. Funk, Roy W. Hoover, and the Jesus Seminar, published by Macmillan in New York. Meanwhile, the Jesus Seminar embarked on a new phase, designed to answer the question, "What did Jesus really do?"

The Five Gospels includes an extensive introduction, followed by the translation of and commentary on the Gospels of Mark, Matthew, Luke, John, and Thomas. After each segment ("pericope") of the gospels in which Jesus is quoted as saying something, commentary is provided explaining why the sayings were colored as they were. Special topics are treated in brief "cameo essays" scattered throughout the book. It should be noted that only 18 percent of the attributed sayings of Jesus are regarded by the Jesus Seminar as authentic (i.e., they received a rating of either red or pink). Thus, a full 82 percent of the sayings tradition is counted

2. See discussion in the introduction to R. W. Funk, R. W. Hoover, and the Jesus Seminar, *The Five Gospels: The Search for the Authentic Words of Jesus* (New York: Macmillan, 1993), 35–37.

3. See *NHLE.* The *Gospel of Thomas* is the second of seven tractates preserved in NH Codex II (*NHLE* 124–38). Greek fragments of three different copies of *Thomas* (P.Oxy. 1, P.Oxy. 654, and P.Oxy 655) were found at Oxyrhynchus in Upper Egypt in 1897 and 1904. For a critical edition of the Coptic and Greek versions, see Layton, *Codex II,* 1:38–128.

as inauthentic (i.e., rated black or gray).[4] Such a surprising result might provide the grounds for some skepticism as to the procedures and methods that led to it. As we shall see, such skepticism is not unjustified.

In the bulk of what follows, I shall assess the work of the Jesus Seminar and its results as published in *The Five Gospels*. This will be done with reference to the seminar's statements in the introduction, in the commentary to individual pericopes, and in some of the "cameo essays." Limitations of space preclude a complete discussion of all of the evidence, but the items chosen for discussion should provide enough of a sample to arrive at a critical assessment and some concluding observations. This discussion will proceed under four headings, considering (1) problems of method, (2) historical premises, (3) examples of mistranslation in the "Scholars Version," and (4) problems of interpretation of the 18 percent of the sayings tradition assigned by the Jesus Seminar to the historical Jesus. But first, it is necessary to situate the work of the Jesus Seminar in its own historical context as part of the ongoing scholarly research on the Gospels and on the "quest of the historical Jesus."

Quests of the Historical Jesus

Historical investigation of the Jesus tradition untrammeled by theological agendas is the product of the eighteenth-century Enlightenment. One of the first to undertake such an investigation was the orientalist Hermann Samuel Reimarus (1694–1768), with whose work Albert Schweitzer begins his classic book *The Quest of the Historical Jesus*.[5] Reimarus saw in Jesus of Nazareth a Jewish messianic revolutionary whose failure led his followers to steal his body and to create a new story of Jesus based on aspects of Jewish messianism. The Christian religion did not grow out of the

---

4. These statistics appear on p. 5 of Funk, Hoover, and the Jesus Seminar, *Five Gospels*. At the end of the book, there is an index of red- and pink-letter sayings (549–53). It should be noted that the results of the Jesus Seminar's work do not reflect unanimity; many of the sayings got red votes from some and black votes from others. Thus, it cannot be assumed that all of the scholars listed in the Roster of the Fellows of the Jesus Seminar (533–37) agree with everything presented in the commentaries to individual pericopes. The presence of their names in the roster, nevertheless, would seem to require them to bear some responsibility for the published results.

5. A. Schweitzer, *The Quest of the Historical Jesus,* with an introduction by J. M. Robinson (New York: Macmillan, 1968), trans. W. Montgomery from the first German edition, *Von Reimarus zur Wrede* (1906); the English translation was first published in 1910.

teaching of Jesus; it is a new creation that gradually unfolded out of a series of failed expectations.[6]

The story of the "quest of the historical Jesus," as told by Schweitzer, includes not only rationalist attempts at discrediting traditional Christian teaching, but also attempts by Christian theologians to fend off such critiques by creating an edifice of critical theological scholarship by which a believable "real Jesus" might emerge to view. The result, often enough, was a "modernized" Jesus, one whose ethical genius and message of a "spiritual kingdom" brought him close to the liberal ideas of nineteenth-century German Protestantism.

Schweitzer's own position on the historical Jesus, present from beginning to end in his famous book but developed especially at the end, is represented by what he calls "thoroughgoing eschatology." This is Schweitzer's lasting contribution to scholarship, even though his own reconstruction of Jesus' short career is open to considerable criticism.[7] Nineteenth-century research had opened up new insights into the study of Palestinian Judaism, on the basis of research into the so-called Pseudepigrapha of the Hebrew Bible that identified a prominent trend in Palestinian Judaism called "Jewish apocalyptic."[8] It was inevitable that the teachings and activity of Jesus would be examined in terms of their rela-

---

6. See the summary in ibid., 13–26. H. S. Reimarus's work *Von dem Zwecke Jesu und seiner Jünger* was published anonymously after his death by G. Lessing in 1778. There is now an English translation of this historic work: *The Goal of Jesus and His Disciples*, intro. and trans. G. W. Buchanan (Leiden: E. J. Brill, 1970).

7. See esp. Schweitzer, *Quest*, 330–97. Cf. A. Schweitzer, *The Mystery of the Kingdom of God: The Secret of Jesus' Messiahship and Passion* (New York: Macmillan, 1914), trans. W. Lowrie from the original German *Das Messianitäts und Leidensgeheimnis: Eine Skizze des Lebens Jesu* (1901). For a critical appraisal of Schweitzer's reconstruction, see Robinson's introduction in Schweitzer, *Quest*, xi–xxxiii. Robinson's critique is theologically oriented and presented from the vantage point of the "new quest of the historical Jesus" grounded in existentialist hermeneutics (discussed in this essay). Robinson does not take issue (in 1968) with Schweitzer's insistence on the eschatological nature of Jesus' ministry: "Schweitzer was correct on the issue of historical criticism, in affirming the eschatological nature of Jesus' ministry" (xx). However, Robinson is now more inclined to opt for a "paradigm shift," a nonapocalyptic Jesus derived from an alleged "preapocalyptic layer lying behind Q" (the hypothetical sayings source shared in common by the Gospels of Matthew and Luke). See Robinson, "The Q Trajectory: Between John and Matthew via Jesus," in Pearson, *Future*, 173–94 (quotation on 189). For a critique of this now popular attempt at finding "layers" in "Q," see R. Horsley, "Logoi Prophetōn: Reflections on the Genre of Q," in Pearson, *Future*, 195–209.

8. See the two volumes of *OTP*, edited by J. H. Charlesworth, esp. vol. 1, *Apocalyptic Literature and Testaments*. One of the most important of the OT Pseudepigrapha for NT study is *1 Enoch*, part of the OT canon of the Ethiopian Orthodox Church.

tionship to Jewish eschatology and to the apocalyptic worldview prominent in first-century Jewish Palestine.[9] Schweitzer's discussion of "the eschatological question" in his *Quest* culminates with his treatment of Johannes Weiss's epoch-making work on "the preaching of Jesus concerning the kingdom of God." Weiss had demonstrated unassailably that "the preaching of Jesus was purely eschatological."[10]

Eschatology as such, involving ideas of the last judgment, resurrection, and supernatural deliverance of the elect from temporal earthly existence, is quite foreign to modern (or "postmodern") ways of thinking, and it was inevitable that a scholarly struggle would be mounted against it as holding the key to Jesus' teachings.[11] Eschatology was equally distasteful to Albert Schweitzer himself, and herein lies his greatness as a scholar: As a critical historian, Schweitzer was constrained by the evidence to situate the historical Jesus squarely within his own temporal-geographic context in first-century Judaism. This Jesus is a foreigner to us: "The historical Jesus will be to our time a stranger and an enigma."[12]

Ever since Schweitzer, the eschatological paradigm, at least until recently, has been dominant in critical scholarship. But in our century, theologians have learned how to deal "hermeneutically" with an eschatological Jesus. Rudolf Bultmann, the preeminent New Testament scholar of the first half of the century, is a case in point. He could resolve in his own work the "either-or" proposition of Schweitzer: either "thoroughgoing skepticism" or "thoroughgoing

---

9. On "apocalypse" as a literary genre and "apocalyptic" or "apocalypticism" as a worldview, see, e.g., the articles in "Apocalypses and Apocalypticism," by P. D. Hanson and J. J. Collins, in *ABD*, 1:279–92, with extensive bibliography. The only "apocalypse" in the Hebrew Bible is Daniel (ca. 164 B.C.E.). The book of Revelation is the only "apocalypse" as such in the NT (cf. the "Little Apocalypse" in Mark 13 and parallels), but much of the NT reflects the apocalyptic worldview.

10. See Schweitzer, *Quest*, 223–41 (quotation on 241). See also J. Weiss, *Die Predigt Jesu vom Reiche Gottes* (Göttingen: Vandenhoeck & Ruprecht, 1892; 3d ed. pub. by Ferdinand Hahn, 1964). An English translation is available: *Jesus' Proclamation of the Kingdom of God*, trans. R. H. Hiers and D. L. Holland (Philadelphia: Fortress Press, 1971; repr. Chico, Calif.: Scholars Press, 1985).

11. See chapter 16, "The Struggle against Eschatology," in Schweitzer, *Quest*, 242–69.

12. Ibid., 399. Schweitzer nevertheless heard this stranger's call "Follow me!" (403). From 1913 until the end of his life in 1965, practicing medicine in French equatorial Africa, he tested the truth of the final words in his book: "To those who obey Him, whether they be wise or simple, He will reveal Himself in the toils, the conflicts, the sufferings which they shall pass through in His fellowship, and, as an ineffable mystery, they shall learn in their own experience Who He is" (403). Schweitzer received the Nobel Peace Prize in 1952.

eschatology."[13] In his classic treatment of the historical Jesus, *Jesus and the Word,* Bultmann asserted that "we can now know almost nothing concerning the life and personality of Jesus, since the early Christian sources show no interest in either, are moreover fragmentary and often legendary."[14] What can be discovered, on the basis of critical assessment of the earliest Palestinian level of tradition, is the essentials of Jesus' message, his "word." This "word" has to do with the coming of the kingdom of God, a "miraculous eschatological event," but one that has to be interpreted existentially: "The Kingdom of God is a power which, although it is entirely future, wholly determines the present . . . because it now compels man to decision."[15] For Bultmann, a scholarly "quest of the historical Jesus" is not only impossible but theologically illegitimate, because it substitutes worldly proof for faith.

This was the dominant position of the Bultmann school until 1953, when one of Bultmann's students, Ernst Käsemann, in a famous address to the annual gathering of the "old Marburgers" (i.e., fellow Bultmannians), proposed that some interest in the historical Jesus is theologically valid, since the Lord of the church cannot be viewed completely as a mythological being, unconnected to his historical existence. Käsemann's statement set in motion what came to be called the "new quest of the historical Jesus."[16] This quest was "new" in the sense that scholarly interest in the historical Jesus, eschewed by Bultmann, was coupled with Bultmann's existentialist hermeneutics. In this view there is, after all, a connection between the eschatological message of Jesus and the christological kerygma ("proclamation") of the church.[17]

It is to be noted that scholars embarking on the "new quest," though not lacking interest in key events of Jesus' life, were, like Bultmann himself, primarily interested in the *message* of Jesus and the essentials of his teaching. To get at this teaching, critical study of the gospel traditions was required, including the applica-

---

13. See chapter 19 of ibid., 330–97.

14. R. Bultmann, *Jesus and the Word* (New York: Scribner's, 1934), trans. L. P. Smith and E. H. Lantero from the original German *Jesus* (1926), 8.

15. Ibid., 45, 51.

16. See esp. J. M. Robinson, *A New Quest of the Historical Jesus,* SBT 25 (London: SCM, 1959). The first book on the historical Jesus produced in the Bultmann school since Bultmann's own *Jesus and the Word* was G. Bornkamm, *Jesus von Nazareth* (Stuttgart: Kohlhammer, 1956), translated as *Jesus of Nazareth* (New York: Harper & Brothers, 1960).

17. Robinson, *New Quest,* esp. 12–13.

tion of form criticism and other critical tools.[18] Criteria also had to be devised for determining the authenticity of individual sayings of Jesus. The most important of these criteria, already used by Bultmann, was dubbed by Norman Perrin "the criterion of dissimilarity": "The earliest form of a saying we can reach may be regarded as authentic if it can be shown to be dissimilar to characteristic emphases both of ancient Judaism and of the early Church."[19] Though it is not denied that Jesus' teaching consisted of "variations on themes from the religious life of ancient Judaism," nevertheless, "if we are to seek that which is most characteristic of Jesus," it will be found in the things wherein he differs from Judaism, such things as would be "new and startling to Jewish ears."[20] An unstated premise here, of course, is that Jesus was unique among his contemporaries.

While the "new quest" was dominating German scholarship and the American scholarship influenced by it, the "old quest" was proceeding as usual in places like Great Britain and North America. More recently there has developed what is sometimes referred to as the "third quest,"[21] exemplified by a spate of books continuing unabated. This "third quest," unlike the "new" one, lacks a unifying theological agenda, but it is also distinguishable from the first two quests in claiming to lack *any* theological agenda. The unifying factor in works of this type is the claim that critical historical research, involving careful sifting of the sources, can lead to positive knowledge about who Jesus was. The most important feature of much of the current work is the attempt to situate Jesus squarely within the context of first-century Palestine and Second Temple Judaism.[22]

---

18. The classic book on the form criticism of the Gospels is R. Bultmann, *History of the Synoptic Tradition*, 2d ed. (Oxford: Blackwell; New York: Harper & Row, 1968), trans. J. Marsh from the 2d edition of *Geschichte der synoptischen Tradition* (Göttingen: Vandenhoeck & Ruprecht, 1958), first published in 1921.

19. N. Perrin, *Rediscovering the Teaching of Jesus* (New York: Harper & Row, 1967), 39.

20. Ibid., 39–40. Perrin goes on to discuss "coherence" and "multiple attestation," criteria subsidiary to that of "dissimilarity" (43–47).

21. See, e.g., N. T. Wright's article "Quest for the Historical Jesus," part of the larger entry "Jesus Christ," in *ABD*, 3:796–802.

22. It is not feasible to try to list here all of the relevant current works representing the "third quest," but I cannot refrain from citing the most ambitious and meticulous of them, J. P. Meier's *A Marginal Jew: Rethinking the Historical Jesus* (New York: Doubleday, 1991–). Two volumes have been published (1991, 1994), and a third is forthcoming. For a good survey of recent work, see B. Chilton and C. Evans, eds., *Studying the Historical Jesus: Evaluations of the State of Current Research*, NTTS 19 (Leiden: E. J. Brill, 1994).

Another interesting aspect of some of the current research is the use of theoretical models drawn from the social sciences to shed light on the sociopolitical context in which Jesus operated. Gerd Theissen, for example, sees Jesus as the founder of a "renewal movement within Judaism" and proceeds to subject this "Jesus Movement" (active 30–70 C.E.) to a functional sociological analysis.[23] Jesus and some of his followers are depicted as "wandering charismatics" dependent on sympathizers in the local villages. At one point in his discussion, Theissen cites an interesting analogy in the larger gentile world: "The wandering Cynic philosophers are in some way analogous to the earliest Christian wandering charismatics. They too seem to have led a vagabond existence and also to have renounced home, families, and possessions."[24]

The Cynics, it will be recalled, were itinerant preachers of a philosophy of freedom from every constraint and a life lived with minimal requirements "according to nature." Flouting social convention, they derived their name (*kynikoi,* "dog-like") from an epithet applied to one of their founders, "the Dog" Diogenes (of Sinope, fourth century B.C.E.), who went about Athens doing in public everything that a dog might do, all the while hurling insults on his contemporaries. The following chreia,[25] among many preserved by Diogenes Laertius, is typical: "One time while masturbating in the market place he said, 'Would that it were possible to relieve hunger simply by rubbing the belly'" (*Lives of Eminent Philosophers* 6.46).[26]

Since virtually anything seems to be possible nowadays in New Testament scholarship, it was almost a foregone conclusion that Gerd Theissen's throwaway analogy would issue in a number of books and articles depicting Jesus as a Cynic. F. Gerald Downing set about assembling what he took to be "parallels" from the Cynic (but also Stoic!) tradition to items in the Jesus tradition,[27] and ar-

---

23. G. Theissen, *Sociology of Early Palestinian Christianity* (Philadelphia: Fortress Press, 1978), translated from the German *Soziologie der Jesusbewegung* (Munich: Kaiser Verlag, 1977).

24. Ibid., 14–15.

25. A chreia ("anecdotal maxim") is a literary or rhetorical form consisting of a pregnant saying provided with a brief narrative context. The form occurs widely in Hellenistic and Jewish literature, including the NT Gospels. Bultmann referred to this form as an "apophthegm." See his *History of the Synoptic Tradition,* 11–69.

26. My translation. Hicks's translation in the LCL edition translates χειρουργῶν (lit. "working by hand") more demurely as "behaving indecently."

27. F. G. Downing, *Christ and the Cynics* (Sheffield: JSOT, 1988). One might just as easily plumb the Epicurean tradition in the same fashion for evidence that Jesus was really an Epicurean. That Jesus' teaching "closely resembles the real teaching

gues in a more recent work that Cynics could have been active in Galilee in Jesus' day because the example of Jesus proves it![28]

This brings us to the recent work of John Dominic Crossan, *The Historical Jesus: The Life of a Mediterranean Jewish Peasant,* whose dust jacket advertises it as "the first comprehensive determination of who Jesus was, what he did, what he said"![29] According to Crossan, the eschatological Jesus was foisted on the tradition by the early church. Jesus himself rejected the eschatological message of John the Baptist and adopted an "egalitarian" and "sapiential" teaching and demeanor appropriate to his peasant background. Crossan's handling of his sources produces an astonishing conclusion in what most people would regard as an oxymoron: "The historical Jesus was, then, a *peasant Jewish Cynic.*"[30]

One can only wonder how Crossan could reach this conclusion, but at least part of the answer is conveniently found in appendix 1 of his book, "An Inventory of the Jesus Tradition by Chronological Stratification and Independent Attestation."[31] Trickster-like, Crossan deftly sets standard critical scholarship on its head by assigning to the earliest stratum (30–60 C.E.) such sources as a supposed "first layer" of the *Gospel of Thomas,* Papyrus Egerton 2 and other papyrus fragments, and the *Gospel of the Hebrews,* writings usually assigned to the second century.[32] He even invents a new gospel of his own, the "Cross Gospel," which he reconstructs out of the second-century *Gospel of Peter* and assigns to this period.[33] To the "second stratum" of tradition (60–80 C.E.) he assigns the *Gospel of the Egyptians,* his "second layer" of the *Gospel of Thomas,* and a hypothetical "Dialogue Collection" embedded in the *Dialogue of the Savior,* one of the Coptic texts of the

---

of Epicurus" was the view of W. Kirchbach (*Was lehrte Jesus? Zwei Urevangelien* [Berlin, 1897]), according to Schweitzer's account (*Quest,* 324). Anyone wanting to update Kirchbach's work will be glad to know about B. Inwood and L. P. Gerson, eds., *The Epicurus Reader: Selected Writings and Testimonia* (Indianapolis: Hacket Publishing, 1991).

28. See F. G. Downing, *Cynics and Christian Origins* (Edinburgh: T. & T. Clark, 1992). For a good critical discussion of this thesis, see P. R. Eddy, "Jesus as Diogenes? Reflections on the Cynic Jesus Thesis," *JBL* 115 (1996): 449–69.

29. J. D. Crossan, *The Historical Jesus: The Life of a Mediterranean Jewish Peasant* (San Francisco: HarperSanFrancisco, 1991).

30. Ibid., 421 (Crossan's italics).

31. Ibid., 427–50.

32. See *NTApoc,* vol. 1, *Gospels and Related Writings.* For the items cited here, see 96–99, 110–33, 172–78, and 216–27.

33. J. D. Crossan makes his case for the "Cross Gospel" in another ponderous tome, *The Cross That Spoke: The Origins of the Passion Narrative* (San Francisco: Harper & Row, 1988). I know of no one who accepts Crossan's reconstruction.

Nag Hammadi corpus (NHC III,5).[34] Thus, items in early Christian literature that betray a de-eschatologization of tradition are now taken as evidence for a "preapocalyptic" Jesus.

Crossan is co-chair of the Jesus Seminar and has obviously played a prominent role in the making of *The Five Gospels*. To this work we now return.[35]

The Methodology of the Jesus Seminar

We have already discussed the procedures by which the Jesus Seminar came to its results as published in *The Five Gospels*. As we saw, the aim of the seminar was to answer the question, "What did Jesus really say?" The second question, "What did Jesus really do?" was put off to a second phase of the project. But this separation of "word" from "deed" is untenable and leads to a distortion of the evidence. Jesus is presented as a "talking head,"[36] one that bears little or no relationship to what the historical Jesus — the head's body — did or what was done to him, from his (highly significant) baptism by John to his (also highly significant) death on a Roman cross. "Actions speak louder than words," and that is especially true of symbolic actions.[37] Thus, a much better case could be made for asking the "deeds" question first and then situating the sayings into that framework, as has been done by E. P. Sanders, for example.[38] The Jesus Seminar's exclusive attention to the sayings tradition, reminiscent of the emphases of the now old "new quest," inevitably issues in skewed results.

34. See *NTApoc*, 1:209–15, 300–311. In the case of *Dial. Sav.*, the existence of an earlier dialogue source is plausible. See esp. the introduction by H. Koester and E. Pagels in *Nag Hammadi Codex III,5: The Dialogue of the Savior*, ed. S. Emmel, NHS 26 (Leiden: E. J. Brill, 1984), 1–17. Koester and Pagels assign a late-first-century date to the dialogue source and a date in the early second century to the tractate as a whole.

35. Subsequent page references to this book are given parenthetically in the text.

36. This expression is used in a highly critical review of the Jesus Seminar by R. B. Hays, "The Corrected Jesus," in *First Things* 43 (May 1994): 43–48, esp. 46.

37. For example, silent burning of the American flag is (at least so far!) protected under the "free speech" amendment of the U.S. Constitution.

38. See E. P. Sanders, *Jesus and Judaism* (Philadelphia: Fortress Press, 1985). Sanders lists eight "almost indisputable facts" that he takes as his starting point (11): Jesus was baptized by John the Baptist; Jesus was a Galilean who preached and healed; Jesus called disciples and spoke of there being twelve; Jesus confined his activity to Israel; Jesus engaged in a controversy about the Temple; Jesus was crucified outside Jerusalem by the Roman authorities; after his death, Jesus' followers continued as an identifiable movement; and at least some Jews persecuted at least parts of the new movement. See also E. P. Sanders, *The Historical Figure of Jesus* (London: Penguin, 1993).

rules of historical inquiry

In its assessment of the sayings tradition, the Jesus Seminar adopted an important rule: "Canonical boundaries are irrelevant in critical assessments of the various sources of information about Jesus" (35). All words attributed to Jesus in extant material from the first three centuries C.E., canonical and noncanonical, were taken into account. This is consonant with the stated intent of the seminar, to act "in accordance with the canons of historical inquiry" (35). This is one of the more laudable aspects of the work of the Jesus Seminar, at least as a statement of intent. Thus, the *Gospel of Thomas,* a collection of sayings of Jesus, is included as the fifth gospel in *The Five Gospels,* and fragmentary sayings material is also often included in the commentary.

The dating of some of these sources, however, is open to criticism. In a "cameo essay" entitled "Stages in the Development of Early Christian Tradition" (128),[39] dates are assigned to the earliest sources, both actual and hypothetical. For example, a supposed "first edition" of the *Gospel of Thomas* is assigned to the same period as the hypothetical sayings source "Q" (50–60 C.E.), and its "surviving edition" (more plausibly) to between 100 and 150. No convincing case can be made, however, for an early "first edition" of the *Gospel of Thomas.* Although some of its 113 sayings may put us in touch with very early tradition independent of the canonical gospels, such a finding can be made only by close analysis of each individual saying. The redacted version of the sayings in the *Gospel of Thomas* represents a de-eschatologization of the tradition and is furthermore completely dominated by a (probably Syrian) type of Christianity oriented to mysticism and informed by a myth of the descent and ascent of the soul.[40] The assumptions about the *Gospel of Thomas* made by the Jesus Seminar are quite naive, though in fact even the seminar found only two of this gospel's singly attested sayings (i.e., sayings lacking canonical parallels) — sayings 97 and 98 — to warrant so much as a pink rating, a judgment with which I have no quarrel.

The seminar's use of the *Gospel of Thomas* reflects a current trend in North American (not European or British) scholarship, that is, among some of those who take the *Gospel of Thomas* seriously as a potential source for Jesus tradition independent of the

---

39. See also the cameo essay "The Discovery of the Gospel of Thomas" (474).

40. On this variety of early Christianity, see Layton, *Gnostic Scriptures,* 359–409. G. J. Riley, in his *Resurrection Reconsidered: Thomas and John in Controversy* (Minneapolis: Fortress Press, 1995), argues for an early date for the beginnings of the "Thomas tradition" but not for *Gos. Thom.* as we know it.

synoptic Gospels, and who see this gospel as closely related to the hypothetical "Q" source.[41] What is often involved in their work is a confusion of categories that results in flawed conclusions regarding both sayings collections: First, judgments made about the early date of "Q" or its supposed "layers" lead to the supposition that the *Gospel of Thomas,* as a collection of Jesus' sayings formally comparable to "Q," is early. Second, the sayings source "Q" is now taken as a sayings "gospel" on the analogy of the (secondary) title of the *Gospel of Thomas;* and then come unfounded assumptions about the "community" for which "Q" served as its "gospel" (more on this to follow). But this begs the question as to the function of "Q" in the communities that used it. The Gospels of Luke and Matthew, at least, show that "Q" was used in their communities not as an alternative "gospel" at all, but together with the story of Jesus. The story tells about the authoritative person who speaks in the collection of sayings attributed to him. But the Jesus Seminar is oblivious to these problems.

Much of the methodology of the Jesus Seminar is standard and is based on the results of two centuries of critical scholarship. The basic critical approach is presented in a discussion of seven "pillars of scholarly wisdom" in the introduction to *The Five Gospels* (3– 5). The first four of these are as follows:

1. The distinction between the historical Jesus and the Christ of Christian faith

2. Preference for the synoptic Gospels (Matthew, Mark, and Luke) over John as sources for the historical Jesus

3. The chronological priority of the Gospel of Mark

4. The hypothetical source "Q" used independently by Matthew and Luke

These four pillars represent findings of nineteenth-century scholarship now commonly accepted. The last three reflect more recent trends:

5. "The liberation of the non-eschatological Jesus...from Schweitzer's eschatological Jesus" (4)

6. The fundamental contrast between an oral culture, such as that of Jesus, and a print culture

---

41. See, e.g., W. E. Arnal, "The Rhetoric of Marginality: Apocalypticism, Gnosticism, and Sayings Gospels," *HTR* 88 (1995): 471–94. Other items are cited in subsequent discussion here.

7. The "burden of proof" on those who argue for authenticity, rather than on those who argue for inauthenticity

The last two "pillars" lead to the development of elaborate "rules of oral evidence" and "rules of attestation" which reflect refinements of older discussions of form-history and criteria for determining authenticity, such as "multiple attestation" (25–30).[42]

One interesting holdover from the old "new quest" is the criterion of dissimilarity, referred to here as "distinctive discourse" (30). The "distinctiveness" of Jesus vis-à-vis the early Christian tradition is, of course, one of the refinements of the first "pillar of scholarly wisdom." That "Jesus was not the first Christian" (24) is a fundamental starting point for critical research in the study of the Jesus tradition, for there can be no denying that early Christian faith has not only preserved but also heavily affected the Jesus tradition. The other side of this criterion, however, is not so obvious. The Jesus Seminar describes Jesus' "distinctive discourse" as follows: "Jesus' characteristic talk was distinctive"; "Jesus' sayings and parables cut against the social and religious grain"; "Jesus' sayings and parables surprise and shock: they characteristically call for a reversal of roles or frustrate ordinary, everyday expectations" (30–31). Although there is some truth to these observations, such as the "call for a reversal of roles" that is prominent in the Jesus tradition, the overall thrust of the application of this emphasis on the "distinctiveness" of Jesus in the work of the Jesus Seminar is that the historical Jesus must be viewed *over against* the Jewish society and religion in which he was reared.

The key feature of the Jesus Seminar's method, which also inevitably results in the rejection of 82 percent of the sayings tradition from the database of Jesus' authentic sayings, is reflected in pillar 5, the rejection of eschatology. The following comments are highly instructive:

> The eschatological Jesus reigned supreme among gospel scholars from the time of Weiss and Schweitzer to the end of World War II. Slowly and surely the evidence began to erode that view.... The creation of the Jesus Seminar coincides with the reemergence of interest in the Jesus of history, which was made possible by the wholesale shift of biblical scholarship away from its earlier academic home in the church, seminaries, and isolated theological enclaves.... As that interest came

---

42. See n. 20.

back to life in the 1970s and 1980s, scholars were surprised
to learn that they no longer labored under the tyranny of
either neo-orthodoxy or an eschatological Jesus.... The liberation of the non-eschatological Jesus of the aphorisms and
parables from Schweitzer's eschatological Jesus is the fifth
pillar of contemporary scholarship. (3–4)

The "evidence" leading to the "erosion" of the eschatological
Jesus paradigm is not cited, for the very good reason that it does
not exist! On the contrary, all of the real evidence that has come
to light since Weiss and Schweitzer — the massive evidence now
available in the Dead Sea Scrolls is probably the most important —
only serves to confirm the fact that the apocalyptic worldview was
pervasive in first-century Jewish Palestine. This evidence is of direct relevance to the study of the historical Jesus.[43] So one begins
to wonder about a possible "hidden agenda" in the rejection of
eschatology by the Jesus Seminar.

With the gospel of "liberation" from the "tyranny" of the eschatological Jesus so fervently embraced, what paradigm does the
Jesus Seminar propose to put in its place? Answer: "the laconic
sage":

Jesus does not as a rule initiate dialogue or debate, nor does
he offer to cure people.... Jesus rarely makes pronouncements or speaks about himself in the first person.... Jesus
makes no claim to be the Anointed, or messiah.... Like the
cowboy hero of the American West exemplified by Gary
Cooper, the sage of the ancient Near East was laconic, slow
to speech, a person of few words. The sage does not provoke
encounters.... As a rule, the sage is self-effacing, modest,
unostentatious. (32)

Obvious questions that the Jesus Seminar has not entertained
in The Five Gospels but would presumably have to be faced in
its second phase of work are these: Who would want to crucify a
laconic sage, even one whose discourse is "distinctive"? And why?

Historical Premises of the Jesus Seminar

The approach taken by the Jesus Seminar brings with it a number
of historical premises, most of them unwarranted or insupportable.

43. See esp. C. A. Evans, *Jesus and His Contemporaries: Comparative Studies,*
AGJU 25 (Leiden: E. J. Brill, 1995), esp. 83–154 on the Qumran material. See also
n. 62.

These premises inform the choice of colors to be assigned to the sayings of Jesus. Some of these premises arise from the seminar's a priori rejection of eschatology; others are based on other factors. Here are my comments on a few of them:

1. John "the Baptist" is one of the more colorful figures in first-century Palestine, as is attested both in the New Testament and in the writings of the Jewish historian Josephus (see *Ant.* 18.116–19). Preaching a message of repentance in preparation for the coming of God in judgment, he offered his hearers a purificatory bath ("baptism") in the waters of the Jordan River as a sign of their repentance and the forgiveness of their sins. This would enable them to escape the wrath of God's coming judgment and the "unquenchable fire" of hell (Matt 3:1–12 and parallels). We do not know the names of very many of the Jews who underwent this baptism and became John's followers, but we do know the name of one: Yeshuʻa bar Yoseph of Nazareth (or "Nazara"), better known as Jesus of Nazareth.

The Jesus Seminar will now have us believe that Jesus, after his baptism by John, rejected John's "mentality" of impending cataclysm, "quit the ascetic desert, and returned to urban Galilee," where he "took up eating and drinking and consorting with toll collectors and sinners, and developed a different point of view" (4), one much like that of "the Cynic philosophers who probably wandered about Galilee in Jesus' day" (316). The apocalyptic worldview characteristic of John the Baptist and early Christians such as Paul was attributed to Jesus by his followers after his death; they, in turn, had learned it from John the Baptist (40–41, 135). Jesus himself did not proclaim "that the end of the age was near"; rather, he "spoke most characteristically of God's rule as close or already present but unrecognized" (40). Accordingly, virtually all of the sayings in the Jesus tradition that refer to the future kingdom of God or judgment, rewards, and punishments after death are colored black by the seminar. By what canon of historiography such a view of Jesus is developed is a mystery, for not only is it intrinsically improbable, but it strains credulity to the breaking point.

That early Christians reinterpreted Jesus' message in the interests of their developing christology is, of course, most probable, but these early Christians also preserved much of Jesus' own teaching. Indeed, a commonsense application of historical method can distinguish between Jesus' eschatology, which focused on the "coming" of God's "kingdom" or "rule," and that of the early church, which focused on the "coming" (i.e., return) of Jesus as the heavenly "Son of Man" (presumably in view of the nonarrival of the kingdom coupled with a belief in his resurrection from the dead). Jesus referred to himself enigmatically as "the Son of Man"; it is probably early Christian interpretation of the Jesus tradition that explicated this self-designation in terms of an interpretation of Daniel 7:13, with its reference to "one like a son of man coming with the clouds of heaven."[44] Thus, there is a clear distinction between the expectation of a coming "kingdom" and the expectation of a coming heavenly "Son of Man."[45] To attribute the latter to early Christian interpretation is fully in accord with intrinsic probability, but it is intrinsically improbable that both are the product of early Christian interpretation. Even more improbable is the notion that early Christians consciously rejected a noneschatological message of Jesus in favor of one gotten from John the Baptist, whose message Jesus himself is supposed to have rejected. But this is the view of the Jesus Seminar and the premise upon which it colors Jesus' eschatological sayings black. Of course, it also has to color black Jesus' depiction of John as "more than a prophet" and as the "messenger" predicted in Malachi 3:1 (Matt 11:9–10 ‖ Luke 7:26–27, a "Q" saying), and similar sayings about John.

2. How did the Jesus tradition get its eschatology? The Jesus Seminar has a ready answer: from "Q people." These are people who carried out some sort of (unspecified) mission in Galilee and who resentfully developed a message of judgment against people of villages there who did not respond positively. For example, the "woes" (which the Jesus Seminar transforms into curses, as I will discuss presently in this essay) against Chorazin, Bethsaida, and Capernaum (Matt 11:20–24 ‖ Luke 10:13–15, "Q") were not pronounced by Jesus but by "prophets" of the "Q community" (181, 320). Jesus' refusal to provide any "sign" except that of Jonah, and his prophecy of judgment against "this generation" (Matt 12:38–42 ‖ Luke 11:29–32, "Q") are likewise attributed to

---

44. The interpretation of the "Son of Man" sayings in the Gospels is one of the most contentious topics in NT research. My own view, reflected here though not elaborated, is only one of many possibilities. See the excellent summary by G. W. E. Nickelsburg in his article "Son of Man," in *ABD*, 6:137–50, with extensive bibliography.

45. An illustration of this distinction is found in a comparison between Mark 9:1, where Jesus predicts the imminent coming of the "kingdom of God," and its parallel in Matt 16:28, where he predicts the imminent "coming in his kingdom" of "the Son of Man." One of the problems in Schweitzer's reconstruction of the historical Jesus is that he failed to notice this distinction. See n. 7.

the "Q community" on the grounds that Jesus "did not share the common apocalyptic view that the end of history was near, nor did he threaten judgment" (332; cf. 188). One finds throughout *The Five Gospels* such references to the "Q community" or "Q people," supposedly active in Galilee in the period ca. 40–60 C.E. Who were these people?

That there were followers of Jesus in Galilee after his death is indeed probable. The problem is that we have no evidence at all about them. The only Galilean followers of Jesus of whom we have any record are the ones referred to in the Acts of the Apostles (chaps. 1–12) as being active in the formation of the church in *Jerusalem,* people like Simon Peter and Jesus' brother James (Jacob). We can suppose (though the Jesus Seminar does not) that the Galileans in Jerusalem were in contact with those back home in Galilee and later with Jesus believers in places like Caesarea and Antioch on the Orontes, but our evidence is scanty (Acts 10–15). The "Q community" of the Jesus Seminar is, in fact, extrapolated from a supposed "apocalyptic" "second layer" of the hypothetical "Q," and lacks any evidentiary support. Indeed, it is not all that obvious that the authors of Matthew and Luke got their copies of "Q" from co-religionists in Galilee or that "Q" was produced there. So the Galilean "Q community" is simply a figment of scholarly imagination.[46]

3. One of the items in the gospel tradition that is usually taken for granted is that Jesus had twelve disciples.[47] The Jesus Seminar would seem to dispute this, although the issue of "the Twelve" as such is not discussed. The seminar grants that Jesus had followers, both men and women, but it argues that Jesus did not actively recruit them. Thus, Jesus' call to Simon and Andrew (Mark 1:17) is colored gray. It is argued that Jesus, as "an itinerant sage without institutional goals," did not recruit people but might have used the metaphor of "fishing for people" in another context (41).

---

46. For two recent examples of imagination run amok in "Q" scholarship, see B. Mack, *The Lost Gospel* (San Francisco: HarperSanFrancisco, 1993); and L. Vaage, *Galilean Upstarts: Jesus' First Followers according to Q* (Valley Forge, Pa.: Trinity Press International, 1994). For a critique of Mack, see J. M. Robinson, "The History and Religious Taxonomy of Q: The Cynic Hypothesis," in *Gnosisforschung und Religionsgeschichte: Festschrift für Kurt Rudolph zum 65 Geburtstag,* ed. H. Preissler and H. Seiwert (Marburg: Diagonal-Verlag, 1994 [1995]), 247–65. For a similar critique of Vaage, see Robinson, "*Galilean Upstarts:* A Sot's Cynical Disciples," *Sayings of Jesus: Canonical and Non-Canonical: Essays in Honour of Tjitze Baarda,* ed. W. L. Petersen, J. S. Vos, and H. J. de Jonge, NovTSup (Leiden: E. J. Brill, 1997), 223–49.

47. This is one of the "almost indisputable facts" cited by Sanders (see n. 38).

Elsewhere the exhortation "Follow me" is colored black, with one exception: "Follow me, and leave it to the dead to bury their own dead" (Matt 8:22 ‖ Luke 9:59–60, "Q"). This reply to a would-be follower who first wants to bury his father is colored pink on the grounds that it "contradicts traditional familial relationships" and advises the potential follower "to dishonor his father," something that was not only socially unacceptable but a violation of one of the Ten Commandments (160, 317). This interpretation of the pericope requires us to assume that the potential follower is actually arranging for, or about to arrange for, the burial of a father who has just died, something that is not given in the text.[48] In any case, Jesus' attitude toward the commandment in question is clearly enough stated in a discussion with some Pharisees in which he brings up their *halakah* (legal interpretation, lit. "walking") of *qorban* (meaning "consecrated to God"), a passage that the seminar regards as inauthentic (Matt 15:3–9, gray ‖ Mark 7:6–8, black).

As Jesus did not recruit followers for a special mission, so also did he not have a "mission" of his own: "He probably did not think of his work as a program he was sent to carry out" (47). Accordingly, all of the "I have come…" pronouncements of Jesus — that is, those announcing his mission (e.g., Mark 2:17; Luke 12: 49–51) — are regarded by the seminar as inauthentic (343).

4. It is usually assumed by critical scholars that Jesus restricted his activity to Israel, that is, to his fellow Jews.[49] The Jesus Seminar, however, believes that "a restricted mission was not characteristic of Jesus." Thus, Jesus' command to his disciples not to go to non-Israelites or Samaritans but to restrict their activity to "the lost sheep of the house of Israel" (Matt 10:5–6) is colored black, as reflecting "the point of view of a Judaizing branch" of the early church (167–68). Jesus himself "is believed to have had frequent contact with gentiles in the towns and cities around the Sea of Galilee" (204), presumably to stay in touch with the (historically unattested) "Cynic philosophers who probably wandered about Galilee in Jesus' day" (316).

---

48. The seminar's interpretation of this passage is a common one, especially in German scholarship, and, surprisingly, is upheld even by E. P. Sanders (*Jesus and Judaism*, 252–55). G. Vermes provides a more plausible scenario: the man's father is not dead yet, and the son's eventual filial responsibility is an excuse for procrastination. See Vermes's *The Religion of Jesus the Jew* (Minneapolis: Fortress Press, 1993), 27–29.

49. This is another of Sander's "almost indisputable facts" (see n. 38).

In fact, there were a number of predominantly gentile cities in Galilee. The most important of these were Tiberias, on the shore of the lake, and Sepphoris, a rather short distance from Jesus' home village of Nazareth (ca. 7 km as the crow flies). But these cities are conspicuous in the gospel tradition by their absence. The geographical information we have, such as it is, suggests that Jesus restricted his activity, for the most part, to the Jewish villages of rural Galilee.

Tyre and Sidon, on the Phoenician coast, are mentioned in the tradition, but it is not reported that Jesus went into these cities, only that he spent some time in their "environs" (μέρη, lit. "parts"; Matt 15:21; par.), where he is reported to have healed a "Canaanite" or "Syrophoenician" woman's daughter (Mark 7:26). Zarephath, a place located between Tyre and Sidon, was the site of a healing miracle reportedly performed by Elijah (1 Kgs 17:17–24), an event mentioned in one of Jesus' sayings (Luke 4:26, colored black by the seminar). But why Jesus went to this district, if he did, we do not know.

Similarly, Caesarea Philippi appears in the sources (Banias in northern Gaulanitis, the site of a sacred grotto dedicated to the god Pan, now part of the Golan), but again Jesus is not represented as going into the city but only its "environs" (μέρη; Matt 16:13) or "villages" (κῶμαι; Mark 8:27). The site of Peter's "confession" (Mark 8:27–30; par.), the area, located at the foot of Mount Hermon, was part of Israel's "sacred geography."[50]

The Decapolis, east of the Sea of Galilee, is also mentioned in the tradition (Matt 4:25; Mark 5:20; 7:31). The well-known story of Jesus' exorcism of demons who entered swine and caused them to plunge into the lake to their deaths (Matt 8:28–34 ‖ Mark 5:1–20 ‖ Luke 8:26–39) is variously located in the "region of the Gadarenes" (χώραν τῶν Γαδαρηνῶν; Matt 8:28) or the "region of the Gerasenes" (χώραν τῶν Γερασηνῶν; Mark 5:1 ‖ Luke 8:26). Gadara, modern Umm Qeis, the home of the Cynic philosopher Menippus (third century B.C.E.) and the Epicurean philosopher Philodemus (first century B.C.E.),[51] and Gerasa, modern Jerash, were both prominent cities of the Decapolis (= "ten cities"). It is noteworthy that the textual variant Γεργεσηνῶν, "of the Gergesenes," appears in all three Gospels, as is attested in numerous

---

50. See G. W. E. Nickelsburg, "Enoch, Levi, and Peter: Recipients of Revelation in Upper Galilee," *JBL* 100 (1981): 575–600, esp. 582–86 and 590–600.

51. Passages from Philodemus's treatise *On Piety* are quoted in chapter 4 of this book.

manuscripts and versions, and this may very well be the correct reading. Gadara is located at a considerable distance from the Sea of Galilee, Gerasa even further. The obscure Gergesa, modern Kursi, is located on the lakeshore, a more likely setting for the exorcism story.[52] The manuscript tradition, with its variants, probably reflects a scribal substitution of more familiar places in the Decapolis — Gadara and Gerasa — for the obscure Gergesa. To be sure, one cannot necessarily take as historically reliable all of the geographical references in the gospel tradition, or the stories associated with them, but it is a telling fact that in no case at all is there any reference to "urban Galilee" (4) or the gentile cities as the locus of Jesus' activity![53]

5. The assumption that Jesus had regular contact with gentiles in their urban centers leads to a gross misunderstanding of Jesus' relationship to the Jewish Law. We have already encountered the claim that Jesus advocated violating one of the Ten Commandments (160, 317). Thus, it is no surprise to find the Jesus Seminar claiming that Jesus set about "undermining a whole way of life" by hurling "a categorical challenge to the laws governing pollution and purity" (69). This claim is based on the saying "It's not what goes into a person from the outside that can defile; rather it's what comes out of the person that defiles" (Mark 7:14 ‖ Matt 15:11 ‖ *Gos. Thom.* 14, colored pink). The saying in question, set in the context of Jesus' challenge to a specific Pharisaic *halakah* regarding hand washing, does not represent "a categorical challenge to the laws," because there were so such "laws" in the Torah, only, in this case, a Pharisaic opinion regarding purity. In Mark 7:19b (without

---

52. For a brief but useful discussion, see J. J. Rousseau and R. Arav, *Jesus and His World: An Archaeological and Cultural Dictionary* (Minneapolis: Fortress Press, 1995), 97–99.

53. There is considerable literature on the question of the extent of Jewish cultural and religious influence in Galilee. For a recent discussion, see S. Safrai, "The Jewish Cultural Nature of Galilee in the First Century," in *The New Testament and Christian Jewish Dialogue: Studies in Honor of David Flusser,* ed. M. Lowe, *Immanuel* 24–25 (1990); 147–86. For recent discussions of the archaeological evidence and its bearing on Jesus research, see J. F. Strange, "First-Century Galilee from Archaeology and from the Texts"; R. A. Horsley, "The Historical Jesus and Archaeology of the Galilee: Questions from Historical Jesus Research to Archaeologists"; and D. E. Oakman, "The Archaeology of First-Century Galilee and the Social Interpretation of the Historical Jesus," in SBLSP (1994), 81–90, 91–135, 220–51. See also S. Freyne, "Jesus and the Urban Culture of Galilee," in *Texts and Contexts: Biblical Texts in Their Textual and Situational Contexts, Essays in Honor of Lars Hartman,* ed. T. Fornberg and D. Hellholm (Oslo: Scandinavian University Press, 1995), 597–622; and R. A. Horsley, *Galilee: History, Politics, People* (Valley Forge, Pa.: Trinity Press International, 1995).

par.) we read (in the RSV) the following parenthetical comment: "(Thus he declared all foods clean)."[54] This is clearly a late gloss, representing a gentile Christian misunderstanding of Jesus' saying. Though the Jesus Seminar takes no notice of this gloss in its translation, its interpretation of the saying is in accord with this gentile misunderstanding and is just as perverse as an interpretation of Jesus' own pronouncement!

Similarly, Jesus' injunction to traveling disciples, "Whenever you enter a town and they welcome you, eat whatever is set before you" (Luke 10:8, colored pink), is taken by the Jesus Seminar as an indication that Jesus advocated a nonobservance of kosher laws (319) or indeed that "Jesus apparently ignored, or deliberately transgressed, food laws" (481, commenting on the [obviously secondary] parallel in *Gos. Thom.* 14). But this interpretation is possible only if we accept the assumption of the Jesus Seminar that Jesus regularly dined in gentile homes, which we have no reason to believe is the case. In fact, there is not a single instance in the Jesus tradition, including the database accepted by the seminar as authentic, in which it can be shown that Jesus violates, or counsels others to violate, the Jewish Law.[55]

Consistent with the Jesus Seminar's portrayal of Jesus as a habitual violator of the Law is its representation of him as a "party animal" with a reputation for being "a glutton and a drunk" (e.g., 49, 180, 303). This view of Jesus, given prominence in *The Five Gospels,* is ultimately based on a saying of Jesus that the scholars color gray: "Just remember, John appeared on the scene neither eating nor drinking, and they say, 'He is demented.' The son of Adam came both eating and drinking, and they say, 'There's a glutton and a drunk, a crony of toll collectors and sinners!' " (Matt 11:18–19 ‖ Luke 7:33–34, "Q"). The contrast set up by Jesus between himself and the ascetic John the Baptist appealed to the

---

54. The SV (Mark 7:19) reads this passage as a comment on the digestive process described in 7:18: " 'Don't you realize that nothing from outside can defile by going into a person, because it doesn't get to the heart but passes into the stomach, and comes out in the outhouse?' (This is how everything we eat is purified)." Considerable liberties have been taken with the text of 7:19b, which reads καθαρίζων πάντα τὰ βρώματα (lit. "purifying [or declaring pure] all foods").

55. This is the view of G. Vermes, a prominent Jewish scholar who, unlike those in the Jesus Seminar, is thoroughly familiar with the ancient Jewish evidence (see *Religion of Jesus the Jew,* esp. chap. 2, "Jesus and the Law: The Judaism of Jesus," 11–45). The strange saying in *Thomas* 14:1–2 "If you fast, you will bring sin upon yourselves, and if you pray, you will be condemned, and if you give to charity, you will harm your spirits" is alien enough to the authentic Jesus tradition that even the Jesus Seminar colors it black.

seminar, but a gray vote resulted because of the presence in the saying of the supposedly "apocalyptic" figure of the Son of Man (which the seminar translates as "son of Adam").

In a cameo essay entitled "Feasting and Fasting," another contrast between Jesus and John is discussed. The claim is made that Jesus did not practice fasting, as did John the Baptist and his followers. Rather, "the early Christian community immediately reverted to fasting as a religious practice," thus departing from the practice of its master (48). Such a view of Jesus fits well the assumption of the seminar that Jesus consistently violated every provision of his religious tradition and taught others to do the same.

6. In the gospel tradition, Jesus is often presented in dialogue with his opponents on points of law, using scripture to buttress his arguments. All such cases are regarded as inauthentic by the seminar on the assumption that the historical Jesus did not invoke scripture, but rather "taught on his own authority" (e.g., 68; cf. 201), presumably because he lacked training in scripture interpretation (e.g., 236). Although one might argue, with some plausibility, that Jesus' education was limited, it is odd that the seminar, while assuming his ignorance of scripture on points of law, also grants him enough knowledge of particular scriptural texts and traditions to create subtle "spoofs" on or "parodies" of them in his parables (examples of which I will presently cite).[56]

7. Among the opponents of Jesus in the gospel tradition, the Pharisees stand out in greatest relief. Thus, it is with some surprise that we find in *The Five Gospels* the suggestion that there were no Pharisees in Galilee in Jesus' time and that Pharisees were active there only after the Jewish War of 66–70 (217, 239, 242, 244, 369). This claim is made despite the fact that the parable of the Pharisee and the toll collector (Luke 18:10–14) is colored pink. Even in the commentary to that parable, the seminar says, "It would be anachronistic to portray Jesus as engaged in polemics with them [the Pharisees] or about them in Galilee during his life" (369).

Here we encounter an astonishing misunderstanding of the

___

56. For a careful analysis of the probable extent of Jesus' education, see Meier, *A Marginal Jew*, 1:268–78 (see n. 22). On Jesus' use of scripture in both Hebrew and Aramaic (Targumic traditions), see B. D. Chilton, *A Galilean Rabbi and His Bible: Jesus' Use of the Interpreted Scripture of His Time* (Wilmington, Del.: Michael Glazier, 1984). It is very strange to see Chilton's name on the roster of Jesus Seminar "fellows" (Funk, Hoover, and the Jesus Seminar, *Five Gospels*, 534)!

facts. It is, of course, true that some of the wholesale denuncia-
tions of Pharisees in the gospel tradition, such as those in Matthew
23, reflect the bitter polemic of Jesus-believing Jews against leading
Jews of the developing normative Judaism of the late first century.[57] But by that time the Pharisees (*perushim* = "separatists")
are no longer a competing party within a variegated Second Temple Judaism. The Pharisaic interpretation of Torah is in the process
of being established as normative ("rabbinic") Judaism both in
Galilee and in Judea, and the term "Pharisee" is falling out of use
as a party designation. In Matthew 23 and similar passages, it is
used, together with "hypocrite," as a code word of reproach in an
intercommunity (but arguably still intra-Jewish) rivalry. As to the
earlier situation in Galilee, there is no reason at all to doubt the
presence of groups of Pharisees there in the Jewish towns and villages, and probably even in the Jewish minority communities living
in the Hellenistic cites.[58] And there is every reason to believe that
Jesus of Nazareth entered into debate with them.

Other examples of the Jesus Seminar's distortion of the historical record could be cited, but enough has been said of this set of
distortions, because there are others yet to take up.

The "Scholars Version" Translation

The intent of "the Scholars Version" (SV, samples of which have
been given in the previous section), as stated in a preface to *The Five
Gospels,* is to "desacralize" the text of the gospels and to make the
translation "sound like a piece of contemporary literature" (xvi)
by using "the common street language of the original" (xiv). The
scholars have succeeded in this effort brilliantly, whatever one
might think of the claim that the original language of the gospels
was "street language." Somewhat incongruously, however, they
also demonstrate their commitment to "political correctness" with
irritating manipulations of grammatical gender and number. For

---

57. See esp. A. J. Saldarini, *Matthew's Christian-Jewish Community* (Chicago:
University of Chicago Press, 1994), esp. chap. 3, "Matthew's Opponents: Israel's
Leaders," 44–67. The "woe" pronouncement at Matt 23:15 may be an authentic saying of Jesus, and the reference to the making of converts may reflect actual
attempts on the part of Pharisees to attract other Jews to Pharisaic teachings. On
this passage, see M. Goodman, *Mission and Conversion: Proselytizing in the Religious History of the Roman Empire* (Oxford: Clarendon, 1994), 69–72. (I owe this
reference to A. T. Kraabel.)

58. A convenient summary of the evidence on the Pharisees, with extensive bibliography, is provided in A. J. Saldarini's article "Pharisees," in *ABD,* 5:289–303.

example, the "child" in Matthew 18:2 (neuter both in Greek and in English) becomes a "she" in the SV rendition. "He who seeks" in *Gospel of Thomas* 2 becomes "those who seek" in the SV.

In what follows, I shall discuss the SV translations of some of the key words or phrases used frequently in the Jesus tradition. As we shall see, "mistranslation" is often a better term for what the scholars are doing.

1. "God's imperial rule" for ἡ βασιλεία τοῦ θεοῦ ("the kingdom of God"; Mark 1:14 and passim). The Greek word usually translated "kingdom" can also mean "reign" or "rule" (Aramaic *malkuta'*, Hebrew *malkut*). Why "imperial" is added is nowhere explained, and is odd in view of the role played by the Roman *imperium* in Jewish Palestine. The SV translates βασιλεύς ("king") in Jesus' parables as "secular ruler" (e.g., Matt 18:23, colored pink).

2. "I swear to God" for ἀμὴν λέγω ὑμῖν (σοι) ("amen" or "truly I say to you [pl. or sg.]"; e.g., John 13:20, colored gray). This use of "amen" (a Hebrew word used in oaths, promises, prayers, etc.) is variously translated in the SV as "I swear to you" (Matt 5:26, pink), "I tell you" (Luke 12:59, pink), "so help me!" (Mark 14:30, black), and "let me tell you" (Luke 22:34, black). Perhaps this use of "amen" in Jesus' discourse was a factor in the seminar's coloring of Jesus' command "Don't swear at all" (Matt 5:34, gray), though this is not stated in the commentary (143). In any case, it seems to have escaped the notice of the scholars that Jesus' use of "amen" is religious language, not "street language."

3. "The son of Adam" for ὁ υἱὸς τοῦ ἀνθρώπου ("the Son of Man"; Mark 2:28 and passim). The scholars explain their translation in a cameo essay, referring to three different senses of "son of Adam" in the Hebrew Bible: as an insignificant human being, as in Job 25:4–6; as next to God in the order of creation, as in Psalm 8:3–6; and as "the Apocalyptic Figure" of Daniel 7:13–14 (76–77). In all three cases the translation "son of Adam" is wrong! In Job 25:6 ("how much less man, who is a maggot, / and the son of man, who is a worm!" [RSV]), *'enosh* ("man") and *ben 'adam* ("son of man") mean essentially the same thing, "a human being." *'Adam* by itself means the same — that is, generic "man." In the poetry of Job, the juxtaposition of the two terms is a case of synonymous parallelism, one of the most common features of Hebrew poetry, and of Semitic diction in general. In Hebrew, "a son of X" means "a man with the quality of X"; a "daughter of X" means "a woman with the quality of X," as, for example, in Hannah's plea in 1 Samuel 1:16 for Eli not to regard her as "a base woman" (*bat*

beli'al, lit. "daughter of worthlessness"). "Son of man" thus means the same as "man" (i.e., human being), though "son of" might be taken to indicate that the human being in question is male (cf. *benot ha-'adam,* "daughters of men" = human women), but this is not necessarily the case (as in Job 25 and Ps 8, where both genders are certainly implied). Psalm 8:4 (8:5 in Hebrew) is another instance of what we see in Job 25:6, with the juxtaposition of *'enosh* and *ben 'adam.*

Daniel 7:13 is translated by our scholars as follows:

> As I looked, in a night vision,
> I saw one like *a son of Adam* coming with heaven's clouds.
> He came to the Ancient of Days and was presented to him.

This passage is construed by the seminar, in its commentary, in terms of Genesis 1:28, where "the human being" (Adam) is depicted as "the agent to exercise control over every living creature" (77). But the Genesis story of Adam is irrelevant to the interpretation of Daniel 7:13, for "son of Adam" does not occur there. No notice seems to be taken by our scholars that the text of Daniel 7:13 is not Hebrew but Aramaic! It is read as though the text has *ben 'adam,* which it does not. It has *kebar 'enash* ("one like a son of man" or "one like a human being").

Aramaic was the language of Jesus. In the gospel sayings, the enigmatic self-designation "the Son of Man" is rendered in the Aramaic *bar 'enasha',* which means essentially "the human being." What Jesus meant by this term, or even if he used it at all, is a matter of considerable controversy in New Testament scholarship.[59] In a discussion of Jesus' usage in the aforementioned cameo essay, three different meanings are assigned to "son of Adam": (1) the heavenly figure who is to come; (2) one who is to suffer, die, and rise, "a roundabout way of saying 'I'" (77), e.g., in the passion predictions in Mark 8:31; 9:31; and 10:33, colored black; and (3) "human beings" in general.

The comment on meaning 1 contains a surprising statement: "On the lips of Jesus those references to the apocalyptic figure of the future are not self-references but allusions to a third person" (77). This is surprising because it seems to suggest that Jesus did, after all, have an eschatological doctrine. The verses quoted as examples (Mark 8:38; 13:26; and 14:62) are all colored black; it is reported in the commentary to Mark 13:26 that some members of

---

59. See n. 44.

the seminar shared the view "that Jesus may have spoken about the son of Adam as a messianic figure other than himself" (113), but those members were decisively outvoted.

One interesting example of meaning 3 in the seminar's interpretation is the one and only "Son of Man" saying in the *Gospel of Thomas*, saying 86 (colored pink): "Foxes have their dens and birds have their nests but human beings have no place to lay down and rest." This translation of "the Son of Man" as "human beings" creates a statement that is absurd on its face: animals and birds have homes, but people don't![60] The point here, finally, is that the Jesus Seminar's "son of Adam" amounts to a mistranslation wherever it is used.

4. "Congratulations" for μακάριος ("blessed"; Matt 5:3 and passim). Macarisms pronounced on "the poor" and other people by Jesus are all rendered this way. But to render "blessed" everywhere as "congratulations" would lead to even more absurd results; so alternatives do occur — for example, "lucky" as applied to Jesus' mother's womb and breasts (*Gos. Thom.* 79) and "fortunate" as applied to the "eyes" of the disciples (Matt 13:16). In general, "congratulations" might be an appropriate translation of μακάριος in certain cases in Greek literature, but Jesus spoke Aramaic and probably read Hebrew. "Congratulations" is an impossible rendering of *'ashar* ("happy") or *berikh* (Heb. *barukh*, "[divinely] blessed"). Even as a translation of the Greek, one wonders what "the poor" would have accomplished for which "congratulations" are in order. In short, this example of "street language" amounts to a distortion of the text.

5. "Damn" for οὐαί ("woe"). Most of the woes pronounced by Jesus, transformed into curses by our scholars, are colored black. But here is a pink one, hurled at the Pharisees: "Damn you, Pharisees! You're so fond of the prominent seat in synagogues and respectful greetings in marketplaces" (Luke 11:43).[61] My only comment on this use of "street language" by the Jesus Seminar is that even first-year biblical students ought to know the difference between a "woe" oracle, or pronouncement of "woe," and a curse. To be sure, the Jesus Seminar could have taken its street language

60. Oddly enough, the same saying in Luke 9:58 (SV) has, instead, "...but the son of Adam has nowhere to rest his head." This is one of a number of inconsistencies in Funk, Hoover, and the Jesus Seminar, *Five Gospels*.

61. As I have already noted, the scholars do not think that there were any Pharisees in Galilee in Jesus' day; here, however, they grant the existence of enough of them for Jesus to curse them.

a little further, with a dose of scatology. Why not "shithouse" instead of "outhouse" (ἀφεδρών, "latrine") at Mark 7:19?

The Jesus Seminar's Interpretation of Its Database

The "authentic" material in the Jesus sayings tradition comprises 18 percent of the total, according to the Jesus Seminar. This, in the view of the scholars, is the noneschatological part of the tradition. But is it really? The fact is that eschatology is there too, willy-nilly, and a hermeneutical juggling act of considerable dexterity is required to remove it. I can treat only some examples of the seminar's juggling act here, and I do so under three different rubrics.

1. "God's imperial rule." In a cameo essay, "God's Imperial Rule: Present or Future?" (136–37), the seminar provides examples of sayings in which God's rule is future (Mark 9:1; 13:24–27, 30) and present (Luke 11:2; 11:20; 17:20–21; *Gos. Thom.* 113). The future-oriented "apocalyptic" sayings are in accord with the views of John the Baptist and the early Christian community. The question is,

> Did Jesus share this view, or was his vision more subtle, less bombastic and threatening?
> The Fellows of the Jesus Seminar are inclined to the second option: Jesus conceived of God's rule as all around him but difficult to discern. God was so real for him that he could not distinguish God's present activity from any future activity. He had a poetic sense of time in which the future and the present merged, simply melted together, in the intensity of his vision. (137)

The seminar takes the following saying as "a key in identifying Jesus' temporal views" (364; cf. 531):

> You won't be able to observe the coming of God's imperial rule. People are not going to say, "Look, here it is!" or "Over there!" On the contrary, God's imperial rule is right there in your presence. (Luke 17:20–21, pink)

> It will not come by watching for it. It will not be said, "Look here!" or "Look there!" Rather, the Father's imperial rule is spread out upon the earth, and people don't see it. (*Gos. Thom.* 113:2–4, pink)

This saying, addressed to "Pharisees" in Luke and to Jesus' "disciples" in *Thomas,* lacks a narrative context in either. But is this saying really a noneschatological saying? Indeed, I would submit that eschatology is "right there in [the scholars'] presence," but they "don't see it."

The key to a proper interpretation of this saying is provided by the next one that the scholars cite as exemplifying Jesus' "poetic sense of time": "But if by God's finger I drive out demons, then for you God's imperial rule has arrived" (Luke 11:20, pink). This saying is set in a larger context in which Jesus has exorcised a demon and is then accused by some as being in league with the devil, referred to here as "Beelzebul" and "Satan" (Luke 11:14–26 ‖ Matt 12:22–32 ‖ Mark 3:22–29). In this context Jesus also says, in a saying our scholars also color pink: "If Satan is divided against himself — since you claim I drive out demons in Beelzebul's name — how will his kingdom endure?" (Luke 11:18).

Jesus' reference to "Satan" is part and parcel of his dualistic apocalyptic worldview, not "some subtle irony," as the scholars would have it (330). In this key passage, Jesus claims that his exorcisms are a sign of the arrival of the kingdom of God and an attack on the domain of Satan — that is, that they are part of an end-time struggle between the forces of God and Satan.[62]

The third saying the scholars cite as illustrating the presence of God's rule is a surprising one, because it does not fit the category: "Father, your name be revered. Impose your imperial rule" (Luke 11:2; "Father" is red, the rest is pink; cf. Matt 6:9–10). This saying is recognizable, even in the SV translation, as the opening address and first two petitions of "the Lord's Prayer": "Father, sanctified [or hallowed, ἁγιασθήτω] be your name, your kingdom come [ἐλθέτω]." The second petition is, in fact, a prayer for the "coming" of God's future (eschatological) kingdom.

In our scholars' commentary (325–27; cf. 148–49), no notice is taken of an ancient Jewish prayer that is certainly reflected in Jesus' own reformulation, the *Qaddish.* This prayer, composed in vernacular Aramaic, was originally associated with the study of Torah as a dismissal prayer, but is now used mainly in connection with mourning for the dead. One of its ancient forms goes like this: "Magnified and sanctified be His great name in the world which

---

62. There is a possible association of the "kingdom of God" and power over "the demons of death" in a recently published fragment from Qumran, 4Q525. Lines 3–4 have [*mlk*]*wt* / '*lwhym,* and line 5 has *reshp*[*y*] *mwt.* For discussion of this fragment, see Evans, *Jesus and His Contemporaries,* 147–48 (see n. 43).

He hath created according to His will. May He establish His kingdom during your life and during your days, and during the life of all the house of Israel, ever speedily and at a near time, and say ye, Amen."[63] This prayer, like that of Jesus, breathes the spirit of the ancient Jewish apocalyptic worldview.

2. Truncated parables. One of the characteristic modes of Jesus' teaching and preaching was his use of parables. Many of Jesus' recorded parables are accepted as genuine by the seminar, but in some cases only with the application of scissors and paste. The parable of the lost sheep (Luke 15:4–7) is colored pink, but only through verse 6, which concludes with " 'Celebrate with me, because I have found my lost sheep.' " The point of the parable, verse 7, is colored black: " 'I'm telling you that it'll be just like this in heaven; there'll be more celebrating over one sinner who has a change of heart than over ninety-nine virtuous people who have no need to change their hearts.' "

The parable of the shrewd manager (Luke 16:1–8) is colored red up to the first part of verse 8: "The master praised the dishonest manager because he had acted shrewdly." The point of the parable is colored black: "for the children of this world [or this age] exhibit better sense in dealing with their own kind than do the children of light." This is like telling a joke and leaving out the punch line! The scholars do not like this parable's punch line because it "moralizes" the story (359).

The scholars have other devices to use in interpreting Jesus' parables that are more inventive than simply applying the scissors. The parable of the sower (Mark 4:3–8 ‖ Matt 13:3–8 ‖ Luke 8:5–8a ‖ Gos. Thom. 9, all pink) is one of the parables in which agricultural imagery occurs, here with special reference to the harvest (an eschatological metaphor) and concluding with reference to a bountiful yield for the seed that fell on good soil. The seminar refers to Thomas's version as the most original (and I am inclined to agree) but offers no interpretation except to situate it in the context of "hellenistic rhetoric" (478). No notice is taken of the supernatural yield referred to in the parable (30–fold, 60–fold,

63. A. E. Millgram, Jewish Worship (Philadelphia: Jewish Publication Society, 1971), 154. The prayer as used in contemporary Judaism is found in the Siddur, the Jewish prayer book. See, e.g., N. Scherman, ed. and trans., The Complete Art Scroll Siddur (Brooklyn: Mesorah Publications, 1984), 800–801. I express my thanks for my copy to my doctoral student Rabbi Harry Manhoff, who presented it to me as a gift.

and 100–fold in Mark and Matt; 100–fold in Luke; 60–fold and 120–fold in *Gos. Thom.*).[64]

Another parable employing agricultural imagery is the one on the mustard seed (Mark 4:30–32 ‖ Matt 13:31–32 ‖ Luke 13:18–19 ‖ *Gos. Thom.* 20; red in *Gos. Thom.*, otherwise pink), in which Jesus compares the growth of the kingdom to that of a small mustard seed that "produces a large plant and becomes a shelter for birds of the sky" (*Gos. Thom.* 20:3). Our scholars view this parable as "a parody of the mighty cedar of Lebanon [Ezekiel 17:22–23] and the apocalyptic tree of Daniel [4:10–12, 20–22]" (194). This parable is said to betray "an underlying sense of humor on Jesus' part. It is also anti-social in that it endorses counter movements and ridicules established tradition" (485). No further comment is required here.

The two singly attested sayings in *Thomas* regarded as genuine by the seminar are both parables. *Thomas* 97 compares the kingdom to a woman carrying a jar of meal home without noticing that it is broken at the handle and all of the meal has spilled out. This parable, which can be compared to that of the wise and foolish maidens in Matthew 25:1–12 (gray), is taken by the scholars as "a parody of the story of Elijah and the widow" (524; cf. 1 Kgs 17:8–16). *Thomas* 98, which compares the kingdom to a would-be assassin who tests his sword before using it, has to do with "reversal," in the view of the seminar: "The little guy bests the big guy by taking the precautions a prudent person would take before encountering the village bully" (525). The parable can more plausibly be viewed alongside such other parables as that of the tower builder (Luke 14:28–30, black) or the warring king (Luke 14:31–32, also black), as a provocative example of the necessity of preparation in anticipation of the kingdom. But once the eschatology is removed, such parables are reduced to pure nonsense.

3. Contextless aphorisms. A well-known saying of Jesus, attested no fewer than six times (Mark 8:35, black; Matt 10:39, gray; 16:25, gray; Luke 9:24, gray; 17:33, pink; John 12:25, gray), is the one on "saving" or "losing" one's life. The Jesus Seminar colors pink the version found in Luke 17:33: "Whoever tries to hang on to life will forfeit it, but whoever forfeits life will preserve it." In Luke 17, it is found in the context in which Jesus is warning

---

64. A fivefold yield was common in first-century Palestine, as has been recently demonstrated by R. K. McIver, "One Hundred-Fold Yield — Miraculous or Mundane? Matthew 13.8, 23; Mark 4.8, 20; Luke 8.8," *NTS* 40 (1994): 606–8.

of fearful events attendant upon the coming of the days of the Son of Man (vv. 22–37). This context is colored black and gray. The pink-colored saying is taken as a "paradoxical" saying supplied by the evangelist with a secondary context. The saying by itself is said to be "a contextless aphorism" (367). But the eschatology in this saying cannot be removed simply by jerking it out of the context in which it appears. It speaks of a *future*, preparation for which may necessitate the giving up of one's own life!

Indeed, the juxtaposition of the present situation with that of the future is a characteristic feature of Jesus' teaching and is part of the chronological dualism of his Jewish apocalyptic worldview ("this age" / "the age to come"). It pervades the supposedly "noneschatological" sayings material assigned by the seminar to Jesus.

Another example of the same thing is also frequently attested: "Many of the first will be last, and of the last many will be first," as mistranslated in the SV of Mark 10:31 (better the RSV: "But many that are first will be last, and the last first"). As found in Mark (and in Matt 19:30 and the first half of *Gos. Thomas* 4:2, as well as in the different form in Luke 13:30), the saying is colored gray. Only the Matthew 20:16 version is colored pink: "The last will be first, and the first last." The other versions are said to be "softened" (224) or "qualified" by the addition of "many" (473). Had our scholars paid attention to the underlying Semitic idiom, they would have seen that the version with "many" is likely to be more original. The meaning is really "[All] those who are first, who are many...," just as in Daniel 12:2, where "many of those who sleep in the dust of the earth shall awake" means "all those, who are many...."[65] Be that as it may, the meaning of the saying is the point at issue. The saying is rightly taken as "a memorable reversal," the basis for which, however, is not understood by the scholars.

We have seen that the seminar scholars have Jesus "congratulating" the poor (Matt 5:3; Luke 6:20; *Gos. Thom.* 54; red in *Gos. Thom.*, otherwise pink). Their comment is interesting:

---

65. This lack of attention to Semitic philology is surprising. A striking example occurs in the scholars' interpretation of Jesus' cry of dereliction "My God, my God, why did you abandon me?" in Mark 15:34 (black), which they take simply as a quotation of Ps 22:1 secondarily attributed to Jesus by the evangelist (125–26). They pay no attention to the fact that the transliterated words in Mark's Greek text (*Eloi, Eloi, lema sabachthani*) are Aramaic, not Hebrew, and that this fact may have a bearing on how the saying should be understood.

Congratulating the poor without qualification is unexpected to say the least, and even paradoxical, since congratulations were normally extended to those who enjoyed prosperity, happiness, or power. The congratulations addressed to the weeping and the hungry are expressed in vivid and exaggerated language, which announces a dramatic transformation. (138)

What the scholars mean by "dramatic transformation" is clarified in their comment on *Thomas* 54 ("Congratulations to the poor, for to you belongs Heaven's domain"):[66] "He announced that God's domain belonged to the poor, not because they were righteous, but because they were poor. This reverses a common view that God blesses the righteous with riches and curses the immoral with poverty" (504). And what consolation might the poor and the hungry derive from this? Jesus announces the dramatic reversal that he expects in the future, in the coming kingdom of God:

Congratulations, you poor! God's domain belongs to you.
Congratulations, you hungry! You will have a feast.
Congratulations, you who weep now! You will laugh.
(Luke 6:20–21, rightly colored red)[67]

Many more examples of the seminar's failure to notice the eschatology in its own database could be cited, but this discussion has gone on long enough. I cannot refrain, however, from citing one more instance, another saying colored pink by the scholars: "There are castrated men who were born that way, and there are castrated men who were castrated by others, and there are castrated men who castrate themselves because of Heaven's imperial rule" (Matt 19:12). This saying about "eunuchs" calls to mind others in which Jesus counsels ripping out an offending eye or cutting off an offending right hand to prevent having one's whole body wind up in hell (Matt 5:29–30 ‖ Mark 9:43–47 ‖ Matt 18:8–9, all gray). The context in Matthew 19 is a discussion of Jesus' prohibition of divorce (19:9, black; cf. 5:31–32, black; Mark 10:11–12, gray; Luke 16:18, gray) and comes as a reply to the disciples' wondering whether, in view of this prohibition,

---

66. "The poor" is a mistranslation of the Coptic. There is no vocative case as such in Coptic; the definite article is used instead (as in Hebrew). Thus, the context determines the translation, and here "you poor" is correct (as in Luke 6:20).

67. The corresponding woes ("damn you") on the rich, the well fed, and the laughing in Luke 6:24–25 are colored black by the seminar.

it were better not to marry at all (19:10). Jesus' colorful saying has to do with voluntary celibacy, which a man might elect for the sake of the coming kingdom, that is, in anticipation of the resurrection life in which "people do not marry" (Matt 22:30, gray). Jesus' provision for becoming "a eunuch for the sake of the kingdom" cannot be understood apart from the eschatological worldview that informs it.

So why do our scholars color this saying pink? In their view the saying is "an attack on a male-dominated patriarchal society in which male virility and parenthood were the exclusive norms." Jesus is also here "undermining the depreciation of yet another marginal group, this time the eunuchs" (226)! At the hands of these interpreters, Jesus becomes, in effect, the prophet of late-twentieth-century "political correctness." As to the possibility that the saying might be about celibacy, this is entertained only to be rejected:

> The Fellows of the Seminar were overwhelmingly of the opinion that Jesus did not advocate celibacy. A majority of the Fellows doubted, in fact, that Jesus himself was celibate. They regard it as probable that he had a special relationship with at least one woman, Mary of Magdala. In any case, the sayings on castration should not be taken as Jesus' authorization for an ascetic lifestyle; his behavior suggests that he celebrated life by eating, drinking, and fraternizing freely with both women and men. (220–21)

The question posed earlier bears repeating: Who would want to crucify a fellow like this, and why? Or was Jesus really crucified after all? The second phase of the Jesus Seminar's work, in which such questions should presumably be addressed, is promised for publication in 1997. Meanwhile, we can expect their answers to be reflected in the new book by the seminar's founder, Robert W. Funk, entitled *Honest to Jesus*. In his chapter "The Death of Jesus" (chap. 12), he states that "the crucifixion of Jesus is not entirely beyond question"[68] but then goes on to concede its likelihood. Yet he never addresses the question of *why* Jesus was crucified.[69] Small

---

68. R. W. Funk, *Honest to Jesus: Jesus for a New Millennium* (San Francisco: HarperSanFrancisco, 1996), 219.

69. J. D. Crossan gets that part right in his most recent book, *Who Killed Jesus? Exposing the Roots of Anti-Semitism in the Gospel Story of the Death of Jesus* (San Francisco: HarperSanFrancisco, 1995), 39–65. As many others have done, Crossan affirms a direct connection between Jesus' demonstration in the Temple

wonder! Such a question is evidently beyond the ability of Funk & Co. even to discuss. It is better for them just to "sweep it under the rug" and hope nobody notices, because their Jesus would never have been crucified at all. He would have died a ruddy-faced, beer-bellied Falstaff.

Concluding Observations

The Jesus of the Jesus Seminar is a non-Jewish Jesus. To put it metaphorically, the seminar has performed a sneak epispasm on the historical Jesus, a surgical procedure removing the marks of his circumcision. The result might arouse some disquiet in the minds of people who know the history of the 1930s and 1940s. But the Jesus of the Jesus Seminar is much too banal to cause us to think that the ideology producing him is like that which produced the "Aryan Jesus" of the 1930s.[70]

Scholars of religion have rightly come to be suspicious of theo-logically driven scholarship. We should be equally suspicious of atheologically driven scholarship or *any* ideologically driven schol-arship, political or otherwise. The "hidden agenda" in the work of the Jesus Seminar is clearly an ideology that drives the group. So what is this ideology? An important clue is found in the frequency with which the word "secular" appears in *The Five Gospels*. For example, Jesus was not interested in "fine points of the Law"; his responses to his contemporaries "were more secular than legal in character" (201). When Jesus illustrates a point with reference to the intrusion by a burglar into a homeowner's dwelling (Luke 12:39, gray), this root metaphor "would have been understood on his lips in a secular sense" (342). Jesus was simply "a secular sage" (287). This obvious anachronism requires explanation, and we find it in the celebration by the Jesus Seminar of the removal of the quest of the historical Jesus from "the church, seminaries,

---

(Mark 11:15–19; John 2:13–17; cf. *Gos. Thom.* 71) and his execution. But that demonstration is hardly the work of a "secular sage"!

70. Probably the most notorious example of the latter ideology is W. Grund-mann, *Jesus der Galiläer und das Judentum,* in the series Veröffentlichungen des Instituts zur Erforschung des jüdischen Einflusses auf das deutsche kirchliche Leben (Leipzig: G. Wigand, 1940). Grundmann argues that Galilee was predominantly gentile and Jesus' ancestry was Aryan, and that Jesus drew on his ancestral Aryan traditions for his anti-Jewish message. Grundmann's career as a churchman and prominent NT scholar lasted into the 1970s. For a useful discussion, see M. John-son, "Power Politics and New Testament Scholarship in the National Socialist Period," *JES* 23 (1986): 1–24, esp. 4–12.

and isolated theological enclaves" (4) to more secular institutional settings. The ideology driving the Jesus Seminar is, I would argue, one of "secularization."

Of course, one should expect that, in secular academic settings (such as a state university in the United States), a nontheological approach to historical evidence, including religious evidence, is standard. In my view, it ought to be the starting point even for theological historical research. This is *not* what we have in the case of the Jesus Seminar. What we have instead is an approach driven by an ideology of secularization, and a process of coloring the historical evidence to fit a secular ideal. Thus, in robbing Jesus of his Jewishness, the Jesus Seminar has finally robbed him of his *religion*.

"Seek — you'll find." This is one of the "authentic" sayings of Jesus (Matt 7:7 ‖ Luke 11:9 ‖ *Gos. Thom.* 92:1, pink) in *The Five Gospels*. A group of secularized theologians went seeking a secular Jesus, and they found him! Rather, they think they found him, but in fact they created him. Jesus the "party animal," whose zany wit and caustic humor would enliven an otherwise dull cocktail party — this is the product of the Jesus Seminar's six years of research. In a sense, the Jesus Seminar, with its ideology of secularization, represents a "shadow image" of the neoorthodox theology of the old "new quest" — and its ultimate bankruptcy.

Chapter 3

1 Thessalonians 2:13–16

A Deutero-Pauline Interpolation

In any discussion of the origins of Christian "anti-Semitism," among a number of New Testament passages that can be adduced, 1 Thessalonians 2:14–16 will inevitably be brought to the fore.[1] The purpose of this article is not to contribute to the current Jewish-Christian "dialogue" per se but to discuss historically and exegetically this important passage in 1 Thessalonians. Nevertheless, such a study, of course, is not completely irrelevant to the contemporary theological scene.[2]

The foundations for an understanding of our passage in its own historical context were laid in the nineteenth century by "the author of historical theology," Ferdinand Christian Baur.[3] Of 1 Thessalonians 2:14–16 he wrote:

> This passage has a thoroughly un-Pauline stamp. It agrees certainly with the Acts, where it is stated that the Jews in Thessalonica stirred up the heathen against the apostle's con-

---

1. See, e.g., H.-J. Schoeps, *The Jewish Christian Argument,* trans. D. Green (New York: Holt, Rinehart & Winston, 1963), 28; and O. Michel, "Fragen zu I Thessalonicher 2, 14–16: Anti-jüdische Polemik bei Paulus," in *Antijudaismus im Neuen Testament? Exegetische und systematische Beiträge,* ed. W. Eckert et al., ACJD 2 (Munich: Kaiser, 1967), 50–59.

2. See especially N. A. Beck, *Mature Christianity in the Twenty-First Century: The Recognition and Repudiation of the Anti-Jewish Polemic in the New Testament,* rev. ed. (New York: American Interfaith Institute/World Alliance and Crossroad, 1994). Beck provides an extensive discussion of 1 Thess 2:13–16 based on my arguments that this passage is an interpolation (76–90).

3. "The Author of Historical Theology" is the title of chapter 1 in P. C. Hodgson's study of Baur, *The Formation of Historical Theology: A Study of Ferdinand Christian Baur* (New York: Harper & Row, 1966), an impressive and sympathetic treatment of that controversial and oft-misunderstood giant of German scholarship. See also Hodgson's general introduction in his *Ferdinand Christian Baur on the Writing of Church History* (New York: Oxford University Press, 1968), 3–40.

verts, and against himself; yet the comparison is certainly far-fetched between those troubles raised by the Jews and Gentiles conjointly and the persecution of the Christians in Judaea. Nor do we ever find the apostle elsewhere holding up the Judaeo-Christians as a pattern to the Gentile Christians. It is, moreover, quite out of place for him to speak of these persecutions in Judaea; for he himself was the person principally concerned in the only persecution to which our passage can refer.... Is this polemic against the Jews at all natural to him; a polemic so external and so vague that the enmity of the Jews to the Gospel is characterized solely in the terms of that well-known charge with which the Gentiles assailed them, the *odium generis humani?* ... And when it is said that after the Jews have continually filled up the measure of their sins, ἔφθασεν δὲ ἐπ’ αὐτοὺς ἡ ὀργὴ εἰς τέλος, what does this suggest to us more naturally than the punishment that came upon them in the destruction of Jerusalem?[4]

Baur concludes that the reproach against the Jews in 2:14–16 reflects a later period, a time when Pauline Christianity was seeking an accommodation with Jewish Christianity and the Jews were regarded on all sides as enemies of the gospel.[5]

Baur saw in this passage a powerful argument against the authenticity of 1 Thessalonians as a whole; this solution is, of course, unsatisfactory. Other nineteenth-century scholars, though by no means all,[6] suggested that the difficulties could be solved by the hypothesis of later interpolation. Albrecht Ritschl proposed to excise 1 Thessalonians 2:16c as a post-70 C.E. scribal gloss referring to the destruction of Jerusalem.[7] He was followed subsequently by a number of other scholars.[8] Paul Schmiedel extended the scope of

---

4. F. C. Baur, *Paul: The Apostle of Jesus Christ,* trans. from 2d German ed. A. Menzies (London: Williams & Norgate, 1875), 87–88.

5. Ibid., 88; see also 320.

6. See, e.g., G. Lünemann, *Critical and Exegetical Handbook to the Epistle of Paul to the Thessalonians* (Edinburgh: T. & T. Clark, 1880), ad loc.

7. Ritschl's proposal appears in an article in *Halle'sche allgemeine Literaturzeitung* (1847), cited in P. Schmiedel, *Die Briefe an die Thessalonicher und an die Korinther,* HKNT (Freiburg: Mohr-Siebeck, 1892), 21. Ritschl is mentioned in the critical apparatus of Nestle-Aland, ad loc.

8. Among the twentieth-century scholars who followed Ritschl were J. Moffat, *An Introduction to the Literature of the New Testament,* 3d ed. (New York: Scribner's, 1918), 73; and J. Bailey, "The First and Second Epistles to the Thessalonians," in IB (New York: Abingdon-Cokesbury, 1955), 11:280.

the interpolation to incorporate verses 15 and 16;[9] Heinrich Julius Holtzmann included verse 14 as well.[10]

In my view, these nineteenth-century scholars were on the right track. Nevertheless, most twentieth-century commentators reject all theories of interpolation at this point in 1 Thessalonians,[11] insisting that one find refuge in interpolation hypotheses only as a last resort.[12] With this methodological principle I would agree. Yet the historical and theological difficulties in 1 Thessalonians 2 are such that one must begin again to entertain such a hypothesis. On the basis of the insights of previous scholars and of my own historical, theological, and form-critical observations, I will here argue that there is indeed an interpolation in 1 Thessalonians 2 as it now

9. Schmiedel, *Briefe*, 21.

10. H. J. Holtzmann, *Lehrbuch der historisch-kritischen Einleitung in das Neue Testament*, 3d ed. (Freiburg: J. C. B. Mohr, 1892), 214, according to J. E. Frame, *A Critical and Exegetical Commentary on the Epistles of St. Paul to the Thessalonians*, ICC 38 (Edinburgh: T. & T. Clark, 1912), 109. According to S. G. F. Brandon, the passage in vv. 14–16 is understandable as "an interpolation made by some Gentile Christians, with an anti-Semitic bias, such as Marcion"; see Brandon's *The Fall of Jerusalem and the Christian Church* (London: SPCK, 1957), 93.

11. E.g., M. Dibelius, *An die Thessalonicher I, II*, HNT (Tübingen: Mohr, 1925); E. von Dobschütz, *Die Thessalonicher-Briefe*, 7th ed., KEK (Göttingen: Vandenhoeck & Ruprecht, 1909); Frame, *Critical and Exegetical Commentary*; C. Masson, *Les deux épîtres de Saint Paul aux Thessaloniciens* (Neuchatel: Delachaux et Niestlé, 1957); G. Milligan, *St. Paul's Epistles to the Thessalonians* (London: Macmillan, 1908); W. Neil, *The Epistle of Paul to the Thessalonians*, MNTC (New York: Harper, 1950); A. Oepke, "Die Briefe an die Thessalonicher," in H. W. Beyer et al., ed., *Die kleineren Briefe des Apostel Paulus*, NTD 8, 10th ed. (Göttingen: Vandenhoeck & Ruprecht, 1965), 157–87; B. Rigaux, *Saint Paul — Les épîtres au Thessaloniennes*, EtB (Paris: Lecoffre, 1956); and G. Wohlenberg, *Der erste und zweite Thessalonicherbrief*, 2d ed., KNT (Leipzig: A. Deichert, 1909). For a more recent report on scholarship, see R. F. Collins, "Apropos the Integrity of 1 Thess," in *Studies on the First Letter to the Thessalonians*, BEThL 66 (Louvain: Louvain University Press, 1984), 96–135. See also R. F. Collins, ed., *The Thessalonian Correspondence*, BEThL 87 (Louvain: Louvain University Press, 1990). In one article in the last-named work (F. Morgan-Gillman, "Jason of Thessalonica [Acts 17,5–9]," 39–49), reference is made to my article as "the classic statement" of the position that 1 Thess 2:13–16 is an interpolation (43 n. 14).

12. See W. Kümmel's sneering comment about the nineteenth-century love of dissecting the Pauline letters, in "Das literarische und geschichtliche Problem des ersten Thessalonicherbriefes," in *Neotestamentica et Patristica: eine Freundesgabe... O. Cullmann*, NovTSup 6 (Leiden: E. J. Brill, 1962), 214. Collins ("Apropos the Integrity") appeals to "the unanimous witness of the manuscript tradition" in arguing that "the thesis of the unity of the present text of 1 Thess enjoys the *jus possessionis* unless a contrary thesis can be established beyond reasonable doubt" (125). But we lack manuscript evidence for precisely that period (first through third centuries) in which the text would most likely have been in the greatest stage of flux. There is not a single MS datable to before the fourth century that contains 1 Thess 2:13–16. According to Nestle-Aland (p. 687), $\mathfrak{P}^{65}$ (third century) has only 1 Thess 1:3–2:1, 6–13.

stands, reflecting a situation in the post-70 church, and that this interpolation extends from verse 13 through verse 16.[13]

1. Verse 16c. This concluding sentence is pregnant with interpretive possibilities. Assuming that ὀργή here is to be taken in an eschatological sense, the possibilities for εἰς τέλος and ἔφθασεν are still to be considered. εἰς τέλος has been taken as meaning "until the end";[14] other possibilities are "finally" or "completely."[15] Indeed, it has recently been suggested that the Septuagint translators intended by the use of this phrase to render the double meaning of the Hebrew נצח in Greek, so that the phrase can mean both "utterly, completely," and "finally, at last, forever."[16] In any case, all of these translations indicate the finality of the wrath that has come upon the Jews in this passage. Johannes Munck's attempt to paraphrase the expression to mean "until the last events at the end of the world" (i.e., the conversion of Israel), thus harmonizing the passage with Romans 11:25–26, is untenable.[17] The passage excludes categorically any possibility for "the Jews" except the naked wrath of God.

The aorist ἔφθασεν is to be retained in the text.[18] How is this aorist to be interpreted? Many of the commentators who have rejected the views of Baur and others and have held to the genuineness of the passage nevertheless have taken over their suggestions as to what the "wrath" refers to, namely, the destruction of Jerusalem. But they are then reduced to the necessity of interpreting ἔφθασεν as a "prophetic aorist": Paul is speaking "im prophetischen Sinne,"[19] either predicting the destruction of Jerusalem or

---

13. To my knowledge, the only previous argument suggesting vv. 13–16 as an interpolation is that of K.-G. Eckart, "Der zweite echte Brief des Apostels Paulus an die Thessalonicher," *ZThK* 58 (1961): 33–34. For criticisms, see Kümmel, "Literarische Problem," 218ff. On Eckart's argumentation, see n. 66.

14. See, e.g., K. Schelkle, *Die Passion Jesu in der Verkündigung des Neuen Testaments* (Heidelberg: F. H. Kerle, 1949), 37. I will discuss the views of E. Bammel presently.

15. For a good discussion, with numerous parallels, see Milligan's *St. Paul's Epistles*, ad loc.

16. See P. Ackroyd, "נצח – εἰς τέλος," *ExpT* 80 (1968–69): 126. Ackroyd cites Ps 73 (74):3 as an example. For the various Hebrew expressions translated in LXX by the phrase εἰς (τὸ) τέλος, see Hatch-Redpath, 1344–45.

17. J. Munck, *Christ and Israel: An Interpretation of Romans 9–11,* trans. I. Nixon (Philadelphia: Fortress Press, 1967), 64.

18. The variant reading ἔφθακεν is only weakly attested and does not commend itself.

19. Von Dobschütz, *Thessalonicher-Briefe;* see also Frame, *Critical and Exegetical Commentary;* Lünemann, *Critical and Exegetical Handbook;* Neil, *Paul to the Thessalonians;* Oepke, "Briefe an die Thessalonicher"; and Wohlenberg,

predicting generally the impending judgment. Martin Dibelius, too, speaks of the "prophetic style" of the passage, but disallows looking for specific events in the *Zeitgeschichte* for the reference.[20]

Ernst Bammel has seen in this passage a reference to Claudius's expulsion of the Jews from Rome in 49 c.e. He argues that this event was enough to set in motion the "apocalyptic machinery" of both Jews and Jewish Christians and a heightening of end-expectation.[21] In Bammel's view, Paul takes over Jewish apocalyptic motifs and reinterprets them, connecting contemporary events in the political sphere with the persecution of Christians by Jews, the "enemies of God." The aorist ἔφθασεν is interpreted with a present meaning, indicating that the events of the times are an indication that God's judgment is proceeding yet another step "in das τέλος hinein."[22]

All of these suggestions fail to do justice to the text as it stands. The aorist ἔφθασεν must be taken as referring to an event that is now past,[23] and the phrase εἰς τέλος underscores the finality of the "wrath" that has occurred. It need only be inquired further what event in the first century was of such magnitude as to lend itself to such apocalyptic theologizing. The interpretation suggested by Baur and others is still valid: 1 Thessalonians 2:16c refers to the destruction of Jerusalem in 70 c.e.[24] Nevertheless, it is not sufficient merely to excise this one sentence as a post-70 gloss, for formally it constitutes the conclusion to the material represented in the participial clauses of verses 15 and 16 modifying τῶν Ἰουδαίων in verse 14.

Thessalonicherbrief. See also O. Michel: "Paulus spricht nicht im Sinn der Liturgie oder einer Geschichtsbetrachtung, sondern im prophetischen Sinn des sich erfüllenden apokalyptischen Gerichtes" ("Fragen," 58 [see n. 1]).

20. Dibelius, *Thessalonicher I, II,* 11.

21. E. Bammel, "Judenverfolgung und Naherwartung," *ZThK* 56 (1959): 294–315. The phrase "apokalyptische Maschinerie" appears on 301.

22. Ibid., 308–9.

23. See B. Bacon, "Wrath 'unto the Uttermost,'" *Expositor,* 9th ser., 24 (1922): 356–76. Bacon thus accepts the past-tense force of ἔφθασεν and finds a whole list of "current events" to which he believes Paul is referring: the death of Agrippa in 44, the insurrection of Theudas, ca. 44–46, the famine in Judea in 46–47, and the expulsion of the Jews from Rome by Claudius in 49. These events are a sign that God's patience with Israel has come to an end. S. Johnson ("Notes and Comments," *ATR* 23 [1941]: 173–76) adds to Bacon's list a riot in Jerusalem between 48 and 51 (Joseph., *Ant.* 20.5.3) and a famine in Greece and Rome, ca. 49.

24. The relationship between 1 Thess 2:16c and *T. Levi* 6.11 is beyond the scope of this paper to define. For discussion, see Rigaux, *Saint Paul,* 456ff.; and Bammel, "Judenverfolgung," 309 n.1. Cf. Dan 11:36; both *T. Levi* 6.11 and Dan 11:36 refer to God's punishment of the persecutors of his people.

2. Verses 15–16. It is universally agreed that much of the material in these verses is traditional and formulaic.[25] The phrase καὶ πᾶσιν ἀνθρώποις ἐναντίων picks up a theme from Greco-Roman anti-Semitism, as Baur noticed in the quotation cited earlier.[26] It is somewhat surprising to find the characteristic gentile charge of "misanthropy" against the Jews reflected in Pauline correspondence, though it is widespread in the Greco-Roman world of the period.[27] The charge of killing the prophets is a reflection of Jewish tradition widespread in New Testament times, as has been thoroughly documented by Hans-Joachim Schoeps,[28] and appears at various points elsewhere in the New Testament.[29] In early Christian literature it becomes standard to interpret the death of Jesus in connection with the murder of the prophets.[30] But precisely when the charge of "killing the Lord Jesus" was leveled against the Jews is problematic. It will certainly not do to use the speeches in Acts as an example of the early origin of this topos.[31] As Ulrich Wilckens has shown, one finds very little of primitive Palestinian Christianity in the speeches of Acts; on the whole, the speeches reflect the work and thought of the author of Luke-Acts.[32] In my view, one must look to a time after 70 C.E. for the development of the topos.

There is ample evidence that post-70 Christians interpreted the

---

25. See the commentaries. For another discussion, see R. Schippers, "The Pre-Synoptic Tradition in 1 Thessalonians II 13–16," *NovT* 8 (1966): 223–34. The notion of "presynoptic" tradition has to be qualified at the point of distinguishing traditional formulae from the way in which these formulae are put together. On this, see my subsequent discussion.

26. See especially Dibelius, *Thessalonicher I, II*, 11, 29–31, for discussion and for a list of texts from Greek and Latin authors illustrating pagan anti-Judaism. See also the texts assembled by T. Reinach, *Textes d'auteurs grecs et romains relatifs au judaisme* (Paris: Ernst Leroux, 1894; repr., Hildesheim: Geo. Olms, 1963), with the aid of the index entry "misoxenie." The relevant texts are also found, with commentary, in M. Stern, *Greek and Latin Authors on Jews and Judaism*, vol. 1, *From Herodotus to Plutarch* (Jerusalem: Israel Academy of Sciences and Humanities, 1976).

27. For discussion, see V. Tcherikover, *Hellenistic Civilization and the Jews*, trans. S. Applebaum (Philadelphia: Jewish Publication Society, 1966), 357ff.

28. H.-J. Schoeps, "Die jüdischen Prophetenmorde," in *Aus frühchristlicher Zeit: Religionsgeschichtliche Untersuchungen* (Tübingen: Mohr, 1950), 126–43.

29. Schoeps (ibid., 126) cites the following passages as representative of all parts of the NT: Matt 23:31ff.; Acts 7:52; Heb 11:36ff.; 1 Thess 2:15.

30. See, e.g., Acts 7:52; Matt 21:34ff. (Matthean allegorization; see my subsequent discussion); Ign., *Magn.* 8.2; *Barn.* 5.11; Justin, *Dial.* 16; *Mart. Pionii* 13.2; Hipp., *De antich.* 30–31, 58; Tert., *De res. carni.* 26; and Clem. Al., *Strom.* 6.15.127.

31. E.g., Rigaux, *Saint Paul*, cites Acts 2:36 (p. 446).

32. U. Wilckens, *Die Missionsreden der Apostelgeschichte*, 2d ed., WMANT 5 (Neukirchen-Vluyn: Neukirchener, 1963); see esp. 120–21.

destruction of Jerusalem as a punishment inflicted by God upon the
Jews for killing the Christ.[33] Indeed, certain of the rabbis connected
the destruction of the nation and the Temple with the theme of the
persecution of the prophets by the fathers.[34] A common origin for
both of these interpretations might be suggested: reflection on and
study of scripture. One particularly applicable passage in such a
situation would be 2 Chronicles 36:15–16: "The LORD, the God of
their fathers, sent persistently to them by his messengers, because
he had compassion on his people and on his dwelling place; but
they kept mocking the messengers of God, despising his words, and
scoffing at his prophets, till the wrath of the LORD rose against his
people, till there was no remedy" (RSV).[35] This passage, in any
case, presents the basic outline of 1 Thessalonians 2:15–16.

Could Paul have written such a statement? In my view, there
are some basic incompatibilities between 1 Thessalonians 2:15–16
and Paul's thought as expressed elsewhere in his epistles. Though
Paul undoubtedly knows the current tradition concerning the persecution of the prophets — he quotes a basic "proof text" for this
tradition, 1 Kings 19:10, 14, in Romans 11:3 — he never attributes
the death of Jesus to the Jews.[36] First Corinthians 2:8 is the best
example of Paul's own view: Jesus was brought to his death by
the demonic "rulers of this age," who did not know that by so
doing they would defeat themselves in the process.[37] And even

33. See, e.g., Justin, *Apol.* 1.47; Tert., *Adv. jud.* 13; *Apol.* 25; Melito, *Pasch. Hom.* 99; Origen, *c. Cels.* 1.48 and 4.23. Cf. *Gos. Pet.* 7.25 and the variant read-ing at Luke 23:48 ("saying, 'Woe to us for the things that have happened today on account of our sins: for the desolation of Jerusalem has drawn near' "). For discus-sion of some of these texts, see Schoeps, "Die Tempelzerstörung des Jahres 70 in der jüdischen Religionsgeschichte," in *Aus frühchristlicher Zeit*, esp. 145ff.

34. R. Meir: "The citizens of Jerusalem were also smitten because they despised the prophets, as it says, 'But they mocked the messengers of God' (2 Chron 36:16), and it is written 'They have made their faces harder than a rock' (Jer 5:3)." *Exodus Rabba* 31.16 (London: Soncino, 1939), cited by Schoeps, *Aus frühchristlicher Zeit*, 150. Schoeps also cites *Pesiq. R. Kah.* 14 (R. Levi).

35. This passage is partially quoted by R. Meir in *Exod. Rab.* 31.16.

36. In Munck's view (*Christ and Israel*, 115), Paul's quotation of Ps 69:22–23 (= LXX 68:23–24) in Rom 11:9–10 implies also a reflection on Ps 69:21 and "a common early Christian interpretation" of the psalm connecting it with the crucifix-ion of Jesus by the Jews. But Paul does not quote Ps 69:21; it is quite unacceptable to read it into the text of Romans. The only other passage in Paul that Munck uses to support the statement that "the Jews had killed the Messiah" (99) is 1 Thess 2:14–16.

37. The passage is interpreted thus by Origen in his commentary on Matthew (13.8, commenting on Matt 17:22). The "Gnostic" interpretation, as argued, e.g., by U. Wilckens (*Weisheit und Torheit*, BHTh 26 [Tübingen: Mohr-Siebeck, 1959], 71ff.), reads too much into the text.

if one wants to take the phrase οἱ ἄρχοντες τοῦ αἰῶνος τούτου in 1 Corinthians 2:8 as a reference to purely human agencies,[38] then one can credit Paul with historical accuracy in pointing to the Roman imperial authorities, rather than the Jewish people, as responsible for the crucifixion.[39]

I also find it impossible to ascribe to Paul the ad hominem fragment of gentile anti-Judaism in verse 15. Paul seems to have been rather proud of his achievements in Judaism prior to his "conversion" (Gal 1:14; Phil 3:5–6). In fact, even after he became a Christian he continued to refer to himself as a Jew (ἡμεῖς ... Ἰουδαῖοι, Gal 2:15; ἐγὼ Ἰσραηλίτης εἰμί, Rom 11:1); indeed, never in his extant writings does he use the term "Christian," either of himself or of anyone else. Moreover, the thought that God's wrath has come upon the Jewish people[40] with utter finality (v. 16) is manifestly foreign to Paul's theology, which, unique in the New Testament, expresses the thought that God has not abandoned his ancient covenant people (Rom 11:1; cf. 9:4f. and 11:29), and indeed "all Israel will be saved" (Rom 11:26).[41]

3. Verse 14. Here, too, historical and theological questions arise. In this verse, the author draws a connection between Jewish persecutions of Christian churches in Palestine[42] and gentile persecution of the church in Thessalonica. Some have sought to explain this with reference to the book of Acts and the troubles Paul and his coworkers are said to have had at the instigation of local Jews

---

38. See, e.g., A. Feullet, "Les 'chefs de ce siecle' et la Sagesse divine d'après 1 Co. II, 6–8," in *Le Christ Sagesse de Dieu d'après les épîtres pauliniennes* (Paris: J. Gabalda, 1966), 25–36.

39. The best discussion of the historical problems connected with the execution of Jesus is still that of P. Winter, *On the Trial of Jesus*, 2d ed., rev. and ed. T. A. Burkill and G. Vermes (Berlin: de Gruyter, 1974).

40. According to H. Månsson (*Paulus och judarna* [Stockholm: Svenska kyrkans diakonistyrelses bokförlag, 1947], 205), οἱ Ἰουδαῖοι in 1 Thess 2:14 does not refer to the Jewish people as a whole, or even to the inhabitants of Judea. They are the "fanatic Torah-Jews [fanatiska lagjudarna]," whom the apostle identifies with Messiah- and prophet-murderers. If indeed there is such a "theological" meaning attached to "the Jews" in 1 Thess 2:14 — see also Michel, "Fragen," 53 — it is that of the interpolator and not of Paul, for such an interpretation of "the Jews" is without parallel in the Pauline epistles.

41. E. Stauffer (*New Testament Theology*, trans. J. Marsh [London: SCM Press, 1955], 190) speaks of "an astonishing *volte face*" from the thoughts expressed in 1 Thess 2 to those expressed in Rom 11.

42. "Judea" here refers to the Roman province, which includes all of the territory formerly ruled by Herod Agrippa I (41–44 C.E.); see Milligan, *St. Paul's Epistles*, 29. In addition to the texts he cites (Luke 4:44; Acts 10:37; Joseph., *Ant.* 1.160), see also Joseph., *Ant.* 19.363.

(Acts 17:5–9).[43] However, 1 Thessalonians 2:14 refers specifically to persecutions in Judea, and it is said there that the persecution in Thessalonica has been caused by συμφυλέται ("compatriots") of the Thessalonians, gentiles, as Theodore of Mopsuestia correctly interpreted the word centuries ago.[44]

With reference to the alleged persecutions in Judea, 1 Thessalonians 2:14 would be the only New Testament text — were it a genuine expression of Paul — to indicate that the churches in Judea suffered persecution at the hands of the Jews between 44 C.E. and the outbreak of the war against Rome.[45] Those who have dealt with this question in some detail argue that, in fact, there was no significant persecution of Christians in Judea before the war.[46] We are told by Josephus that the execution of James, the brother of Jesus, by the Sadducean priesthood so angered those who were "strict in observance of the law" (the Pharisees) that some of them went to meet the incoming Roman governor with the news and had Ananus deposed from his high priesthood (*Ant.* 20.200). This would indicate that the Christians in Judea, at least up until 62 C.E., were living in harmony with their fellow Jews. Of course, Paul himself encountered quite a bit of hostility in the Diaspora synagogues,[47] but there is a serious question as to how friendly the Christians in Judea were toward Paul (Rom 15:31). Indeed, a careful reading of the available evidence would seem to

---

43. See Frame, *Commentary,* 110; Milligan, *St. Paul's Epistles,* 29; and J. Munck, *Paul and the Salvation of Mankind,* trans. F. Clarke (Richmond: John Knox Press, 1959), 120.

44. Theodore of Mopsuestia, " 'Contribulibus' ut dicat 'Gentibus' "; see H. B. Swete, ed., *Theodori Episcopi Mopseuesteni in Epistolas S. Pauli commentarii* (Cambridge: Cambridge University Press, 1880), ad loc.

45. Bacon ("Wrath 'unto the Uttermost,' " 370) interprets the account of the death of James in Acts 12:1ff. as referring to a systematic pogrom against the Christians. But there is no evidence that it was any such thing. See on this D. Hare, *The Theme of Jewish Persecution of Christians in the Gospel According to St. Matthew,* SNTSMS 6 (Cambridge: Cambridge University Press, 1967), 30ff. M. Goguel (*The Birth of Christianity,* trans. H. Snape [New York: Macmillan, 1954], 123) suggested that 1 Thess 2:14 refers to the persecution of the "Hellenists" (Acts. 8:1; cf. 6:1ff.), but that event probably occurred some 15–20 years prior to the time of the writing of 1 Thess.

46. See Hare, *Theme of Jewish Persecution;* Brandon, *Fall of Jerusalem;* and L. Goppelt, *Jesus, Paul and Judaism,* trans. E. Schroeder (London: T. Nelson, 1964), 105ff.

47. On 2 Cor 11:23ff., see Hare, *Theme of Jewish Persecution,* 62. L. Brun (*Segen und Fluch im Urchristentum,* Skrifter Norsk videnskaps-akademi i Oslo 11–Hist.-filos. klasse 1932, no. 1 [Oslo: Jacob Dybwad, 1932], 127) argues, with reference to Rom 9:3, that Paul was under a curse by the Diaspora Jews, and sees a hint of this also in 1 Cor 4:12. This interesting theory goes beyond the evidence. On the *Birkhath ha-Minim,* see n. 74.

indicate some real hostility on the part of the Judean Christians toward Paul.[48] With respect to the situation in Thessalonica at the time of the writing of 1 Thessalonians, Paul speaks generally — this is a theological topos, revealing his eschatologically oriented theology — about his and his congregation's undergoing "tribulation" (θλίψις, 1:6, recapitulated at 3:3), but that the Thessalonian Christians were actually suffering systematic persecution in the apostolic period is very much in doubt.[49]

Mention should also be made of the "mimesis" terminology that occurs in verse 14. Not only is it improbable that Paul would cite the Judean Christians as examples for his gentile congregations,[50] but also the use of the mimesis theme in this verse does not cohere with Paul's usage elsewhere. It is a very interesting fact that when Paul uses the terminology of "imitation," he uses it with reference to the imitation of himself (1 Cor 4:16; 11:1; Phil 3:17; 1 Thess 1:6; cf. 2 Thess 1:7–9).[51] Nor does he counsel his congregations to "imitate Christ" directly.[52] Characteristic of his usage is 1 Corinthians 11:1: "Be imitators of me, as I am of Christ." In 1 Thessalonians 1:6, Paul uses the expression in the indicative mood: "You became imitators of us [= me] and of the Lord." Here too I see an expression of the intermediary function of the apostle in the mimesis process.[53] What is involved in this usage is nothing less than an intense apostolic self-understanding on the part of Paul. He and no one else — surely not the Judean churches — is, under the Lord, the supreme authority and "model" for his congregations.[54] Given this unique understanding of Paul's own apostolic

---

48. See G. Lüdemann, *Opposition to Paul in Jewish Christianity,* trans. M. E. Boring (Minneapolis: Fortress Press, 1989), esp. 25–115.

49. See Hare, *Theme of Jewish Persecution,* 64.

50. B. Gerhardsson asserts that 1 Thess 2:14 implies that Paul expects the Thessalonian congregation to "receive" from the Judean churches the word of God and to "imitate their halakic practice." See *Memory and Manuscript,* ASNU 22 (Lund: Gleerup, 1961), 274. I am unable to understand how such a conclusion could be suggested by the text. In any case, Paul has his own "halakah," on which see P. J. Tomson, *Paul and the Jewish Law: Halakha in the Letters of the Apostle to the Gentiles,* CRINT 3.1 (Assen/Maastricht: Van Gorcum; Minneapolis: Fortress Press, 1990).

51. For a full-scale treatment of this terminology, see W. De Boer, *The Imitation of Paul* (Kampen: J. H. Kok, 1962). See also D. Stanley, " 'Become Imitators of Me': The Pauline Conception of Apostolic Tradition," *Biblica* 40 (1959): 859–77; and E. Eidem, "Imitatio Pauli," in *Teologiska Studier tillägnade Erik Stave* (Uppsala, 1922), 67–85, unfortunately unavailable to me.

52. On the "imitation of Christ," see H.-D. Betz, *Nachfolge und Nachahmung Jesu Christi im Neuen Testament,* BHTh 37 (Tübingen: Mohr-Siebeck, 1967).

53. Against Betz, ibid., 143.

54. W. Michaelis understands Paul's use of μιμεῖσθαι to imply a claim to obe-

role and authority, and given the otherwise coherent picture of the "mimesis" terminology in the Pauline letters, 1 Thessalonians 2:14 stands out as not only historically incongruous but theologically incongruous as well. What it is, in fact, is a secondary extension on the part of a later editor of the mimesis motif that occurs in 1 Thessalonians 1:6.

4. Verses 13–16. Formally, verse 13 introduces a "thanksgiving" section, indicated by εὐχαριστοῦμεν.[55] The thanksgiving form in the Pauline letters was delineated and described form-critically in the pioneering work of Paul Schubert.[56] There is an apparent anomaly in 1 Thessalonians (and 2 Thess, which is deutero-Pauline and in structure a slavish imitation of 1 Thess),[57] in that it has, as now constituted, two thanksgiving sections (1:2ff. and 2:13ff.),[58] or even three, if one counts 3:9 as a further instance. The εὐχαριστῶ formula does not occur at 3:9, but the clause εὐχαριστίαν δυνάμεθα τῷ θεῷ ἀνταποδοῦναι could be taken as parallel to it. Schubert decided that, in fact, there is only one thanksgiving period in 1 Thessalonians (1:2ff.), which is simply repeated in 2:13ff. and 3:9ff., these repetitions "serving to unify formally the entire section from 1:2–3:13."[59]

Subsequently, Jack Sanders analyzed the transition from "thanksgiving" to "body" in the Pauline letters.[60] He pointed out that in 1 Thessalonians, the opening thanksgiving period is rounded off with an "eschatological climax" in 1:10, and that

---

dience ("μιμέομαι," *TDNT,* 4:668–69). De Boer argues against this interpretation (*Imitation of Paul,* 138, 185–86, 209–10), but Michaelis's view is preferable. On Paul's apostolic consciousness, see especially H. Windisch, *Paulus und Christus: Ein biblisch-religionsgeschichtlicher Vergleich,* UNT 24 (Leipzig: J. C. Hinrichs, 1934), still a very important study on "imitation," see 250ff.; and cf. Betz, *Nachfolge,* 154ff.

55. K. Thieme, in his structural analysis of 1 Thess, places v. 13 at the end of a subsection beginning in 2:1; see "Die Struktur des ersten Thessalonicherbriefes," in *Abraham unser Vater...Festschrift für O. Michel,* ed. O. Betz et al. (Leiden: E. J. Brill, 1963), 45–58. I cannot see any merit at all in his analysis.

56. P. Schubert, *Form and Function of the Pauline Thanksgiving,* BZNW 20 (Berlin: A. Töpelmann, 1939). For a study of the liturgical background of the thanksgiving formula, see J. M. Robinson, "Die Hodajot-Formel in Gebet und Hymnus des Frühchristentums," in *Apophoreta: Festschrift für Ernst Haenchen...,* ed. W. Eltester, BZNW 30 (Berlin: Töpelmann, 1964), 194–235.

57. I find W. Wrede's thorough study of 2 Thess entirely convincing. See *Die Echtheit des zweiten Thessalonicherbriefs,* TU 24.1 (Leipzig: J. C. Hinrichs, 1903).

58. Wrede (ibid., 20) already remarked about this peculiarity in 1 and 2 Thess.

59. Schubert, *Form and Function,* 18ff. He further concluded that in 1 Thess, the thanksgiving period itself constitutes the main "body" of the letter (26).

60. J. T. Sanders, "The Transition from Opening Epistolary Thanksgiving to Body in the Letters of the Pauline Corpus," *JBL* 81 (1962): 348–62.

the following verse, 2:1, is an opening formula introducing the "body" of the letter. This body draws to a close at 2:12, and with 2:13, strangely enough, a second thanksgiving period begins, which continues up to 4:1. "Thus," he writes, "these two thanksgiving periods may be more concisely delineated, on the basis of formal considerations, than is done by merely uniting them functionally into one."[61]

Robert Funk has also done form-critical work on the Pauline corpus and has delineated an entirely new form, the "travelogue,"[62] more recently defined as the "apostolic *parousia*."[63] This form has as its function the effective application in a letter, as a substitute for personal presence, of the apostle's authority in his churches. The form includes such items as the apostle's travel plans, his desire to be with his congregation, and so on. In the case of 1 Thessalonians, Funk has defined the "apostolic *parousia*" as constituting the verses from 2:17 through 3:13.[64]

Funk's analysis now allows us to solve the apparent difficulty of the double thanksgiving in 1 Thessalonians, for it is clear that the "apostolic *parousia*" is introduced formally not by verses 13–16 at all, but by the apostle's remarks in verses 11–12: "For you know how, like a father with his children, we exhorted each one of you and encouraged you and charged you to lead a life worthy of God, who calls you into his own kingdom and glory" (RSV). Note how naturally the transition to apostolic *parousia* takes place by means

---

61. Ibid., 356. For theories dividing 1 Thess into two separate letters, see K.-G. Eckart, "Zweite echte Brief" (see n. 13); and W. Schmithals, "Die Thessalonicher-briefe als Briefcompositionen," in *Zeit und Geschichte: Dankesgabe an Rudolf Bultmann...*, ed. E. Dinkler (Tübingen: Mohr, 1964), 295–315. Eckart, rejecting the authenticity of 2 Thess, deals only with 1 Thess; he divides it into two genuine letters and marks as non-Pauline interpolations 2:13–16; 4:1–8; 4:10b–12; and 5:12–22. Schmithals finds four genuine Pauline letters in 1–2 Thess. Neither study demonstrates any form-critical control. For criticism of Eckart, see Schmithals; and Kümmel, "Literarische und geschichtliche Problem" (see n. 12). For criticisms of Schmithals, see C. Bjerkelund, *Parakalô: Form, Funktion und Sinn der parakalô-Sätze in den paulinischen Briefen*, BTN 1 (Oslo: Universitetsforlaget, 1967), 125ff.; and R. Funk, "The Apostolic *Parousia*: Form and Significance," in *Christian History and Interpretation: Studies Presented to John Knox*, ed. W. Farmer et al. (Cambridge: Cambridge University Press, 1967), 249–68, esp. 263 n. 1. More recently, E. J. Richard (*First and Second Thessalonians*, Sacra Pagina Series 11 [Collegeville, Minn.: Liturgical Press, 1995], 111–27) has isolated 2:13–4:2 as constituting Paul's earliest extant letter to the Thessalonians, except for 2:14–16, which he regards as an interpolation.

62. R. Funk, *Language, Hermeneutic, and Word of God* (New York: Harper & Row, 1966), 263ff.

63. Funk, "Apostolic *Parousia*."

64. Ibid., 250.

of these verses, the apostle continuing in verse 17: "But since we were bereft [ἀπορφανισθέντες] of you, brethren, for a short time, in person not in heart. ... "

Now, we are able to solve Schubert's *aporia* in his discussion of the thanksgiving period in 1 Thessalonians, for he noted the absence of a formal transition from 2:16 to 2:17 and remarked that 2:17 "follows most naturally upon the reminiscences of his [Paul's] former relations to the church (2:1–12)."[65] The conclusion, therefore, that form-critical analysis suggests is this: verses 13–16 do not belong to Paul's original letter at all, but represent a later interpolation into the text.[66] What, then, are the modus operandi and the motivation of our hypothetical interpolator?

If one now compares the passage 2:13ff. with the opening thanksgiving in 1:2ff., one immediately notices that both passages begin by saying the same thing! Identical or equivalent words and phrases are used. The divergence occurs at 1:6 and 2:14: In 1:6, Paul commends the Thessalonians for imitating him and therefore the Lord in that they have received the word joyfully and faithfully, albeit with concomitant "affliction." In 2:14, the author commends the church for imitating the churches in Judea, which have suffered persecution at the hands of the Jews; then follows

---

65. Schubert, *Form and Function*, 23. O. Michel ("Fragen," 51) and P. Richardson (*Israel in the Apostolic Church*, SNTSMS 10 [Cambridge: Cambridge University Press, 1969], 105 n.3) see a connection between the anti-Jewish polemic of vv. 14–16 and v. 18, "but Satan hindered us." I find their interpretation quite impossible: Paul is undoubtedly referring to his illness in v. 18, whatever it was (cf. 2 Cor 12:7). There may indeed be a connection between v. 16 and v. 18, but it is to be explained in a different way. See my subsequent discussion.

66. As indicated in nn. 13 and 61, K.-G. Eckart has also suggested that vv. 13–16 are an interpolation. He sees in vv. 15–16 a programmatic "Judenpolemik" that exhibits a quasi-poetic parallelism. V. 13, too, shows "einen ähnlich straffen Satzparallelismus," which in content is general and unspecific. V. 14 deals generally with suffering and is not specific enough for the Thessalonian situation (32–34). However, Paul may have used "traditional" material just as easily as a later interpolator, and there is lacking in Eckart's study both form-critical control and *sachkritik*. Incidentally, I wish to point out that my own study of the text had led me to the conclusion that vv. 13–16 are an interpolation before I was aware of Eckart's article. See also H. Boers, "The Form-Critical Study of Paul's Letters: 1 Thessalonians as a Case Study," *NTS* 22 (1976): 140–58. Boers accepts my argumentation, provides a useful comment on καὶ ἡμεῖς in 2:13 (150–51), and states in his conclusion: "The problem of the structure of I Thess. finds a simple resolution when ii,13–16 is recognized as an interpolation" (158). See also H. Koester, "1 Thessalonians — Experiment in Christian Writing," in *Continuity and Discontinuity in Church History: Essays Presented to G. K. Williams*, ed. F. F. Church and T. George (Leiden: E. J. Brill, 1979), 33–44, esp. 38; and Koester, *Introduction*, 2:113. D. Schmidt has added linguistic arguments in "1 Thess 2:13–16: Linguistic Evidence for an Interpolation," *JBL* 102 (1983): 269–79.

the anti-Jewish polemic. The method of our hypothetical interpolator is strikingly similar to that of the author of 2 Thessalonians, namely, to use Pauline words and phrases from a genuine letter to provide a putative "Pauline" framework for a new message. In 2 Thessalonians, the new message is contained especially in the eschatological passage, chapter 2.[67] In 1 Thessalonians 2:13ff., the new message has as its purpose, in circumstances of persecution, to encourage the readers with reference to the embattled Christians in Palestine and to underscore now, in a post-70 situation, the "united front" of all Christians against the Jews who have at last suffered in the destruction of their city and Temple the ultimate rejection and judgment from God. The position of the interpolation is suggested by the structure of the original letter, at the end of the thanksgiving period beginning in 1:6 (it thus serves as a repetition of the thanksgiving) and before Paul's discussion of his travel plans. The author of the interpolation has "Paulinized" the anti-Jewish polemic by means of 16a, κωλυόντων ἡμᾶς τοῖς ἔθνεσιν λαλῆσαι ἵνα σωθῶσιν, possibly under the influence of a misinterpretation of Paul's reference to Satan in 2:18,[68] and probably with reference to the memory of what happened to Paul upon his arrival in Jerusalem (see Acts 21:30ff.; Rom 15:31).

As has already been noted, much of the material in the interpolation is traditional and formulaic;[69] yet it constitutes a new message as it is incorporated into the Thessalonian epistle. The importance of a proper historical understanding of this "traditional" material can hardly be overstated, for what is reflected here is the fact that traditional building blocks are given new form in a post-70 historical situation. This thesis can be tested with reference to the parallels in the Gospel of Matthew, quoting the relevant passages from Matthew 23 and 24:[70]

"Woe to you, scribes and Pharisees, hypocrites! ... You are sons of those who murdered the prophets. *Fill up* [(ἀνα-) πληροῦν], then, the measure of your fathers. You serpents,

---

67. In addition to Wrede, *Thessalonicherbriefs*, see R. J. Petersen's unpublished doctoral dissertation "The Structure and Purpose of Second Thessalonians" (Harvard Divinity School, 1968).

68. See my remarks about Michel and Richardson in n. 65. Only in a time of intense Jewish-Christian polemic could such a connection be made.

69. R. Schippers, "Pre-Synoptic Tradition," 224 (see n. 25), refers to the quasitechnical language of *paradosis* in v. 13 and interprets the phrase παραλαβόντες λόγον ἀκοῆς to mean "tradition," the substance of what is contained in vv. 14–16.

70. I use the work of J. Orchard ("Thessalonians and the Synoptic Gospels," *Biblica* 19 [1938]: 20ff.), but I disagree fundamentally with his conclusions.

you brood of vipers, how are you to escape being sentenced
to hell? Therefore I send you *prophets* [προφῆται] and wise
men and scribes, some of whom you will *kill* [ἀποκτείνειν]
and crucify, and some you will scourge in your synagogues
and *persecute* [(ἐκ-) διώκειν] from town to town, that upon
you may come all the righteous blood shed on earth.... Truly,
I say to you, all this will come upon this generation.
   "O Jerusalem, Jerusalem, *killing* the *prophets* and stoning
those who are sent to you!... Behold, your house is forsaken
and desolate.... Truly, I say to you, there will not be left
here one stone upon another, that will not be thrown down."
(23:29–24:2, RSV; my italics)

It is, of course, probable that Jesus had disputes with opponents,
some of whom may have been Pharisees. He may have referred
to the stock idea current in Judaism concerning the persecution
of the prophets. He may even have prophesied the destruction of
Jerusalem.[71] But it is the author of the Gospel of Matthew who
must be credited (or debited!) with putting these motifs together
in the way in which they now stand in the passage quoted. His
work reflects a historical situation that did not pertain prior to
the destruction of Jerusalem: relations between the church and
the synagogue are on the breaking point.[72] In the years since the
destruction, the Pharisaic leaders, at first under the leadership of
R. Johannan ben Zakkai, have assembled at the coastal town of
Jamnia and have begun the task of consolidating the practice of
Judaism so as to require a new uniformity.[73] Christians are being cursed in the synagogues and excommunicated therefrom;[74]

71. On Matt 24:2b, see R. Hummel, *Die Auseinandersetzung zwischen Kirche
und Judentum im Matthäusevangelium*, BEvTh 33 (Munich: Chr. Kaiser, 1966), 85.
Cf. *Gos. Thom.* 71.
   72. In my earlier version of this essay, I wrote, "The final break between the
church and the synagogue has taken place," and I cited Hare, *Theme of Jewish Persecution*, 167ff. and passim; W. Trilling, *Das wahre Israel: Studien zur Theologie
des Matthäus-Evangeliums*, 3d ed., SANT 10 (Munich: Kösel-Verlag, 1964), 75ff.;
and K. Stendahl, *The School of St. Matthew*, 2d ed. (Philadelphia: Fortress Press,
1968), xiff. But A. J. Saldarini has recently made a strong case for understanding the Matthean community as still a part of first-century Judaism; see *Matthew's
Christian-Jewish Community* (Chicago: University of Chicago Press, 1994).
   73. See J. Parkes, *The Foundations of Judaism and Christianity* (Chicago: Quad-
rangle Books, 1960), 224ff. For a full discussion of the developments in Jamnia,
see W. Davies, *The Setting of the Sermon on the Mount* (Cambridge: Cambridge
University Press, 1964), 256ff. See also S. Sandmel, *The First Christian Century in
Judaism and Christianity* (New York: Oxford University Press, 1969), 58ff.
   74. On the *Birkhath ha-Minim*, the twelfth "benediction" of the synagogue

their prophets and teachers are being persecuted and denounced as "children of hell."[75] These developments are not limited only to Palestine but are apparently also felt in the Diaspora.[76] In short, the final break between church and synagogue is about to occur, if it has not already happened, and the relations between Jews and Christians (including Christian Jews) are now acutely polemical.

It is only in this situation that the author of the Gospel of Matthew (and other New Testament writers) can speak of the Jewish nation as culpable not only for the death of the prophets but also for the death of Jesus. This is graphically portrayed in the Matthean passion narrative with the chilling words "His blood be on us and on our children" (27:25). Even the parables of Jesus are the subject of creative rehandling so as to connect the death of Jesus and the prophets to the destruction of Jerusalem. In the parable of the marriage feast (Matt 22:2–14; cf. Luke 14:16), the king's servants are mistreated and murdered, with the result that "the king was angry [ὠργίσθη], and he sent his troops and destroyed those murderers and burned their city" (v. 7).[77] For Matthew, the church, now increasingly of gentile constituency,[78] is in every respect the inheritor of the promises of God; the church is the "true Israel."[79] The non-Christian Jews, on the other hand, are denounced as "children of hell" (Matt 23:15; cf. John 8:44).

In speaking, then, of parallel traditions between 1 Thessalonians 2:14–16 and the Gospels, one must also consider the parallel mode of handling these traditions, reflecting a common historical situation. For it is only in the post-70 period that an editor working

---

prayer *Shemoneh Esreh* cursing Christians and heretics, composed by Samuel the Small under the direction of R. Gamaliel II, ca. 85 C.E. (*Ber.* 28b), see Davies, *Setting,* 275–76. As this relates to ἀποσυνάγωγος in John 9:22, see especially the brilliant treatment by J. Martyn, *History and Theology in the Fourth Gospel,* 2d rev. ed. (Nashville: Abingdon, 1979), 38–62.

75. This according to H.-J. Schoeps's interpretation of *'Abod. Zar.* 17a, in *Jewish Christianity,* trans. D. Hare (Philadelphia: Fortress Press, 1969), 33. See also *t. Sanh.* 13.4, 5, qtd. in R. T. Herford, *Christianity in Talmud and Midrash* (Clifton, N.J.: Reference Book Publishers, 1966), 118–19.

76. See Justin, *Dial.* 108.

77. On this and other redactional elements in Matthew, see Hummel, *Auseinandersetzung,* 82ff.

78. Stendahl, *School of St. Matthew,* xiii.

79. See especially the treatment by W. Trilling, *Wahre Israel.* That the church is the "true Israel" seems to be a universal assumption in the Christian literature of this and subsequent periods.

with the text of Paul's letter to the Thessalonians, in a situation of local (presumably gentile) persecution against the church in Thessalonica,[80] could hold up as a shining example "the churches of God which are in Judea." And very possibly one of these churches has in its leadership the author of the Gospel of Matthew.

---

80. For general remarks on how Christians fared in the Roman world of the period, see W. H. C. Frend, *Martyrdom and Persecution in the Early Church* (New York: New York University Press, 1967), 155ff.

Chapter 4

A Reminiscence of
Classical Myth at 2 Peter 2:4

Of all of the books of the New Testament, 2 Peter is the only
one whose author goes out of his way specifically to deny any
dependence upon "cleverly devised myths" (1:16) in the message
that he wishes to convey.[1] It is all the more ironic, then, that a
careful reader of his work can detect exactly that which he so
vehemently denies, namely, his reliance upon a myth prominent
in Greco-Roman paganism in the framing of his argumentation.
Our detective work will focus upon a single verse, indeed a single
word within that verse, but we shall also have occasion to consider
in passing some other examples of the impact of Greco-Roman
mythology on the author of 2 Peter.

The focus here is on the background of the reference to the
fallen angels in 2 Peter 2:4. The passage reads as follows:

εἰ γὰρ ὁ θεὸς ἀγγέλων ἁμαρτησάντων οὐκ ἐφείσατο, ἀλλὰ
σιροῖς ζόφου ταρταρώσας παρέδωκεν εἰς κρίσιν τηρουμέ-
νους, ...[2]

For if God did not spare the angels when they sinned, but cast
them into hell and committed them to pits of nether gloom to
be kept until the judgment; ... (RSV)

The parallel passage in the Epistle of Jude (v. 6) is considerably
different:

---

1. Reliance upon "myths" is attributed to opponents of Christian truth in the
Pastoral Epistles, the only other writings in the NT that use the term (see 1 Tim
1:4; 2 Tim 4:4; Titus 1:14). Perhaps the author of 2 Peter is of the same opinion,
though this is not stated explicitly.

2. Here I prefer the 25th ed. of Nestle-Aland (1963) to the 27th, which reads
σειραῖς instead of σιροῖς. The NRSV presupposes the newer reading, "chains"
instead of "pits." See my subsequent discussion.

ἀγγέλους τε τοὺς μὴ τηρήσαντας τὴν ἑαυτῶν ἀρχὴν ἀλλὰ ἀπολιπόντας τὸ ἴδιον οἰκητήριον εἰς κρίσιν μεγάλης ἡμέρας δεσμοῖς ἀϊδίοις ὑπὸ ζόφον τετήρηκεν.

And the angels that did not keep their own position but left their proper dwelling have been kept by him in eternal chains in the nether gloom until the judgment of the great day;... (RSV)

These two passages have in common the words ἄγγελοι, ζόφος, and τηρεῖσθαι, and the phrase εἰς κρίσιν. I am completely in accord with the usual view of the relationship between Jude and 2 Peter, namely, that the author of 2 Peter knew and used the Epistle of Jude.[3] Nevertheless, the differences between 2 Peter 2:4 and Jude 6 require explanation. Especially of interest to us here is the use in 2 Peter 2:4 of the verb ταρταροῦν, a hapax legomenon in the New Testament.

The myth of the fallen angels and their fate is dealt with at length in *1 Enoch,* especially in chapters 6–21, and commentators quite rightly refer to *1 Enoch* in illuminating the background of these passages in Jude and 2 Peter.[4] At least in the case of Jude, there can be no question about the influence of that apocalyptic pseudepigraphon. *1 Enoch* 1.9 is actually quoted in Jude 15 with a formula crediting the quotation to the prophet Enoch.[5] And Jude 6 surely reflects the influence of *1 Enoch* in its formulation, especially *1 Enoch* 10.4ff., as is duly noted in the margin of the Nestle-Aland text.

The Old Testament stimulus for the myth in *1 Enoch* is that intrusive passage in Genesis 6:1–4 describing the adventures of the "sons of God" (בני האלהים) with the "daughters of men" (האדם בנות).[6] Nevertheless, it is clear that Enoch's enlargement of the Gen-

---

3. For a good discussion of the four possible explanations for the relationships between Jude and 2 Peter, see R. J. Bauckham's commentary *Jude, 2 Peter,* WBC 50 (Waco: Word Books, 1983), 141–43. Bauckham, too, prefers the usual view. See also the more recent commentaries: H. Paulsen, *Der zweite Petrusbrief und der Judasbrief,* KEK 12:2 (Göttingen: Vandenhoeck & Ruprecht, 1992), 97–100; J. H. Neyrey, *2 Peter, Jude,* AB 37C (New York: Doubleday, 1993), 120–22; and A. Vögtle, *Der Judasbrief / Der zweite Petrusbrief,* EKKNT 22 (Düsseldorf: Benziger; Neukirchen-Vluyn: Neukirchener, 1994), 122–23.

4. See esp. Paulsen, *Zweite Petrusbrief,* 73–78, 130–33, and literature cited therein.

5. Note the introductory formula in v. 14: ἐπροφήτευσεν δὲ καὶ τούτοις ἕβδομος ἀπὸ Ἀδὰμ Ἐνὼχ λέγων.

6. On this passage, see E. A. Speiser, *Genesis,* AB 1 (Garden City, N.Y.: Doubleday, 1964), 44–46.

esis myth includes some new elements not dependent upon Genesis 6 at all, and which can be accounted for only on the basis of extra-biblical influences. Specifically, it has been shown by T. F. Glasson that the myth of the fallen angels in *1 Enoch* has been molded under influences from the theogonic myths of the Greeks,[7] especially those stories dealing with the Titanomachia, the war between Zeus and the Titans.[8]

The doom of the fallen angels is described in the following passages in *1 Enoch:*

> And to Raphael he [the Lord] said, "Go, Raphael, and bind 'Asael hand and foot, and cast him into the darkness. And make an opening in the wilderness that is in Doudael. And there cast him, and lay beneath him sharp stones and jagged stones. And cover him with darkness, and let him dwell there forever. And cover up his face, and let him not see the light. And on the day of the great judgment, he will be led away to the burning conflagration. And heal the earth which the watchers have desolated; and announce the healing of the earth, that they may heal the plague, and all the sons of men may not perish because of the mystery which the watchers told and taught their sons. And all the earth was desolated by the deeds of the teaching of 'Asael. And over him write all the sins." (10.4–8)

> And to Michael he said, "Go, Michael, bind Shemihaza and the others with him, who have united themselves with the daughters of men, so that they were defiled by them in their uncleanness. And when their sons perish and they see the destruction of their beloved ones, bind them for seventy generations in the valleys of the earth, until the day of their judgment and consummation, until the eternal judgment is consummated. Then they will be led away to the fiery abyss, and to the torture, and to the prison where they will be confined forever. And everyone who is condemned and de-

---

7. See T. F. Glasson, *Greek Influence in Jewish Eschatology* (London: SPCK, 1961), esp. 62ff.

8. The word τιτάνες is used in the LXX at 2 Sam 5:18, 22 to translate רפאים; see also Jdt 16:6, where the "giants" (γίγαντες) are referred to as υἱοὶ τιτάνων. The τιτάνες in the latter passage are probably to be taken as referring to the "sons of God" in Gen 6:2. See ibid., 65.

stroyed henceforth will be bound together with them until the consummation of their generation." (10.11–14)[9]

The angels are accused of two crimes. In 10.8, reference is made to the disclosures of secrets to men by 'Asael; in 8.1ff., these secrets consist especially of the arts of civilization and the use of the metals of the earth. This motif is absent from Genesis 6 and is probably influenced by the myth of the Titan Prometheus.[10] In 10.11ff., defilement with women is the crime, and this is developed out of Genesis 6. At 15.3ff., this theme is elaborated: the angels have left their proper "dwelling" (i.e., heaven) and have lain with the daughters of men. In these passages from *1 Enoch* are to be found the sources of Jude 6: the angels have abandoned their proper dwelling place (15.3, 7) and have been placed in chains (10.4, 11; see also 54.3–5) and darkness (10.4–5) until the judgment of the great day (10.6, 12).

In turn, the myth of the fallen angels in *1 Enoch* shows some remarkable points of similarity with the Greek myth of the Titanomachia. The earliest complete source for the latter is Hesiod's *Theogony*.[11] In this myth, the Titans are the children born to Uranos and Gaia, the youngest of whom is Kronos (*Th.* 132ff.).[12] The kingship among the gods falls to Kronos after he has succeeded

---

9. I quote from the eclectic translation of the Ethiopic, Greek, and Aramaic versions prepared by G. W. E. Nickelsburg for his forthcoming commentary on *1 Enoch* (to be published in the Hermeneia Series); I am grateful to him for allowing me to use it. See also the translation of the Ethiopic version by M. A. Knibb, *The Ethiopic Book of Enoch*, 2 vols. (Oxford: Clarendon, 1978). For the Greek fragments, see M. Black, *Apocalypsis Henochi Graece*, PVTG 3 (Leiden: E. J. Brill, 1970). For the Aramaic fragments, see J. T. Milik, *The Books of Enoch: Aramaic Fragments of Qumran Cave 4* (Oxford: Clarendon, 1976). The passages quoted here are partially extant in three of the seven fragmentary copies of the Aramaic version of *1 Enoch* found in the DSS (4QEn[a], 4QEn[b], 4QEn[c]).

1 Enoch 6–11 as we now have it is a conflation of two cycles of tradition in which 'Asael and Shemihazah respectively are identified as chief of the fallen angels. See esp. Nickelsburg, "Apocalyptic and Myth in 1 Enoch 6–11," *JBL* 96 (1977): 383–405. On the use and reinterpretation of *1 Enoch* 6–11 in the Gnostic *Apocryphon of John*, see my article "*1 Enoch* in the *Apocryphon of John*," in *Texts and Contexts: Biblical Texts in Their Textual and Situational Contexts: Essays in Honor of Lars Hartman*, ed. T. Fornberg and D. Hellholm (Oslo: Scandinavian University Press, 1995), 355–67; cf. chapter 7 of this book.

10. See Glasson, *Greek Influence*, 65; and Nickelsburg, "Apocalyptic and Myth," 399–404. Cf. Hes., *Th.* 565ff.; and esp. Aesch., *PV* 445ff. For his defiance Prometheus is bound to rocks (ἀδαμαντίνων δεσμῶν ἐν ἀρρήκτοις πέδαις [*PV* 6]).

11. The myth is presupposed already in Homer. See esp. *Il.* 8.479; 14.274–79; 15.225.

12. It is perhaps only a coincidence that the fallen angels in *1 Enoch* are called "sons of heaven" (*ouranos* = Uranos), as, for example, at 6.2. Cf. Gen 6:2 (LXX): οἱ υἱοὶ τοῦ θεοῦ.

in castrating his father, Uranos (*Th.* 176ff.).[13] Zeus, in turn, conspires against Kronos and the rest of the Titans, aided especially by the "hundred-handed" giants[14] Cottus, Briareos, and Gyes, sons of Uranos who were previously banished to the underworld by their father *(Th.* 147ff.; 617ff.). The battle rages furiously until finally the Titans are vanquished and banished to nether Tartarus:

> And amongst the foremost Cottus and Briareos (= Greek Βριάρεως) and Gyes insatiate for war raised fierce fighting; three hundred rocks, one upon another, they launched from their strong hands and overshadowed the Titans with their missiles, and hurled them beneath the widepathed earth, and bound them in bitter chains [καὶ δεσμοῖσιν ἐν ἀργαλέοισιν ἔδησαν] when they had conquered them by their strength for all their great spirit, as far beneath the earth as heaven is above earth; for so far is it from earth to Tartarus.... There by the counsel of Zeus who drives the clouds the Titan gods are hidden under misty gloom [ὑπὸ ζόφῳ ἠερόεντι], in a dank place where are the ends of the huge earth. And they may not go out; for Poseidon fixed gates of bronze upon it, and a wall runs all round it on every side. There Gyes and Cottus and great-souled Obriareus (Greek = Ὀβριάρεως) live, trusty warders of Zeus, who holds the aegis. (*Th.* 713–35)[15]

The similarities between the fate of the fallen angels in *1 Enoch* and that of the Titans in Hesiod are striking. The angels are bound in chains by the archangels of God, just as the Titans are bound in chains by the henchmen of Zeus, the hundred-handed giants. The fallen angels have rocks heaped upon them by the archangels of the Lord, just as the Titans are overwhelmed with rocks hurled by the giants. The evil angels are consigned to nether darkness in *1 Enoch,* and the Titans are consigned to the nether gloom of Tartarus in Hesiod.[16] The one main feature of the myth in *1 Enoch* that is

---

13. These myths of the succession of kingship among the gods are ultimately derived from ancient Near Eastern sources. For a brief discussion, see A. Lesky, *A History of Greek Literature,* trans. J. Willis and C. de Heer (New York: Thomas Y. Crowell, 1966), 94–96 and literature cited therein. On the general question of the impact of Semitic culture on Mycenaean and archaic Greece, see M. C. Astour, *Hellenosemitica* (Leiden: E. J. Brill, 1965).

14. The "hundred-handed" giants were called οἱ ἑκατόνχειρες in later literature; see, for example, Apollod., *Bibl.* 1.1.1; and other texts cited in this essay.

15. H. Evelyn-White's translation in the LCL edition. In the text both "Briareos" and "Obriareus" are used for the same giant.

16. The word used in the Greek fragment of *1 Enoch* 10.5 is σκότος. The usual

absent from the Greek myth is reference to the future judgment of fire.[17]

These similarities are such that one can safely assert that *1 Enoch* was profoundly influenced by Greek mythology. Jude 6 reflects this influence, but there the influence of Greek mythology is indirect, coming via the Jewish book of *1 Enoch*.[18] But the case of 2 Peter 2:4 is a different matter. Although 2 Peter 2:4 is partially indebted to Jude 6 for the theme of the doom of the sinful angels, it is my contention that 2 Peter 2:4 was formulated under *direct* influence from Greek mythology, with no independent use of *1 Enoch* at all in evidence. This can be seen especially in the phrase σιροῖς ζόφου ταρταρώσας.

The verb ταρταροῦν does not occur in the Greek fragments of *1 Enoch*. The noun Τάρταρος occurs once:[19] in *1 Enoch* 20.2, the archangel Uriel is described as "one of the holy angels who is over the world and Tartarus" (ὁ εἷς τῶν ἁγίων ἀγγέλων ὁ ἐπὶ τοῦ κόσμου καὶ τοῦ Ταρτάρου).[20] The question thus arises as to the source of the verb ταρταροῦν in 2 Peter 2:4, its precise meaning, and the contexts in which it is used elsewhere in Greek literature.

In Hesiod and the older classical writers, the verb ταρταροῦν does not occur. Instead one finds the noun "Tartarus" used in a prepositional phrase together with a verb, as, for example, in the phrase ῥίπτειν (or βάλλειν) ἐς Τάρταρον. By analogy, the precise meaning of ταρταροῦν is "to cast into Tartarus."[21]

From the first century B.C.E. onward, the verb ταρταροῦν does occur, sometimes in compound form as καταταρταροῦν. A study of

---

word in Greek literature that describes the darkness of Tartarus is ζόφος, as, for example, in Hes., *Th.* 729. But see Aesch., *Eum.* 71–72, where κακὸς σκότος is used in connection with Tartarus.

17. In addition to the texts quoted earlier, see *1 Enoch* 21.7–10; 54.1–6.

18. Jude 13 may be a different case; see J. P. Oleson, "An Echo of Hesiod's Theogony vv. 190–2 in Jude 13," *NTS* 25 (1979): 492–503.

19. The word Τάρταρος occurs in the LXX at Job 40:20; 41:24; and Prov 30:16. For a survey of the use of the word "Tartarus" "from Greek mythology to the Christian liturgy," see G.-H. Baudry, "Le Tartare: De la mythologie grecque à la liturgie chrétienne," *MScRel* 52 (1995): 87–104. *1 Enoch* 20.2 is not preserved in any of the Qumran fragments.

20. The Ethiopic text of this verse is corrupt; see Knibb's note to 20.2 in his *Ethiopic Book*, 106–7. The angel Uriel as warder of Tartarus performs a function similar to that of the hundred-handed giants at Hes., *Th.* 734ff. Uriel's function is later attributed in apocryphal literature to a separate angel who goes under the name Ταρταροῦχος. See, e.g., *Apoc. Paul* 18; and the *Book of Thomas the Contender* (NHC II,7) 142, 42.

21. Hom., *Il.* 8.13; *Hymn. Hom. Merc.* 256, 374; Hes., *Th.* 868; cf. Lycoph., *Alex.* 1197: ἐμβαλεῖν ταρτάρῳ.

the contexts in which the verb is found is instructive, and I present here all of the occurrences in Greek literature through the early third century c.e. that I have been able to find.[22]
Apparently, the first occurrences of the verbs ταρταροῦν and καταταρταροῦν occur in the treatise *On Piety* (Περὶ εὐσεβείας) by the Epicurean philosopher Philodemus, preserved in very fragmentary condition among the famous papyri from Herculaneum (P.Herc.). The second part of his treatise[23] consists of criticism of the poets and previous philosophers for their views of the gods and their myths.[24] Our first example of the use of ταρταροῦν apparently occurs (if the reconstructions of lacunae are correct) in a discussion of punishments meted out by Zeus, in this case on the Titan Prometheus: he is bound and, in addition, "is thrown down by him [Zeus] to Tartarus" (ὑπ᾽] αὐτοῦ τα[ρταροῦται]; P.Herc. 1088 III, ll. 6–8).[25]
The binding of Prometheus is brought up again a little later, and Aeschylus is cited in this context. After reporting on the deeds of Kronos in imprisoning his own brothers, Philodemus adds the following:

Αἰσχύλος ἐν τῶι λυομ[έ]ν[ωι Προ]μη[θ]εῖ [φησιν ὑπ]ὸ Διὸς δεδ[έσθαι.] καὶ πάντες [καταταρτα]ρωθέντες [ἤδη πρὶν ὑπ᾽] Οὐρανοῦ κ[αταδέδεντ]αι.

Aeschylus, in his *Prometheus Bound,* says that he [Kronos] was bound by Zeus, and all those who had already previ-

---

22. These findings have recently been confirmed by a search of the *TLG*.
23. Until the recent work on this treatise by D. Obbink, part 2 was regarded as part 1, and part 1 as part 2, ever since the edition of T. Gomperz, *Philodem über Frömmigkeit,* Herkulanische Studien 2 (Leipzig: Teubner, 1866). Obbink has used a new method of reconstructing the papyrus rolls and has published a critical text of the first (philosophical) part of the text: *Philodemus on Piety, Part 1: Critical Text with Commentary* (Oxford: Clarendon, 1996 [1997]). The passages quoted here from part 2 are from the edition prepared by A. Schober, *Philodemi de pietate pars prior,* a dissertation submitted to the University of Königsberg in 1923 but not published until a photo-offset reproduction appeared in the journal *Cronache ercolanesi* 18 (1988): 67–125. (Schober's edition is not in the *TLG* database.) I have also consulted R. Philippson's improvements to Gomperz's edition, "Zu Philodems Schrift über die Frömmigkeit," *Hermes* 55 (1920): 225–78, 364–72; 56 (1921): 355–410. Translations are my own.
24. According to Philippson ("Philodems Schrift," 225), the critique of the traditional gods of antiquity from the second century B.C.E. onward, including that of the Christian apologists, is based on Epicurean foundations; Philodemus is the most important witness to this Epicurean topos.
25. See Schober, *Philodemi,* 90.

ously been thrown down to Tartarus by Uranos are bound fast. (P.Herc. 1088 III, ll. 21–28)[26]

In another passage, Philodemus uses the verb ταρταροῦν with reference to the story of the banishment of the hundred-handed giants to Tartarus by Uranos:

τ[ὸν δ Οὐρα]νὸν Ἀ[κο]υσίλαος δείσαντα τοὺς [ἑκατ]όγχειρας, μὴ [ἐπιθῶ]νται, ταρτ[αρῶσαι], διότι τοι[οῦτος εἶ]δε.

But Uranos, [as reported by] Acusilaus, fearing that the hundred-handed ones might attack, hurled them down to Tartarus because he saw what sort they were. (P.Herc. 433 V, ll. 15–21)[27]

Apollodorus (or Pseudo-Apollodorus)[28] the Mythographer uses the verb three times in the *Bibliotheca*. At 1.1.4, he refers to the accession of Kronos as follows: τῆς δὲ ἀρχῆς ἐκβαλόντες τούς τε καταταρταρωθέντας ἀνήγαγον ἀδελφοὺς καὶ τὴν ἀρχὴν Κρόνῳ παρέδοσαν ("And, having dethroned their father, they [the Titans] brought up their brethren [the Cyclopes] who had been hurled down to Tartarus [by Uranus], and committed the sovereignty to Cronus").[29] At 1.2.1, he refers to the help given to Zeus in the Titanomachia by the Cyclopes who "had been thrown down to Tartarus" (καταταρταρωθέντας). And, at 1.2.3, Apollodorus refers to Menoetius, the son of Japetus, as one ὃν κεραυνώσας ἐν τῇ τιτανομαχίᾳ Ζεὺς κατεταρτάρωσεν ("whom Zeus in the battle with the Titans smote with a thunderbolt and hurled down to Tartarus").

In the *Theologia Graeca* of the Stoic philosopher L. Cornutus occurs the following passage (from chap. 7):

Τελευταῖον δὲ ὁ μὲν Κρόνος ἱστορεῖται συνεχῶς κατιόντα ἐπὶ τῷ μίγνυσθαι τῇ Γῇ τὸν Οὐρανὸν ἐκτεμεῖν καὶ παῦσαι

---

26. See ibid. Aeschylus (*PV* 221–23) refers to Kronos and his allies' banishment to the gloom of Tartarus but does not use the verb καταταρταροῦν.

27. Philodemus cites Acusilaus (fifth century B.C.E.), but I doubt that Acusilaus used this verb. For the fragments of Acusilaus, see *FGH* 1:2, Akusilaos von Argos (pp. 47–58). Frag. 8 (50–51) is our Philodemus text (using Philippson's reconstructions [see "Philodems Schrift"]).

28. The attribution of the *Bibliotheca* by Photius to Apollodorus the Grammarian (second century B.C.E.) is surely wrong, and the author does not identify himself. Frazer (in his introduction to the LCL edition [xi]) assigns the *Bibliotheca* to the first century B.C.E.

29. Frazer's translation in the LCL edition; the brackets are mine.

τῆς ὕβρεως, ὁ δὲ Ζεὺς ἐκβαλὼν αὐτὸν τῆς βασιλείας καταταρταρῶσαι.

But finally Kronos, for his part, upon encountering the intercourse of Uranos with Ge, is reported to have castrated him, thus bringing an end to his offense. Zeus, in turn, deposed Kronos from his reign and threw him down into Tartarus.[30]

In the *Hypotyposes* (*Outlines of Pyrrhonism*) of Sextus Empiricus, in a section wherein he seeks to prove that there is no absolute good, he refers to the custom of the Scythians of cutting the throats of their fathers when they get older than the age of sixty, and then remarks:

καὶ τί θαυμαστόν, εἴγε ὁ μὲν Κρόνος τῇ ἅρπῃ τὰ αἰδοῖα ἐξέτεμε τοῦ πατρός, ὁ δὲ Ζεὺς τὸν Κρόνον κατεταρτάρωσεν, ἡ δὲ Ἀθηνᾶ μετὰ Ἥρας καὶ Ποσειδῶνος τὸν πατέρα δεσμεύειν ἐπεχείρησεν...

And what wonder, seeing that Cronos cut off his father's genitals with a sickle, and Zeus plunged Cronos down to Tartarus, and Athena with the help of Hera and Poseidon attempted to bind her father with fetters? (3.210)[31]

The Christian apologist Athenagoras utilizes the philosophical traditions of criticism against the gods of mythology in his defense of the Christian faith. In chapter 20 of his *Supplicatio pro Christianis,* he recounts the succession myths, including the story of how Zeus bound Kronos and hurled him down to Tartarus (κατεταρτάρωσεν), and then adds this sneering comment in chapter 21:

οὐ καταβάλλουσι τὸν πολὺν τοῦτον ἀσεβῆ λῆρον περὶ τῶν θεῶν; Οὐρανὸς ἐκτέμνεται, δεῖται καὶ κατατατταροῦται Κρόνος,...

Do they not pour out at length such impious nonsense about the gods? Uranos is castrated, Kronos is bound and hurled down to Tartarus,...[32]

---

30. C. Lang, ed. (Leipzig: Teubner, 1881); my translation. Cornutus goes on to interpret the myth allegorically according to Stoic convention.
31. Bury's translation in the LCL edition.
32. C. Richardson, trans., in *Early Christian Fathers,* LCC 1 (New York: Macmillan, 1970), 320. Cf. Ps.-Clem. *Homil.* 4.16.2: αὐτὸς δὲ ὁ Ζεὺς τὸν αὐτοῦ πατέρα δήσας καθείρξεν εἰς Τάρταρον καὶ τοὺς ἄλλους κολάζει θεούς.

Athenagoras also uses the verb καταταρταροῦν in chapter 18 in connection with the hundred-handed giants and the Cyclopes, οὓς καὶ δήσας κατεταρτάρωσεν, ἐκπεσεῖσθαι αὐτὸν ὑπὸ τῶν παίδων τῆς ἀρχῆς μαθών ("[whom] he [Uranos] bound and hurled to Tartarus, because he had learned from the beginning that he would be dethroned by his children").

Origen, at *Contra Celsum* 8.68, takes note of the charges of Celsus that Christians do not honor the emperor. Referring sarcastically to Celsus's quotation from Homer ("Let there be one king, him to whom the son of crafty Kronos gave the power" [*Il.* 2.205]), Origen replies:

> Kings are not appointed by the son of Kronos who drove his father from his rule and, as the Greek myths say, cast him down to Tartarus [οὐκ ὁ τοῦ καταταρταρωθέντος], not even if anyone were to interpret the story allegorically; but by God who governs all things and knows what He is doing in the matter of the appointment of kings.[33]

In the curious treatise *On Rivers* that has come down as part of the corpus of Plutarch's *Moralia* (Pseudo-Plutarch, *De fluviis,* date uncertain),[34] the myth about Zeus and Kronos appears: ὁ δὲ Ζεὺς ἐπιφανεὶς τὸν μὲν πατέρα δήσας πλεκτῷ ἐρίῳ κατεταρτάρωσε ("But Zeus appeared to his father, bound him with twisted wool, and threw him down to Tartarus"; *De fluviis* 5.3). And a scholiast comments on *Iliad* 14.296 as follows:

> ... λάθρα οὖν ἐμίγη. ὅτε δὲ ἐταρταρώθη ὁ Κρόνος, ὡς παρθένος ὑπνοουμένη ἐξεδόθη Διὶ παρὰ Τηθύος καὶ Ὠκεανοῦ.

> Therefore she [Hera] had intercourse in secret. But when Kronos was thrown into Tartarus, she was given away to Zeus as a supposed virgin by Tethyos and Okeanos.[35]

---

33. H. Chadwick, trans., *Origen: Contra Celsum* (Cambridge: Cambridge University Press, 1980), 504.

34. G. Bernardakis, ed., *Plutarchi Chaeronensis Moralia*, vol. 7 (Leipzig: Teubner, 1896). I missed this reference in the earlier version of this essay.

35. W. Dindorf, ed., *Scholia Graeca in Homeri Iliadem* (Oxford: Clarendon, 1877), 4:59. Cf. *Il.* 295–96: "even as when at the first they [Zeus and Hera] had gone to the couch and had dalliance together in love, their dear parents knowing naught thereof" (Murray's translation in the LCL ed.). The scholion is attributed to Porphyry's *Homeric Questions* by H. Schrader, *Porphyrii Quaestionum Homericarum ad Iliadem pertinentium reliquias* (Leipzig: Teubner, 1880), 1:196.

There are still other texts, dating from the sixth century and later, in which the verb (κατα)ταρταροῦν occurs.[36] In Olympiodorus's commentary on Plato's *Phaedo* (61C), the verb καταταρταροῦν is used in the context of a reference to the Orphic tradition of four divine kingships, those of Uranos, Kronos, Zeus, and Dionysos: μετὰ δὲ τὸν Κρόνον ὁ Ζεὺς ἐβασίλευσε καταταρταρώσας τὸν πατέρα ("After Kronos Zeus assumed kingship, having thrown his father down to Tartarus").[37] In John Lydus's *De mensibus* 4.158, it is stated that the Saturnalia (Κρόνια) in December is celebrated at night ὅτι ἐν σκότει ἐστὶν ὁ Κρόνος ὡς ταρταρωθεὶς ὑπὸ τοῦ Διός ("because it is in darkness that Kronos is, as it were, thrown into Tartarus by Zeus"). In the next section (159), he compares the downward flow of water to the mythical stories that "throw Kronos down to Tartarus" (τὸν Κρόνον καταταρταροῦσιν). In all of these cases, the verb (κατα)ταρταροῦν is used with very narrow reference, namely, to the theogonic myths involving Uranos; Kronos; the Titans, Cyclopes, and others; and Zeus. It seems clear to me that the verb as it occurs in 2 Peter 2:4 cannot be interpreted apart from an understanding of its use in these other contexts. In light of the concinnity of these contexts, it is evident that the author of 2 Peter 2:4 framed his description of the fate of the fallen angels under direct influence from the Greek theogonic myths, unmediated either by his primary source, Jude, or by *1 Enoch,* with which he shows no familiarity.

The use of σιρός in the same context in 2 Peter requires some comment, since it too is a hapax legomenon in the New Testament and at first glance appears to be an unusual word to be used with ταρταροῦν. There is a textual problem here, for some manuscripts read σειραῖς (or σιραῖς).[38]

Since it makes better sense to take σειραῖς as a corruption of σιροῖς (under the influence of δεσμοῖς in Jude 6) rather than vice versa, σιροῖς is the preferable reading.[39] Indeed, I find in the use

---

36. In addition to the texts given here, the *TLG* search turned up numerous others, found in patristic and Byzantine sources. These include citations of 2 Pet 2:4 itself, by Amphilochius, Basil, Didymus the Blind, John Chrysostom, John of Damascus, John Philoponus, and Photius. Comments on the relevant Greek myths are found in Epiphanius, Eustathius, Hesychius, and Photius, and in scholia to Aeschylus, Apollonius of Rhodes, Aratus, Euripides, Hesiod, and Homer.

37. In O. Kern, *Orphicorum Fragmenta* (Berlin: Weidmann, 1922), no. 220; my translation.

38. See n. 2. Noteworthy support for σειραῖς is 𝔓[72] (P.Bodmer 8). Among the witnesses for σιροῖς are the important uncials אAB.

39. So also Paulsen, *Zweite Petrusbrief;* and Vögtle, *Judasbrief* (see n. 3). But

of the word σιρός in 2 Peter 2:4 another indication that the author's description of the fate of the fallen angels is independent of
1 *Enoch* and betrays no Jewish influences in its reformulation of
Jude 6.[40]

σιρός is a word capable of expressing connotations of both "underworld" and "punishment," and so fits well in context with
ταρταροῦν (though 2 Peter 2:4 is apparently the only place in
Greek literature where these two words occur together). The word
σιρός means "pit" or its cognate "silo." In some parts of the
Mediterranean world, σιροί were used for grain storage. Pliny, for
example, suggests that the best method of storing grain is by keeping it "in holes, called *siri*, as is done in Cappadocia and Thrace,
and in Spain and Africa" (*HN* 18.73.306).[41] The use of such σιροί
in Greece can be documented from the fifth century B.C.E. An important Athenian decree from ca. 418 (IG I² 76)[42] provides for the
gathering of firstfruits from the Greek cities for the cult of Demeter
and Kore at Eleusis and for the building of three σιροί at Eleusis in which to house the offerings. The storage of firstfruits and
seed grains in such underground silos[43] corresponds to the descent
(καταγωγή) into the underworld of Kore in the Eleusinian cult legend, and her sojourn in Hades for one-third of the year (from June
to October).[44] The word σιρός can, therefore, by association with
the myth of Kore in the Mysteries, connote "underworld." Such a
connotation and association is made all the more probable in view
of the use of the Eleusinian cult term ἐπόπτης in 2 Peter 1:16.

The word σιρός is occasionally used as a substitute for βάραθρον,
"cleft" or "pit." In ancient Athens, there was a βάραθρον into
which criminals were thrown for punishment.[45] Diodorus Siculus
(19.44.1) uses the word σιρός instead of βάραθρον in his description
of the death of Eumenes at the hands of Antigonus: Eumenes was

---

Paulsen (133) inexplicably refuses to acknowledge the author's indebtedness to
Greek mythology at 2 Pet 2:4; Vögtle (190) gets it right.

40. The word σιρός does not occur in the Greek fragments of 1 *Enoch*, and is
also absent from LXX.

41. Rackham's translation in the LCL ed.

42. The text, with bibliography and discussion, is published in M. N. Tod,
A Selection of Greek Historical Inscriptions, 2d ed. (Oxford: Clarendon, 1946),
1:179–85. The relevant lines of the inscription are 10–13.

43. This must reflect an earlier custom, as can be seen in the phrase κατὰ τὰ
πάτρια in line 11.

44. See M. P. Nilsson, *Geschichte der griechischen Religion*, 2d ed., Handbuch
der Altertumswissenschaft 5.2.1 (Munich: C. H. Beck, 1955), 1:473.

45. See, e.g., Ar., *Nub.* 14; and Pl., *Grg.* 516D (ref. in LSJ erroneous). Demosthenes uses the words σιρός and βάραθρον together in Or. 8.45 and 10.16.

thrown into a pit (εἰς σειρόν) and burned alive. The word βάραθρον is also used by Lucian as a metaphorical equivalent of Tartarus;[46] thus, in view of the interchangeability of the two words, it should come as no surprise to find Lucian's contemporary, the author of 2 Peter, using σιρός in precisely the same way.

That the word σιρός is used at all in 2 Peter is, in all likelihood, an indication that the author was at work in an area of the Mediterranean world in which σιροί were used in the manner described by Pliny in the preceding discussion. Asia Minor is one of those areas, and the results of our little study might serve to bolster the arguments of those commentators who would place the origins of 2 Peter there.[47]

In sum, we have seen how illuminating a comparison of the parallel passages in Jude and 2 Peter can be, especially the verses here treated. Whereas the author of Jude derives most, if not all,[48] of his mythological traditions from Jewish sources — mainly from such Apocrypha or Pseudepigrapha as *1 Enoch* — the author of 2 Peter seems to avoid any reference or allusion to these writings, either because he does not know them or, perhaps, because he finds them unacceptable.[49] Instead, despite the disclaimer in 1:16, he is clearly influenced by pagan mythology in the formulation of his message. Whether his use of "myths" is intentional or not cannot finally be decided.

---

46. In *Icaromenippus* 33, the assembly of the gods tells Zeus what he should do with the philosophers: κεραύνωσον, κατάφλεξον, ἐπίτριψον, ἐς τὸ βάραθρον, ἐς τὸν Τάρταρον, ὡς τοὺς Γίγαντας.

47. So, e.g., J. N. D. Kelly, *A Commentary on the Epistles of Peter and of Jude*, BNTC (London: Adam & Charles Black, 1969), 237, on the basis of 2 Pet 3:1. Bauckham, *Jude, 2 Peter* (see n. 3) uses the same verse to argue for Rome (159). Another frequent suggestion is Alexandria; see, e.g., Paulsen, *Zweite Petrusbriefe*, 95. That Asia Minor is the most likely place of composition (i.e., the author's "social location") has been argued quite forcefully by Neyrey, *2 Peter, Jude*, 132 (see n. 3); Neyrey refers in this context to the previous version of this essay, in *GRBS* 10.

48. See n. 18.

49. This is a long-standing opinion; see Kümmel, *Introduction*, 431.

Chapter 5

The *Apocalypse of Peter* (NHC VII,3) and Canonical 2 Peter

In our discussion of 2 Peter 2:4 in the preceding chapter, reference was made to the epistle's author and his use of Greek mythological traditions. It was taken for granted that the author in question was not the historical Peter, Simon bar Jonah. To be sure, Peter looms very large in the early history of the church — the book of Acts presents him as the founder of the church in Jerusalem — and it might be expected that the church would have preserved some of his writings. As it is, we have nothing from him. We have, instead, a number of writings purporting to come from his pen, including the two canonical epistles, pseudepigrapha all. Was the historical Peter illiterate, or barely literate? (We might expect a Galilean fisherman to be able to write at least short receipts.) However that may be, we now have a fair number of texts, some only partially preserved, that were penned in his name. One interesting, if inconvenient, feature of the pseudo-Petrine writings is that they do not in any wise represent a single "Petrine" tradition. On the contrary, these writings are theologically diverse, some even "heretical."

In what follows, I shall take up for discussion two of the Petrine pseudepigrapha, one an "orthodox" text treated already in chapter 4, and the other a "heretical" (Gnostic) text. I want to propose a new way of looking at the relationship between them. The "heretical" text treated here is the *Apocalypse of Peter* preserved in Coptic in Nag Hammadi Codex VII.[1]

---

1. Pearson, *Codex VII*, 201–47, introduction by M. Desjardins, transcription and translation by J. Brashler. This apocalypse is to be distinguished from the *Apocalypse of Peter* partially preserved in Coptic and Ethiopic; see *NTApoc*, 1:620–38.

That 2 Peter is an "orthodox" writing is taken for granted by everyone. For some, indeed, it is *too* orthodox, if by "orthodox" is meant "early catholic." The views expressed by Ernst Käsemann in a famous article are a case in point: 2 Peter's consistent "early catholicism" makes it "the most dubious writing in the canon."[2] The Protestant slant in this opinion is, of course, obvious and will be ignored here.

As for the *Apocalypse of Peter,* no one can doubt that it is a Gnostic work and therefore, from the standpoint of early catholic orthodoxy, thoroughly "heretical." What, then, do these two "Petrine" texts have in common, except a bald attempt to capture the legacy of the apostle Peter for their respective, thoroughly opposite worldviews?

Indeed, one of the reasons that the *Apocalypse of Peter* is such a fascinating text is that it presents the apostle Peter as the founder of the Gnostic community and the chief protagonist in a struggle against orthodox ecclesiastical Christianity.[3] Not Paul, the *haereticorum apostolus* ("apostle of the heretics"),[4] but Peter! What is also of interest, by the way, is that the Gospel of Matthew, which alone of the Gospels contains the dominical pronouncement on which the Petrine structure of the Roman papacy is putatively built,[5] is a key authority for the *Apocalypse of Peter* and is extensively quoted and paraphrased throughout the text in support of its antiecclesiastical stance.[6] The *Apocalypse of Peter* has even

2. E. Käsemann, "An Apologia for Primitive Christian Eschatology," in *Essays on New Testament Themes,* trans. W. J. Montague, SBT 41 (London: SCM Press, 1964), 169–95; quotation on 169.

3. See esp. Koschorke, *Polemik der Gnostiker,* 11–90. See also Desjardins's introduction to the critical edition in Pearson, *Codex VII;* and J. Brashler, "The Coptic 'Apocalypse of Peter': A Genre Analysis and Interpretation" (Ph.D. diss., Claremont Graduate School, 1977), 197–238.

4. Tert., *Adv. Marc.* 3.5. Tertullian refers to the appropriation of Paul by the Marcionites, but he could equally well have included the Gnostics, especially the Valentinians. See E. Pagels, *The Gnostic Paul: Gnostic Exegesis of the Pauline Letters* (Philadelphia: Fortress Press, 1975).

5. Matt 16:17–19 was used, from the third century on but not before, to bolster the authority of the bishop of Rome. See O. Cullmann, *Peter: Disciple, Apostle, Martyr* (London: SCM Press; Philadelphia: Westminster, 1953), esp. 234; cf. R. E. Brown, K. Donfried, and J. Reumann, eds., *Peter in the New Testament* (Minneapolis: Augsburg; New York: Paulist, 1973), 83–101.

6. See esp. A. Werner, "Die Apokalypse des Petrus: Die dritte Schrift aus Nag-Hammadi-Codex VII," *ThLZ* 99 (1974): 575–84, esp. 575–77, 582–83; P. Perkins, "Peter in Gnostic Revelation," SBLSP (1974), 2:1–13, esp. 5–6; C. M. Tuckett, *Nag Hammadi and the Gospel Tradition: Synoptic Tradition in the Nag Hammadi Library* (Edinburgh: T. &. T. Clark, 1986), 117–24; and J.-D. Dubois, "L'Apocalypse de Pierre (NHC VII,3) et le Nouveau Testament," in *Écritures et traditions dans la*

been cited as evidence for the persistence of a special "Matthean" community of ascetic and charismatic Christians into the second century and beyond.[7] Be that as it may, the authoritative position of the apostle Peter in the Gnostic apocalypse is undeniably tied to an interpretation of the Gospel of Matthew. Could it not be the case that canonical 2 Peter was also put to good use by the author of the *Apocalypse of Peter?*

That the author of the *Apocalypse of Peter* knew and used canonical 2 Peter is precisely what I intend to argue here.[8] In this argument lies an anomaly of supreme irony: 2 Peter consists essentially of an attack on heretical opponents and warnings against heresy, the *Gnostic* character of which is widely assumed![9]

Terence V. Smith, in his important study of the use of Peter and Petrine writings in the early church, has devoted considerable attention to the problem of the relationship between 2 Peter and the Gnostic *Apocalypse of Peter*.[10] He presents an impressive list of similarities between the two writings: similarities of language in describing opponents, anthropological ideas, the Parousia expectation, and the authority of Peter. Even so, he does not argue for a "literary relationship" between them. Instead, he situates the two documents in the context of a "Petrine controversy" and suggests that "in the Apocalypse of Peter we come face to face with the *type* of Gnostic opposition encountered by the writer of 2 Peter." The two documents, according to Smith, reflect a "situation in which two pro-Peter groups were polemicizing against each other as rivals."[11]

Smith's analysis is, prima facie, quite plausible. But is it finally correct? I would like to suggest here another way of assessing the evidence. Inasmuch as both the *Apocalypse of Peter* and 2 Peter

littérature copte: Journé d'études coptes Strasbourg 28 mai 1982, ed. J.-E. Ménard (Louvain: Peeters, 1983), 117–25, esp. 118 and n. 15.

7. See E. Schweizer, "The 'Matthean' Church," *NTS* 20 (1974): 216; and G. Stanton, "5 Ezra and Matthean Christianity in the Second Century," *JTS* 28 (1977): 67–83, esp. 80–83.

8. Possible use of 2 Peter by the author of *Apoc. Pet.* has been suggested before. See Perkins, *Gnostic Dialogue*, 117; Perkins, "Peter in Gnostic Revelation," 6 (crediting G. MacRae); and Dubois, "L'Apocalypse de Pierre," 119.

9. See, e.g., Käsemann, "Apologia"; Kümmel, *Introduction*, 532; and Koester, *Introduction*, 1:296. For a good statement of the problem, see T. S. Caulley, "The Idea of 'Inspiration' in 2 Peter 1:16–21" (Th.D. diss., Tübingen, 1982), 50–82.

10. T. V. Smith, *Petrine Controversies in Early Christianity: Attitudes towards Peter in Christian Writings of the First Two Centuries*, WUNT 15 (Tübingen: Mohr-Siebeck, 1985), 137–41.

11. Ibid., 141.

are highly polemical, we shall look first at how the opponents
are presented in the respective writings,[12] and then examine some
other points of connection between them before coming to our
conclusions.

The core of the polemical material in the *Apocalypse of Peter*
is found in the context of the Savior's interpretation of the first of
three visions accorded to Peter in the text.[13] The Savior prophesies
apostasy from the truth on the part of many, and sure destruction
at the Parousia for those who are enemies of the truth (73,19–
80,23). The following points of contact with 2 Peter are especially
noticeable:[14]

> "For many will accept our teaching in the beginning. But they
> will turn away again in accordance with the will of the father
> of their error" (73,23–28; cf. 74,15–17; 77,25–26. Cf. πλάνη
> ["error"] in 2 Pet 2:18; 3:17; and on apostasy, especially
> 2:2, 21.)

> "propagation of falsehood" (74,11. Cf. "false teachers,"
> 2 Pet 2:1.)

> "defiled" (74,15–16. Cf. "blemishes," 2 Pet 2:13; "licentious
> ways," 2:2.)

> "For some of them will blaspheme the truth" (74,22–24. Cf.
> 2 Pet 2:2: "and because of them the way of truth will be
> maligned.")

> "they will be ruled heretically" (ϨⲚ ⲞⲨⲘⲚ̄ⲦϨⲈⲢⲈⲤⲒⲤ)
> (74,20–22. Cf. αἱρέσεις, 2 Pet 2:1.)

> "they will be given destruction" (ⲠⲒⲦⲀⲔⲞ) (75,6. Cf.
> ἀπώλεια, 2 Pet 2:1, 3; 3:7, 16.)

> "not every soul comes from the truth" (75,12–13. Cf. 2 Pet
> 2:14: "unsteady souls.")

---

12. Some of the following items are noted in ibid., 138–39; and Dubois,
"L'Apocalypse de Pierre," 119. Surprisingly, neither Koschorke, *Polemik der Gnostiker,* nor Brashler, "Coptic 'Apocalypse of Peter' " (see n. 4), makes anything of the
connection between *Apoc. Pet.* and 2 Peter.

13. See Brashler's structural analysis, "Coptic 'Apocalypse of Peter,' " 144–47.

14. Quotations from the *Apoc. Pet.* in what follows are from J. Brashler's translation in Pearson, *Codex VII,* 219–47 (omitting the parentheses supplying Greek
words occurring in the Coptic text). Quotations from 2 Peter are from the NRSV,
except where otherwise noted.

"For every soul of these ages has death assigned to it . . . since it is created for its desires [ⲉⲡⲓⲑⲩⲙⲓⲁ] and their eternal destruction [ⲧⲁⲕⲟ]" (75,15–20. Cf. 2 Pet 1:4: "that . . . you may escape from the corruption that is in the world because of lust." Cf. also ἐπιθυμία, 2:10, 18; 3:3; and ἀπώλεια, 2:1, 3; 3:7, 16.)

"material creatures" (lit. "creatures of matter") (75,24–25. Cf. 2 Pet 2:12: "irrational animals, mere creatures of instinct.")

"everything that does not abide will dissolve [ⲃⲱⲗ ⲉⲃⲟⲗ] into that which does not exist" (76,18–20. Cf. 2 Pet 3:10: "the elements will be dissolved" [λυθήσεται].)

"deaf and blind ones" (76,21–22; cf. 72,12,14; 73,12–13; 81,30. Cf. 2 Pet 1:9: "nearsighted and blind.")

"evil words and deceptive mysteries" (76,25–27. Cf. "cleverly contrived myths," 2 Pet 1:16; "deceptive words," 2 Pet 2:3.)

"they speak of these things which they do not understand" (76,29–30. Cf. 2 Pet 2:12: "they slander what they do not understand.")

"the way" (77,13. Cf. 2 Pet 2:2, 15, 21.)

"messengers [ⲁⲅⲅⲉⲗⲟⲥ] of error" (77,24. Cf. 2 Pet 2:4: "the angels when they sinned.")[15]

"They do business in my word" (77,33–78,1. Cf. 2 Pet 2:3: "in their greed they will exploit you with deceptive words.")

"until my return [ⲡⲁⲣⲟⲩⲥⲓⲁ]" (78,6. Cf. παρουσία, 2 Pet 1:16; 3:4, 12.)

"slavery . . . freedom" (78,13–15. Cf. 2 Pet 2:19.)

"unrighteousness [ⲁⲇⲓⲕⲓⲁ]" (78,19. Cf. ἀδικία, 2 Pet 2:13, 15.)

"will be cast into the outer darkness" (78,24–25. Cf. 2 Pet 2:17: "for them the deepest darkness has been reserved.")

"punishment [ⲕⲟⲗⲁⲥⲓⲥ]" (79,17. Cf. κολάζειν, 2 Pet 2:19.)

---

15. Good angels also occur in both texts: *Apoc. Pet.* 82,12 and 2 Pet 2:11.

"Those people are dry canals" (79,30–31. Cf. 2 Pet 2:17: "these are waterless springs.")

The last item listed, "dry canals" || "waterless springs," is a key item leading to the supposition that the author of the *Apocalypse of Peter* knew and used 2 Peter.[16] The author of the Gnostic apocalypse, however, has adapted the expression "waterless springs" (πηγαὶ ἄνυδροι)[17] to fit an Egyptian geographical environment, with the substitution of "waterless canals" (ⲚⲒⲞⲞⲢ ⲚⲀⲦⲘⲞⲞⲨ). In the process, he has picked up a motif from native Egyptian apocalyptic tradition.[18]

What is most striking, however, is the strong eschatological expectation found in the *Apocalypse of Peter*. Its pronouncement of the judgment that is to come upon false teachers at the Parousia of Christ is very similar, at least on the surface, to the message of 2 Peter. It used to be thought that the eschatological teaching of 2 Peter marks it as an anti-Gnostic text, in that a denial of the Parousia (cf. 2 Pet 3:3–7) is supposedly a characteristic of Gnostic doctrine.[19] But now we have a Gnostic text that not only contains a vigorous eschatological expectation but even uses 2 Peter itself in giving expression to it! The Gnostic author of the *Apocalypse of Peter* has evidently found 2 Peter to be a very congenial piece of Petrine teaching, one that can freely be used in his own presentation of Petrine gnosis.

There are numerous other points of contact between the *Apocalypse of Peter* and 2 Peter in addition to those already noted as part of the polemical features of the two writings. The most important feature of the *Apocalypse of Peter* is, after all, its christology, expressed in a docetic interpretation of the crucifixion of Christ. Indeed, the entire document consists of a series of visions and revelations whose setting is the Temple in Jerusalem on Good Friday.[20]

---

16. See n. 8.

17. The author of 2 Peter makes an analogous adjustment in the use of his source, Jude 12: νεφέλαι ἄνυδροι, "waterless clouds."

18. The drying up of the Nile and its canals is a standard feature in the description of apocalyptic woes on Egypt in such Hellenistic texts as the *Oracle of the Potter* (see P.Oxy. 2332, ll. 73–74; and NHC VI,8: *Asclepius* 71,16–19). It is a very ancient motif; see, e.g., the *Prophecies of Neferti* (M. Lichtheim, *Ancient Egyptian Literature* [Berkeley: University of California Press, 1975], 1:139): "Dry is the river of Egypt." For a good discussion of the Hellenistic material, see J. G. Griffiths, "Apocalyptic in the Hellenistic Era," in Hellholm, *Apocalypticism*, 273–93, esp. 287–91.

19. See Käsemann, "Apologia," 171–72.

20. On the difficult opening passage of *Apoc. Pet.*, see Brashler's notes to

The crucifixion that takes place on that day is of a fleshly substitute for the real Jesus, who stands apart laughing at the ignorance of those who think that they are destroying him. The "living Savior" is really immune from suffering.[21] Now, it can hardly be argued that this docetic doctrine is derived from 2 Peter. Even so, there are some interesting points of contact between the two documents precisely in their descriptions of Christ.

The key text in 2 Peter, in terms of both its christology and its doctrine of the Parousia, is 1:16–18, describing the transfiguration of Christ:

> For it was not by following cleverly contrived myths that we made known to you the *power and Parousia* [δύναμιν καὶ παρουσίαν] of our Lord Jesus Christ, but it was by becoming eyewitnesses [or "initiates," ἐπόπται][22] of his *majesty* [μεγαλειότητος]. For when he received honor and glory from God the Father, and such a voice as this was borne down upon him from the majestic Glory: "This is my beloved son, with whom I have been well pleased" — even we heard this voice borne from heaven when we were with him on the holy mountain.[23]

In the *Apocalypse of Peter,* Peter is with the Savior in the Temple (70,13–15), that is, on the Temple Mount, a "holy mountain"; there he receives visions and revelations. The first vision is described thus: "I saw a new light greater than the light of day. Then it came down upon the Savior" (72,23–27). The Savior tells Peter that he has been chosen to "know him" (71,26), including the "body of his radiance" (71,32–33), and his "honorable reward" (72,1–2). The experience here recounted has to do with divine "majesty" (†ⲘⲚ̄ⲦⲚⲞϬ = μεγαλειότης, 70,19).[24]

The language employed here is certainly "resurrection appearance" language, as James Robinson has noted.[25] The Gnostic

his translation in Pearson, *Codex VII;* and J.-D. Dubois, "Le Préambule de l'Apocalypse de Pierre (Nag Hammadi VII,70,14–20)," in Ries, *Gnosticisme et monde hellénistique,* 117–25.

21. On the christology of *Apoc. Pet.* and its relation to that of the *Second Treatise of the Great Seth* (NHC VII,2), see Brashler, "Coptic 'Apocalypse of Peter,'" 158–96; and G. Riley's introduction to *Treat. Seth* in Pearson, *Codex VII,* 129–44, esp. 135–38.

22. See chapter 4 of this book.

23. My translation and italics.

24. In the Sahidic version of 2 Pet 1:16, ⲘⲚ̄ⲦⲚⲞϬ is used to translate μεγαλειότης.

25. J. M. Robinson, "Jesus — From Easter to Valentinus (or to the Apostles'

apocalypse uses this resurrection language as part of a narrative of the (apparent) crucifixion of Christ, replacing the (orthodox) doctrine of Christ's crucifixion and resurrection with what Robinson refers to' as "the idea of his bifurcation at the time of the passion into 'the living Jesus' (81,19) that did not suffer and 'his fleshly part' (81,20), 'the body' (83,5) that was crucified."[26] Of special interest to us in this case is the apparent use, on the part of the Gnostic author, of the transfiguration passage in 2 Peter. This Gnostic writer has found the language of 2 Peter in describing the transfiguration quite compatible with his own understanding of Christ's true nature. It might also be observed here that the rest of 2 Peter presents no obstacle to the use of the transfiguration passage in an explication of the (apparent) crucifixion of Christ, for in fact the Pauline doctrine of "Christ crucified" is not a feature of 2 Peter's teaching.[27]

But what of the Gnostic views in the *Apocalypse of Peter* concerning the true nature of the elect? Could we not expect to see here a basic incompatibility with what is taught in an "orthodox" writing like 2 Peter? Let us look at the texts.

For the author of the *Apocalypse of Peter* — and this is typical of Gnosticism in general — the elect, that is, those who have received gnosis, share the divine nature of the Savior, being "consubstantial" (ⲚϢⲂⲎⲢ ⲚⲞⲨⲤⲒⲀ = ὁμοούσιος, 71,14–15) with him.[28] The true "nature" (φύσις) of the elect soul is "immortal" (75,26–76,4), though it must "receive power in an intellectual spirit" (77,18–19). Those so constituted live in a "brotherhood" (79,1) "rooted in fellowship" (κοινωνία, 79,4). What holds the brotherhood together is not only "gnosis" (73,22–23 and passim) but "faith" (76,2) and "renunciation" (76,3) of the world. This community of faith and knowledge has its grounding in the apostle Peter, whom the Savior has "chosen" and from whom he has "made a beginning for the remnant whom [he has] summoned to knowledge" (71,19–21).

Creed)," *JBL* 101 (1982): 5–37, esp. 13. Robinson ties this account to the original resurrection appearance of Jesus to Peter mentioned in 1 Cor 15:5 and Luke 24:34 (pp. 8–9).

26. Ibid., 13.

27. The closest 2 Peter comes to such a doctrine is at 2:1, "denying the Master who bought them," but even this passage is not explicitly related to the crucifixion. As for Paul, his letters are considered by the author of 2 Peter to contain "some things hard to understand" (3:16).

28. The term *homoousios* is probably a Gnostic coinage; see G. C. Stead, *Divine Substance* (Oxford: Clarendon Press, 1979), 190–222.

Virtually all of this the author of the *Apocalypse of Peter* could have read out of 2 Peter — and apparently did.[29] Second Peter is addressed by its author to those who have "faith" equal to his own, as well as "knowledge" (ἐπίγνωσις, 1:1–2). It is indeed the divine *power* (δύναμις) that has granted the elect the things that pertain to life (1:3), by means of "knowledge" (ἐπίγνωσις, 1:3),[30] thus enabling them to become "participants of the divine nature" (θείας κοινωνοὶ φύσεως) and to "escape from the corruption that is in the world because of lust" (ἀποφυγόντες τῆς ἐν τῷ κόσμῳ ἐν ἐπιθυμίᾳ φθορᾶς, 1:4). The "brothers and sisters" (ἀδελφοί, 1:10), united in "knowledge" (1:8), are exhorted by the apostle to "confirm (their) call and election" (1:10).

There is yet more in 2 Peter that can, at least on the surface, be taken as quite congenial to the views reflected in the *Apocalypse of Peter*. "Peter's" statement that he will soon be "putting off" his "tent," that is, his earthly body (1:14), seems quite compatible with the Gnostic anthropology (and christology) found in the Gnostic apocalypse. Terminology employed in 2 Peter in reference to God ("Father," 1:17) and Christ ("Savior," 1:1, 11; 2:20; 3:2, 18) is that commonly used by Gnostics and is found also throughout the *Apocalypse of Peter*. Even material in 2 Peter that is evidently inimical to the views of the author of the *Apocalypse of Peter* — for example, the Old Testament prophets are valued in 2 Peter (1:19–21) and devalued in the *Apocalypse of Peter* (71,6–9) — could easily be resolved with mental recourse to the mention of "false prophets" in 2 Peter 2:1.

In short, what I am arguing here is that 2 Peter could have been, and indeed was, freely used by the Gnostic author of the *Apocalypse of Peter*. That is not, of course, to say that 2 Peter is really a Gnostic text! In fact, it probably was an anti-Gnostic text, so far as the original intention of its author is concerned.[31] But it can be read "gnostically," and so it was in its use by the author of the *Apocalypse of Peter*. That writer was also able to read the Gospel of Matthew "gnostically," as we have seen. This would also indicate that the two books would have occupied a prominent place among the "New Testament" writings treasured by the Gnostic

---

29. In the last-cited passage there are also echoes of Matt 16:13–20. See esp. Koschorke, *Polemik der Gnostiker*, 27–29.
30. ἐπίγνωσις occurs in 2 Pet at 1:2, 3, 8; 2:20. γνῶσις occurs at 1:5, 6; 3:18.
31. See n. 9.

community to which our apocalypse was addressed, a community that clearly honored the apostle Peter as its founder.[32]

I referred earlier to Terence Smith's views on the relationship between the *Apocalypse of Peter* and 2 Peter, and now I want to specify more clearly my points of agreement and disagreement with him. I disagree with him on the basic nature of the relationship; that is, I think that there is a literary dependence of the *Apocalypse of Peter* on 2 Peter. I do agree with his view that the two texts reflect "a situation in which two pro-Peter groups were polemicizing against each other as rivals."[33] His elaboration of that situation, however, pits 2 Peter against the *Apocalypse of Peter* as representing the two opposing stances. Although it may be true that certain features of the Gnostic writing, such as its strong anticlericalism — note especially its attack on the use of the titles "bishop" and "deacon" (79,25–26) — are typical of the Gnostic opponents of 2 Peter (e.g., 2:10), it is also the case that 2 Peter itself could easily have been appropriated by the author of the *Apocalypse of Peter* and given a Gnostic reading, as I think I have shown here. There is some indication, too, that the Gnostic author was aware of the use of 2 Peter (and/or other Petrine literature) on the part of his ecclesiastical opponents. In the *Apocalypse of Peter,* the Savior tells Peter that he "will be despised" by "the children of this age," "since they are ignorant of [him]" (73,18–21). In other words, the (ecclesiastical) opponents of the Gnostic elect will also appeal to the authority of Peter in their propagation of error.

There is considerable indication in the text of the *Apocalypse of Peter* that its Petrine-Gnostic community, probably located somewhere in Egypt, is an embattled one, facing a mounting ecclesiastical opposition. The Gnostic author is not able to provide any hope for his co-religionists in this age of "harsh fate." Instead, he holds out the hope of vindication for the Gnostic elect at the future Parousia of the Savior (78,1–14), when the opponents will get their just deserts. And, as we have seen, it is 2 Peter's very teaching on the Parousia that provides the ground for this delicious hope!

The results of this investigation offer no help to those who like to keep their categories neat and tidy. But study of the real data

32. A number of "pro-Peter" Gnostic groups existed in the early centuries. See Perkins, *Gnostic Dialogue,* 113–30; and Smith, *Petrine Controversies,* 117–42 (see n. 10).

33. Smith, *Petrine Controversies,* 141. See also G. MacRae, "Nag Hammadi and the New Testament," in Aland, *Gnosis,* 144–57, esp. 157.

of Christian history, and history in general, always produces surprises. This is especially true when we are confronted with new data, such as the *Apocalypse of Peter* and the other writings from the Nag Hammadi collection, texts that still have a lot of surprises waiting for students of early Christianity who are willing to study them.

_____ *Chapter 6* _____

Old Testament Interpretation in Gnostic Literature

It used to be thought that one of the chief characteristics of Gnosticism, as "the acute hellenization of Christianity,"[1] was a rejection of the Old Testament.[2] However, even before the publication of new source material for Gnosticism, such as the Nag Hammadi corpus,[3] that view was hardly tenable, for the ancient heresiologists themselves complained not so much that the Gnostic heretics rejected the Old Testament but that they interpreted it incorrectly.[4] The fact is, the Gnostic interpretation of the Old Testament (Mikra) is a very complicated matter, and there is great variety in the range of attitudes adopted by Gnostics vis-à-vis the Bible. Now that the new source material is available, a comprehensive assessment of the use, authority, and exegesis of Mikra in Gnostic literature is possible. Unfortunately, no such comprehensive assessment exists, and such a project is beyond the purview of the present study.[5] In this essay, I shall try instead to summa-

---

1. This was the famous dictum of A. Harnack, *History of Dogma*, trans. N. Buchanan (London: Williams & Norgate, 1900), 1:227. Harnack's position still has its defenders; see further discussion and n. 18 (W. Beltz).

2. See ibid., 1:227, 169–73; and Bauer, *Orthodoxy and Heresy*, 195–202. This view is rightly rejected by H. von Campenhausen, *The Formation of the Christian Bible*, trans. J. Baker (Philadelphia: Fortress Press, 1972), 75.

3. See *NHLE*. Unless otherwise indicated, all English translations of the Nag Hammadi Coptic texts in this chapter are taken from that volume. Citations in each case are according to page and line of the MS.

4. See von Campenhausen, *Formation*, 76.

5. A number of articles on the problem have been published. See, for example, those in Tröger, *Altes Testament*, esp. R. Haardt, "Schöpfer und Schöpfung in der Gnosis" (37–48); P. Nagel, "Die Auslegung der Paradieserzählung in der Gnosis" (49–70); H.-F. Weiss, "Das Gesetz in der Gnosis" (71–88); H.-G. Bethge, "Die Ambivalenz alttestamentlicher Geschichtstraditionen in der Gnosis" (89–109); W. Beltz, "Elia redivivus: Ein Beitrag zum Problem der Verbindung von Gnosis und Altem Testament" (137–41); A. Szabó, "Die Engelvorstellung vom

rize the present state of scholarship on this issue and, concentrating chiefly on some of the sources from Nag Hammadi, attempt some conclusions of my own.

Basic Issues

Although it is no longer argued by serious scholars that the Gnostics completely rejected the Old Testament, it is still occasionally stated that they were concerned only with the opening passages of Genesis.[6] Such an assertion is easily refuted. Robert M. Wilson has effectively challenged it simply by referring to the index of scripture citations in the two-volume anthology of Gnostic texts edited by Werner Foerster.[7] The statistics Wilson assembles do show a predilection on the part of the Gnostics for the early chapters of Genesis, but most other parts of the Old Testament are represented as well, seventeen books in all.[8]

A more complete statistical analysis has been put forward by Giovanni Filoramo and Claudio Gianotto, using a database that includes all of the heresiological sources as well as the Coptic texts from Nag Hammadi and other Coptic sources.[9] Around 600 biblical references have been assembled. Again, the opening passages of Genesis predominate — 200 of 230 references to Genesis are

Alten Testament bis zur Gnosis" (143–52); J. Maier, "Jüdische Faktoren bei der Entstehung der Gnosis?" (239–58); and W. Schenk, "Textverarbeitung in Frühjudentum, Frühkirche und Gnosis" (299–313). See also W. Beltz, "Gnosis und Altes Testament–Überlegungen zur Frage nach dem jüdischen Ursprung der Gnosis," *ZRGG* 28 (1976): 353–57; M. Krause, "Aussagen über das Alten Testament in z. T. bisher unveröffentlichten gnostischen Texten aus Nag Hammadi," in *Ex Orbe Religionum: Studia G. Widengren,* ed. J. Bergman, et al., SHR 21 (Leiden: E. J. Brill, 1972), 1:449–56; R. M. Wilson, "The Gnostics and the Old Testament," in *Proceedings of the International Colloquium on Gnosticism, Stockholm, August 20–25, 1973* (Stockholm: Almqvist & Wiksell, 1977), 164–68; M. Simonetti, "Note sull' interpretazione gnostica dell' Antico Testamento," *Vetera Christianorum* 14 (1977): 301–30; and F. Filoramo and C. Gianotto, "L'interpretazione gnostica dell' Antico Testamento: Posizioni ermeneutiche e techniche esegetiche," *Augustinianum* 22 (1982): 53–74. Additional studies, such as articles on individual Gnostic tractates, are cited in subsequent notes.

6. See, e.g., O. Betz, "Was am Anfang geschah: Das jüdische Erbe in den neugefundenen koptisch-gnostischen Schriften," in *Abraham unser Vater: Juden und Christen im Gespräch über die Bibel, Festschrift für Otto Michel,* ed. O. Betz et al. (Leiden: E. J. Brill, 1963), 24–43, esp. 43; and E. Yamauchi, *Pre-Christian Gnosticism: A Survey of the Proposed Evidences,* 2d ed. (Grand Rapids, Mich.: Baker Book House, 1983), 144–45.

7. Wilson, "Gnostics and the Old Testament," 165; Foerster, *Gnosis,* 2:350–52.

8. These are Gen, Exod, Lev, Num, Deut, Josh, 1 Sam, 2 Sam, 1 Kgs, Job, Pss, Prov, Isa, Jer, Ezek, Dan, and Hos. See Wilson, "Gnostics and the Old Testament."

9. Filoramo and Gianotto, "L'interpretazione gnostica."

concentrated on Genesis 1–11 — but other parts of the Bible are represented as well.[10]

More important, of course, is the question as to *how* the Old Testament is utilized and interpreted in the Gnostic literature. It is at this point that the issues become complicated, for there is a bewildering variety of interpretive methods and attitudes displayed in the sources.

Some useful attempts have been made to classify the varieties of Gnostic use of the Old Testament with reference to examples drawn from the Gnostic sources. Peter Nagel, for example, identifies the following six categories, providing examples for each:

1. Openly disdainful rejection of figures and events from the Old Testament: NHC VII,2: *Treat. Seth;* NHC IX,3: *Testim. Truth.*

2. Exposition in a contrary sense, through changes in roles and functions: NHC II,4: *Hyp. Arch.;* NHC II,5 and XIII,2: *Orig. World;* NHC V,2: *Apoc. Adam;* the "Peratae."

3. Corrective exposition, closely related to group 2: NHC II,1; III,1; IV,1; and BG,2: *Ap. John;* the "Ophites."

4. Appropriation of "neutral" passages by means of allegorical interpretation: Justin, *Baruch;* the "Naassenes"; *Pistis Sophia.*

5. Eclectic references to individual passages of the Old Testament in support of certain doctrines or cult practices: the Valentinians; "libertine" Gnostics.

6. Etiological and typological interpretation of the Old Testament, in part with a soteriological tendency: NHC I,5: *Tri. Trac.;* NHC I,3 and XII,2: *Gos. Truth;* NHC II,3: *Gos. Phil.;* NHC II,6: *Exeg. Soul; Pistis Sophia.*[11]

Nagel points out that there is some overlapping in this classification and that more than one of these categories can be reflected in a single text. He regards the first three categories as closely related to one another, and sharply distinguishes them from the other three.[12]

---

10. Ibid., 55–56. See now also C. Evans, R. Webb, and R. Wiebe, eds., *Nag Hammadi Texts and the Bible: A Synopsis and Index,* NTTS 18 (Leiden: E. J. Brill, 1993).

11. Nagel, "Auslegung," 51. See also Simonetti, "Note sull' interpretazione"; and Filoramo and Gianotto, "L'interpretazione gnostica."

12. Nagel, "Auslegung," 51. Nagel goes on to analyze the various Gnostic interpretations of the Paradise narrative in Gen 2–3.

It is to be noted that virtually all of the Gnostic texts cited by Nagel as examples of the six categories of Old Testament interpretation, with the arguable exception of the *Apocalypse of Adam*,[13] are Christian Gnostic texts, or at least texts that show Christian influences. Questions thus arise concerning the role played by Christian doctrine in the development of Gnostic Old Testament interpretation, as well as the existence of an originally non-Christian *Jewish* Gnosticism[14]. Some of the scholars who have studied the problem of Gnostic Old Testament interpretation have expressed strong skepticism as to the existence of a Jewish Gnosticism and a Gnostic interpretation of the Bible unmediated by Christianity. For example, Hans-Friedrich Weiss, in his study of the Torah in Gnosticism, suggests that the various Gnostic attitudes adopted toward the Torah all reflect the basic Christian contrast between the Law and the gospel.[15] Hans-Gebhard Bethge, in his study of Gnostic interpretation of the historical traditions in the Old Testament, concludes that Gnostic biblical interpretation is a feature of Christian Gnosticism and did not arise in "heterodox" Judaism.[16]

The strongest stand on this issue has been taken by Walter Beltz, in a short article devoted to "Gnosis and the Old Testament" and the "question of the Jewish origin of Gnosis." He states in this article that there are no Old Testament passages used in the Gnostic texts from Nag Hammadi that are not already found in the New Testament.[17] He also argues in support of Adolph Harnack's

---

13. On *Apoc. Adam* as a "Jewish Gnostic" text, see my discussion in chapter 7. *Apoc. Adam* is the only Gnostic text included in *OTP* (1:707–19; trans. and intro. G. MacRae).

14. For discussion of the problem, see, e.g., Pearson, *Gnosticism*, esp. chaps. 1–9; see also chapter 7 in this book.

15. See Weiss, "Gesetz," esp. 73. Somewhat anomalously, Weiss goes on to acknowledge that Mandaeism, with its negative picture of Moses as the prophet of the wicked Ruha, stands "outside the scope of early Christian Gnosticism," and cites K. Rudolph's studies on the Jewish origins of Mandaean Gnosticism (in ibid., 80 and nn. 46–51).

16. Bethge, "Geschichtstraditionen," esp. 109. See also Maier, "Jüdische Faktoren."

17. Beltz, "Gnosis und Altes Testament," 355, repeated on 356 with reference to the index of biblical passages in the Nestle edition of the Greek New Testament. Beltz's argument is cited with approval by E. Yamauchi, "Jewish Gnosticism? The Prologue of John, Mandaean Parallels, and the Trimorphic Protennoia," in van den Broek-Vermaseren, *Studies-Quispel*, 467–97, esp. 487. Beltz repeats his assertion as to the Christian mediation of "Jewish elements" in Gnosticism in "Elia redivivus" (141, citing his earlier study). In that article, he makes much of the absence from the Gnostic material of the Jewish eschatological tradition of the appearance of Elijah and Enoch in the end of days (*Apocalypse of Elijah*, etc.). But this tradition is

view of Gnosticism as the "acute hellenization of Christianity," on the grounds that the church was stronger than Judaism and that the "anti-Jewish" strain in the Gnostic materials can therefore be attributed better to Christians than to disaffected or heretical Jews.[18]

Both of Beltz's assertions are manifestly wrong, as has been pointed out by Wolfgang Schenk. As to the first, it suffices simply to say that the key biblical text used in the Gnostic parody of the foolish Creator ("I am God and there is no other," Isa 45:22 = 46:9) is absent from the New Testament. Even if it were there, the important question would be *how* the scriptural text is used in the respective cases.[19] As to the second assertion, it is unlikely that the Christian population in the Roman Empire exceeded that of the Jews until well into the fourth century.[20] But even if the church had been numerically stronger than Judaism much earlier, Beltz's statistical argument is irrelevant to the issue of the existence of a Jewish Gnosticism. After all, Christianity itself began as a Jewish sect![21]

Three Hermeneutical Presuppositions

In exploring further the question as to how the Gnostics used the Old Testament, it will be useful to explore the "hermeneutical presuppositions,"[22] or attitudes toward the Old Testament, held by the Gnostics. There are three main possibilities, and all of them are found in the sources: a wholly negative attitude toward the Old Testament; a wholly positive attitude; or intermediate positions.[23]

It will be noted that the question of the methods used in interpreting the biblical texts is bound up with these presuppositions, especially the presence or absence of allegorical interpretation and the application or nonapplication of literal interpretation. Referring to Nagel's six categories of interpretation, we can provisionally associate the negative stance with category 1, the positive

---

possibly present in the fragmentary tractate *Melchizedek* (NHC IX,*1*), p. 13 of the MS. See Pearson, *Codices IX and X*, 25, 63–65.

18. Beltz, "Gnosis und Altes Testament," 357.

19. Schenk, "Textverarbeitung," 301–2. On the "blasphemy of the Demiurge," see my subsequent discussion.

20. So Schenk, "Textverarbeitung," 304.

21. See chapter 8 of this book, and n. 52 of that chapter, for traditions concerning pre-Christian Jewish sects.

22. The term is that of Filoramo and Gianotto in "L'interpretazione gnostica," 56.

23. Ibid., 56–57. Cf. Krause, "Aussagen." Krause cites as examples of the three stances the same three texts from Nag Hammadi discussed in what follows.

stance with category 6, and the intermediate positions with categories 2 to 5 (and partially with 6). Although a detailed account
is not possible here, I shall treat first the three basic stances with
reference to selected examples from Christian Gnostic texts.

Wholly Negative Stance: *Second Treatise of the Great Seth* (NHC VII,2)

The *Second Treatise of the Great Seth*[24] is a revelatory exhortation
purportedly addressed to an embattled group of Gnostic Christians
by Jesus Christ in an attempt to bolster their steadfastness in the
face of persecution by a more powerful group. Strongly polemical,
this text attacks adversaries who are easily identifiable as catholic
Christians associated with a growing ecclesiastical establishment.
As part of its attack, the document advances a radical dualist doctrine of antagonism and separation between the highest God and
the Creator, between Christ and the world, and between the true
Christians and those who are attached to the Old Testament. This
tractate contains the most violent attack against the Old Testament
and its heroes that can be imagined:

> For Adam was a laughingstock, and he was created from
> the image of a pattern of a man by the Hebdomad [= the
> Creator], as though he had become stronger than I [Christ]
> and my brethren.... Abraham was a laughingstock, and Isaac
> and Jacob, since they were given a name by the Hebdo-
> mad, namely "the fathers from the image," as though he
> had become stronger than I and my brethren.... David was
> a laughingstock since his son was named the Son of Man,
> having been activated by the Hebdomad.... Solomon was a
> laughingstock, since he thought that he was Christ, having
> become arrogant through the Hebdomad.... The 12 prophets
> were laughingstocks, since they have come forth as imita-
> tions of the true prophets.... Moses was a laughingstock, a
> "faithful servant," being named "the Friend"; they bore wit-
> ness concerning him in iniquity, since he never knew me.
> Neither he nor those before him, from Adam to Moses and
> John the Baptist, none of them knew me nor my brethren.
> (62,27–64,1)

---

24. For other discussions of the *Treat. Seth,* see Krause, "Aussagen, 450–51;
Bethge, "Geschichtstraditionen," 104–6; Weiss, "Gesetz," 78–79; and Filoramo
and Gianotto, "L'interpretazione gnostica," 59–60. The translation used here is
that of G. J. Riley in the critical edition, in Pearson, *Codex VII,* 147–99, omitting
the Greek words in parentheses; the brackets are mine.

The text goes on to attack the "doctrine of angels" (= the Torah)[25] associated with these figures, with its "dietary rules" and "bitter slavery." The climax is reached with a virulent attack on the God of the Bible:

> For the Archon was a laughingstock because he said, "I am God, and there is none greater than I. I alone am the Father, the Lord, and there is no other beside me. I am a jealous God, bringing the sins of the fathers upon the children for three and four generations,"[26] as though he had become stronger than I and my brethren. But we are innocent with respect to him; for we did not sin. Though we mastered his doctrine in this way, he lives in conceit, and he does not agree with our Father. And thus through our friendship we prevailed over his doctrine, since he is arrogant in conceit and does not agree with our Father. For he was a laughingstock [with] his judgment and false prophecy. (64,17–65,2).

Here is a wholesale rejection of the Old Testament — its heroes of faith, its history of salvation, its legal demands, and its God. The text's inclusion of John the Baptist in the list of biblical figures serves to strengthen the denial of any suggestion that Christ had any human forerunners at all, much less that he came in fulfillment of biblical prophecy. Yet this text should not be considered necessarily "anti-Jewish," for in fact the opponents attacked in it are not Jews but ecclesiastical Christians for whom the Old Testament is still holy scripture.[27]

The closest analogy to this tractate's rejection of the Old Testament in the history of Christian heresy is the attitude adopted by Marcion and his followers.[28] The closest analogy in the history of the Gnostic religion is the Mandaean tradition, in which Moses is the prophet of the evil Ruha, and the Creator of the biblical tradition is the chief of the demons.[29] The analogies break down in each

---

25. Cf. Gal 3:19.
26. Cf. Isa 45:5, 22; 46:9; Exod 20:5. These passages are part of a Gnostic traditional complex, the "blasphemy of the Demiurge." The author of *Treat. Seth* is probably using the Gnostic tradition, rather than quoting the OT directly, as suggested by Schenk ("Textverarbeitung," 305–6). On the "blasphemy of the Demiurge" in Gnostic tradition, see subsequent discussion in this chapter.
27. See Bethge, "Geschichtstraditionen," 106.
28. On Marcion's rejection of the OT and his role in the development of a NT canon, see von Campenhausen, *Formation*, 148–67 (see n. 2).
29. See Weiss, "Gesetz," 80.

case, however. Marcion, though undoubtedly influenced by Gnosticism, was not a Gnostic but a Christian who carried to radical extremes the Pauline doctrine of justification by faith (not gnosis) apart from the works of the Law.[30] The Mandaeans were both anti-Jewish and anti-Christian, though they probably originated as a splinter group of Palestinian Judaism[31] and share a number of traditions with the Gnostics known to us from the Nag Hammadi sources.[32] The community behind *Treat. Seth* was an embattled group of Christian Gnostics (or Gnostic Christians) whose attitude toward the Old Testament was forged out of controversy with other Christians. In their total rejection of the Old Testament, they may have been influenced by Marcionites,[33] though, as the Mandaean case shows, their own Gnostic presuppositions could also have led them to this stance.

Another Nag Hammadi tractate, *The Testimony of Truth* (NHC IX,3), has been brought into close association with *Treat. Seth* in respect to its aggressive attitude toward the Old Testament.[34] This tractate, too, is a polemical attack on other Christians, in this case directed not only against the ecclesiastical establishment but also against other Gnostics.[35] Its use of the Old Testament is multifaceted, and although the Law and the biblical Creator are vigorously attacked, it is evident that the author looks upon the Old Testament as a source of Gnostic revelation that can be ferreted out by means of allegorical interpretation. *Testim. Truth* is an especially interesting tractate in that it contains two extended "midrashim," a Gnostic one on the serpent in Paradise (45,30–46,2) and one that is not necessarily Gnostic, on David and Solomon (69,32–70,24). Both midrashim are subjected to allegorical interpretation by the Christian Gnostic author.

I have commented extensively on *The Testimony of Truth* else-

---

30. See the classic work of A. Harnack, *Marcion: Das Evangelium vom fremden Gott* (Leipzig: J. C. Hinrichs, 1924); and the more recent work by R. J. Hoffmann, *Marcion: On the Restitution of Christianity* (Chico, Calif.: Scholars Press, 1984).

31. On the Mandaeans, see Rudolph, *Gnosis*, 343–66, and literature cited there. For a convenient selection of Mandaean texts in English translation, with valuable discussion by Rudolph, see Foerster, *Gnosis*, 2:121–319.

32. See esp. K. Rudolph, "Coptica-Mandaica: Zu einigen Übereinstimmungen zwischen koptischen und mandäischen Texten," in *Gnosis: Aufsätze*, 433–57.

33. See von Campenhausen, *Formation*, 77.

34. See Nagel, "Auslegung," 51; cf. preceding discussion.

35. See, for example, B. A. Pearson, "Anti-Heretical Warnings in Codex IX from Nag Hammadi," chap. 12 in Pearson, *Gnosticism;* and Koschorke, *Polemik der Gnostiker,* esp. 91–174.

where.[36] Suffice it to say here that its use of the Old Testament is not the same as that of *Treat. Seth.*

Wholly Positive Stance: *The Exegesis on the Soul* (NHC II,6)

The *Exegesis on the Soul* (NHC II,6)[37] is devoted to an exposition of the divine origin, fall, and reintegration of the human soul. The doctrine of the descent and ascent of the soul was widespread in the Hellenistic Roman world and is part and parcel of the popular Platonism of the period. *Exeg. Soul* presents this doctrine with a Gnostic twist, depicting the (female) soul's descent as a fall into prostitution. Its ascent requires "repentance" and consists in a restoration of the soul, as a renewed virgin, to her Father's house.

Of interest to us here is the use made of the Old Testament in this remarkable text. Scriptural passages are cited extensively as "proof texts" for the various aspects of the soul's experience, as set forth by the tractate's author.[38] The following examples are taken from the first part of the tractate:

> Now concerning the prostitution of the soul the Holy Spirit prophesies in many places. For he said in the prophet Jeremiah, "If the husband divorces his wife and she goes and takes another man..." (Jer 3:1–4)

36. See Pearson, *Codices IX and X,* 101–20. On the serpent midrash, see B. A. Pearson, "Jewish Haggadic Traditions in *The Testimony of Truth* from Nag Hammadi (CG IX,3)," chap. 3 in Pearson, *Gnosticism.* On the David-Solomon midrash, see "Gnostic Interpretation of the Old Testament in the *Testimony of Truth* (NHC IX,3)," *HTR* 79 (1980): 311–19; and "Jewish Sources in Gnostic Literature," in Stone, *Jewish Writings,* 443–81, esp. 457.

37. For discussion of *Exeg. Soul,* see Krause, "Aussagen," 452–56; R. M. Wilson, "Old Testament Exegesis in the Gnostic Exegesis of the Soul," in Krause, *Essays-Labib,* 217–24; R. Kasser, "Citations des grands prophètes bibliques dans les textes gnostiques coptes," in Krause, *Essays-Labib,* 46–64; P. Nagel, "Die Septuaginta-Zitate in der koptisch-gnostischen 'Exegese über die Seele' (Nag Hammadi Codex II)," *APF* 22/23 (1974): 249–69; and A. Guillaumont, "Une citation de l'Apocryphe d'Ezéchiel dans l'Exégèse au sujet de l'âme: Nag Hammadi II,6," in Krause, *Essays-Labib,* 35–39. For critical editions, see Layton, *Codex II,* 2:135–69 (intro. and trans. W. C. Robinson Jr.); and J.-M. Sevrin, *L'Exégèse de l'âme* (NH II,6), BCNH "Textes" 9 (Québec: Université Laval, 1983). See also M. Scopello's important monograph *L'Exégèse de l'âme: Introduction, traduction et commentaire,* NHS 25 (Leiden: E. J. Brill, 1985).

38. As Nagel has shown ("Septuaginta-Zitate"), the LXX text is closely followed in the OT passages quoted in *Exeg. Soul.* See also Kasser, "Citations." Scopello (*L'Exégèse,* 13–44) and Sevrin (*L'Exégèse,* 13) both argue for the author's use of an anthology.

Again it is written in the prophet Hosea, "Come, go to law with your [pl.] mother, for she is not to be a wife to me nor I a husband to her...." (Hos 2:2–7)

Again he said in Ezekiel, "It came to pass after much depravity, said the Lord.... You prostituted yourself to the sons of Egypt, those who are your neighbors, men great of flesh." (Ezek 16:23–26) (129,5–130,20)

The author is not content simply to cite scriptural proof texts, but he (or she)[39] offers specific interpretive commentary on key words and phrases in the scriptural text, as can be seen in the passage immediately following the material previously quoted:

But what does "the sons of Egypt, men great of flesh" mean if not the domain of the flesh and the perceptible realm and the affairs of the earth, by which the soul has become defiled here, receiving bread from them, as well as wine, oil, clothing [cf. Hos 2:5], and other external nonsense surrounding the body — the things she thinks she needs. (130,20–28)

The author then proceeds to fortify his argument with additional teaching, with scriptural proofs from the Old and New Testaments, and in one case (135,31–136,4) with an apocryphal passage from Pseudo-Ezekiel.[40] The author's fund of revelatory scripture is larger than usual, however, for he quotes Homer in the same way that he does the Bible: "Therefore it is written in the Poet, 'Odysseus sat on the island weeping... [Od. 1:48–59]' " (136, 27–35). This is followed by two quotations from Odyssey 4. Our author evidently regards the Bible and "the Poet" as equal sources of revelation, specifically as allegories of the soul's fall and restoration. His pagan contemporaries were already treating Homer in this way,[41] so it was simply a matter of adding the Chris-

---

39. *Exeg. Soul* is one of the Nag Hammadi tractates for which a female author could easily be posited. See Scopello's discussion of the role of the feminine in this and other texts (*L'Exégèse*, 49–55). Scopello, however, does not argue for a female author, referring to the author as "il" (55). For convenience, I also use the masculine gender in what follows, although I leave the question as to the sex of the author completely open.

40. This passage, formerly associated with *1 Clem.* 8:3, was first identified as Pseudo-Ezekiel by Guillaumont, "Une citation." On Pseudo-Ezekiel (*Apocryphon of Ezekiel*), see *OTP*, 1:487–90.

41. See esp. Porphyry, *De antr. nymph.*, a commentary on *Od.* 13.102–12; and Plotinus's interpretation of the flight of Odysseus from Circe and Calypso, *Enn.* 1.6.8. On the allegorical interpretation of Homer in Hellenistic antiquity, see esp. F. Buffière, *Les mythes d'Homère et la pensée grecque* (Paris: Belles Lettres, 1956).

tian scriptures to the fund of revelation concerning the nature and destiny of the human soul. In the process, some new (Gnostic) features were added to the doctrine, including material related to the Valentinian myth of Sophia.

The *Exegesis on the Soul* is clearly a "late" product of Christian Gnosticism, as is particularly evident from its eclecticism. Its affinities with Valentinian Gnosticism have been noted.[42] Its affinities with the Naassene Gnostic system are also noteworthy.[43] The Naassenes interpreted Homer in much the same way as the author of *Exeg. Soul.*[44] The Old Testament is also treated in a notably positive way in the Naassene material, with the application of allegorical interpretation.[45] Indeed, the Naassene use of the Old Testament is exceedingly sophisticated, ranging from the use of proof texts — for example, Isaiah 53:8 is quoted with reference to the Divine Man, Adamas[46] — to the poetic elaboration of a biblical psalm as an allegory of the soul's salvation as a result of the descent of Jesus the Savior.[47]

The last-named example deserves further comment, involving as it does one of the most beautiful examples of Gnostic poetry preserved from antiquity. I refer, of course, to the so-called Naassene Psalm (Hippol., *Haer.* 5.10.2), in which the soul is presented as a "hind" weeping in her wanderings in the cosmic labyrinth until Jesus asks his Father to send him down to help the soul "escape

---

42. According to Krause ("Aussagen," 456), it is a Valentinian product; according to Sevrin (*L'Exégèse,* 58–60), it is pre-Valentinian; according to Scopello (*L'Exégèse,* 48, passim), it relies on Valentinian traditions and much else besides.

43. These affinities are noted by W. Robinson, "The Exegesis on the Soul," *NovT* 12 (1970): 102–17, esp. 116–17. For the Naassene material, see esp. Foerster, *Gnosis,* 1:261–82, providing a translation of Hippol., *Haer.* 5.6.3–11.1. See also J. Frickel's important work *Hellenistische Erlösung in christlicher Deutung: Die gnostische Naassenerschrift,* NHS 19 (Leiden: E. J. Brill, 1984). Another Gnostic work preserved by Hippolytus, *Baruch,* by the Gnostic Justin, presents an interesting contrast to *Exeg. Soul* in its interpretation of the prophet Hosea, citing Hos 1:2 as referring to the "mystery" of the ascent of "Elohim" to "the Good" (= Priapus!) and his divorce from "Eden" (*Haer.* 5.27.4). For a translation of *Baruch,* with discussion by E. Haenchen, see Foerster, *Gnosis,* 1:48–58. See also R. Batey, "Jewish Gnosticism and the *hieros gamos* of Eph. V,21–33," *NTS* 10 (1963/64): 121–27; and K. Kvideland, "Elohims Himmelfahrt," *Temenos* 10 (1974): 68–78.

44. Hippol., *Haer.* 5.7.30–39 (*Od.* 24.1–12); 5.8.35 (*Od.* 4.384–85); 5.7.36 (*Il.* 4.350); 5.8.3 (*Il.* 15.189).

45. See Nagel, "Auslegung," 51; and earlier discussion herein.

46. Hippol., *Haer.* 5.7.2. The passage is introduced with the formula "It is written."

47. Unfortunately, no extended analysis of the Naassene use of the OT exists, and space does not allow for such an analysis here.

the bitter chaos" by transmitting "the secrets of the holy way...
Gnosis."[48] As Martin Elze has brilliantly demonstrated, this beautiful poem is a Gnostic interpretation of Psalm 41 (LXX): "As a
hind longs for the springs of the waters, so longs my soul for you,
O God...."[49]

Biblical psalms are included among the scriptural passages utilized in *Exeg. Soul.* Psalm 45:10–11 (LXX 44:11–12) is quoted
to show the Father's desire for the soul's repentance (133,15–20).
Psalm 103 (102):1–5 is quoted with reference to the ascent of the
soul to the Father (134,16–25). Psalm 6:6–9 (7–10) is quoted at
the end of the tractate as part of a final exhortation to repentance
(137,15–22).

A similar use of the biblical psalms, with the same positive
stance toward the scriptural text, is found in *Pistis Sophia,* one of
the Coptic Gnostic writings known before the discovery of the Nag
Hammadi corpus.[50] In that text, the heroine, Pistis Sophia ("Faith
Wisdom"), whose mythic fall and restoration are paradigmatic of
the fall and restoration of the Gnostic soul, cries out in "repentance" to the world of light and is ultimately restored by Jesus.
There are thirteen such "repentances," accompanied by extended
quotations from the Psalms and the *Odes of Solomon* as proof
texts of the experience of salvation.[51] Geo Widengren, in an important article, has analyzed the use of the Old Testament in *Pistis
Sophia,*[52] and I shall therefore forgo any further comment here, ex-

---

48. The best edition of the Greek text of the Naassene Psalm, with English
translation and commentary, is M. Marcovich, "The Naassene Psalm in Hippolytus (*Haer.* 5.10.2)," in Layton, *Rediscovery,* 2:770–78. I have used his translation here.

49. My translation of v. 1. See M. Elze, "Haresie und Einheit der Kirche in
2. Jahrhundert," *ZThK* 71 (1974): 389–409, esp. 402–3.

50. For the critical edition of *Pistis Sophia,* with English translation, see
C. Schmidt, ed., and V. MacDermot, trans., *Pistis Sophia,* NHS 9 (Leiden: E. J.
Brill, 1978).

51. Ps 102 (LXX):1–5 is quoted in *Pistis Sophia* 2.75; the same passage is quoted
in *Exeg. Soul* (as noted earlier). The Coptic translation of parts of *Odes Sol.* 1, 5,
6, 22, and 25 in *Pistis Sophia* was the only version of the *Odes* known until the
discovery of the Syriac version and then a Greek MS of Ode 11. *Odes Sol.* is not
a Gnostic composition, contrary to the opinion of some scholars. For an English
translation, with introduction and bibliography, see *OTP,* 2:725–71.

52. G. Widengren, "Die Hymnen der Pistis Sophia und die gnostische Schrift-
auslegung," in *Liber Amicorum: Studies in Honour of Professor Dr. J. C. Bleeker*
(Leiden: E. J. Brill, 1969), 269–81." See also A. Kragerud, *Die Hymnen der Pistis
Sophia* (Oslo: Universitetsforlaget, 1967); and C. Trautman, "La citation du Psaume
85 (84): 11–12 et ses commentaires dans la Pistis Sophia," *RHPhR* 59 (1979):
551–57.

cept to say that the affinities between that text and the *Exegesis on the Soul* are manifest.[53]

Intermediate Positions: Ptolemaeus's *Letter to Flora* and Other Texts

The *Letter to Flora* by the Gnostic teacher Ptolemaeus, a disciple of the famous Valentinus, is one of the few precious Gnostic texts coming down to us from antiquity in its original Greek form (as quoted by Epiphanius, *Panarion* 33.3.1–7.10).[54] In this letter, Ptolemaeus addresses a certain lady, presumably an uninitiated seeker, on the subject of the Law of Moses and the extent of its continuing relevance to the (Gnostic) Christian life. Ptolemaeus's starting point is "the words of the Savior" (Jesus), from which it is concluded that the Law is divisible into three parts: a part attributed to God and his legislative activity, a part attributed to Moses himself, and a part added by "the elders of the people" (4.1–14). The Law of God, in turn, is divided into three parts: the Decalogue, fulfilled by the Savior; an imperfect part, abolished by the Savior; and a third (cultic) part that must be interpreted "spiritually," that is, allegorically (5.1–7.1). Ptolemaeus finally reveals his Gnostic stance by identifying the "God" who gave the Law as the Demiurge, the Creator of the world, who is actually inferior to the perfect God, the Father (7.2–7). The import of his previous discussion, however, is that the Law is, to some extent, still authoritative, as defined by "the words of the Savior." Even its cultic legislation contains revelation of value when it is subjected to allegorical interpretation.

This important text of the Valentinian school, though dealing especially with the Law (i.e., the Pentateuch), can be seen to express the typical Valentinian Gnostic position vis-à-vis the Old Testament as a whole: even though the Old Testament is inspired by an inferior deity, its text contains valuable truth, which "the Savior" fulfills, or which, when subjected to allegorical interpretation, reveals gnosis. The Valentinian use of the Old Testament thus derives not only from Gnostic religious presuppositions (e.g., regarding

---

53. See esp. Krause, "Aussagen," 450, 452; and Filoramo and Gianotto, "L'interpretazione gnostica," 65–69.

54. The standard edition of the *Letter to Flora* is G. Quispel, *Ptolémée: Lettre à Flora*, 2d ed., SC 24 (Paris: Cerf, 1966). For good English translations, with introductions, see Foerster, *Gnosis*, 1:154–61; and Layton, *Gnostic Scriptures*, 306–15. For an important discussion, see von Campenhausen, *Formation*, 82–87; see also Weiss, "Gesetz," 82–83.

the inferior Creator) but also from general, nonheretical Christian tradition.

One of the Valentinian texts from Nag Hammadi, the *Tripartite Tractate* (NHC I,5),[55] presents a discussion of the biblical prophets comparable to that on the Law in Ptolemaeus's letter. In the framework of a general discussion of various philosophies and theologies existing in the world (108,13–114,30),[56] the author discusses the various "heresies" that existed among the Jews as a result of their differing interpretations of scripture (112,14–113,1)[57] and offers the following assessment of the prophets:

> The prophets, however, did not say anything of their own accord, but each one of them [spoke] of the things which he had seen and heard through the proclamation of the Savior. This is what he proclaimed, with the main subject of their proclamation being that which each said concerning the coming of the Savior, which is this coming. Sometimes the prophets speak about it as if it will be. Sometimes [it is] as if the Savior speaks from their mouths, saying that the Savior will come and show favor to those who have not known him. They [the prophets] have not all joined with one another in confessing anything, but each one thinks on the basis of the activity from which he received power to speak about him.... Not one of them knew whence he would come nor by whom he would be begotten, but he alone is the one of whom it is worthy to speak, the one who will be begotten and who will suffer. (113,5–34)

---

55. For critical editions of *Tri. Trac.*, see R. Kasser et al., *Tractatus Tripartitus,* 2 vols. (Bern: Francke, 1973, 1975); H. Attridge, *Nag Hammadi Codex I (The Jung Codex),* 2 vols., NHS 22–23 (Leiden: E. J. Brill, 1985), 1:159–337 and 2:217–497; and E. Thomassen, *Le Traité Tripartite (NH I,5),* BCNH "Textes" 19 (Québec: Université Laval, 1989). For a discussion of its use of the OT, see J. Zandee, "Das Alte Testament im Urteil des Gnostizismus," in *Symbolae Biblicae et Mesopotamicae: Francisco Mario Theodoro de Liagre Böhl dedicatae,* ed. M. Beek et al. (Leiden: E. J. Brill, 1973), 403–11.

The other Valentinian texts are *Pr. Paul* (I,1); *Gos. Truth* (I,3 and XII,2); *Treat. Res.* (I,4); *Gos. Phil.* (II,3); *Interp. Know.* (XI,1); and *Val. Exp.* (XI,2). Still other Nag Hammadi texts betray Valentinian influences.

56. For an important discussion and commentary, see Attridge, *Nag Hammadi Codex I,* 1:185–86 and 2:417–35.

57. On this passage in relation to rabbinic discussions of "heresy," see A. H. B. Logan, "The Jealousy of God: Exodus 20:5 in Gnostic and Rabbinic Theology," in *Studia Biblica 1978* (Sixth International Congress on Biblical Studies, Oxford, 3–7 April 1978), ed. E. A. Livingstone, vol. 1, *Papers on Old Testament and Related Themes,* JSOTSup 11 (Sheffield: University of Sheffield, 1979), 197–203, esp. 199–200.

This passage sounds perfectly "orthodox" until we realize that, in the context, the "race of the Hebrews," including the prophets, is a "psychic" people attached to the inferior Creator, who himself is only an "image of the Father's image" (110,22–36).

The Valentinians were by no means the only Gnostics who developed this "intermediate" position vis-à-vis the Old Testament. Another of the Nag Hammadi texts, the *Concept of Our Great Power* (NHC VI,4),[58] not a Valentinian text but perhaps influenced by Valentinian Gnosticism, adopts such a stance in presenting a Gnostic-apocalyptic presentation of world history. In this interesting text, which has been referred to as an "epitome of a Christian Gnostic history of the world,"[59] history is divided into three epochs or "aeons": the "aeon of the flesh" (38,13; 41,2), brought to an end by the flood; the "psychic aeon" (39,16–17; 40,24–25), during which the Savior appears and which will end in a conflagration (46,29–30); and a future "aeon of beauty" (47,15–16), which is an "unchangeable aeon" (48,13). The Creator is referred to as "the father of the flesh," who "avenged himself" by means of the water of the flood (38,19–32). Yet, in contrast to most Gnostic treatments, Noah is presented as "pious and worthy," a preacher of "piety" (*eusebeia,* 38,26).[60]

Many more examples could be cited here, but we can conclude this part of our discussion with the observation that an "intermediate" stance vis-à-vis the Old Testament is the most characteristic attitude toward the scriptures displayed in the Gnostic sources in general. Scripture is viewed largely as the product of a lower power (or lower powers), but it is nevertheless capable of revealing gnosis so long as the proper exegetical method is adopted. In the case of the Christian Gnostic documents, the proper method involves allegorical exegesis and/or a christocentric approach according to which Christ perfects or fulfills the Old Testament or parts thereof.

There remains another question to consider: Does the Christian Gnostic material exhaust our available evidence? That is to

---

58. For critical editions of the *Concept of Our Great Power,* see D. Parrott, *Nag Hammadi Codices V,2–5 and VI with Papyrus Berolinensis 8502,1 and 4,* NHS 11 (Leiden: E. J. Brill, 1979), 291–326; and P. Cherix, *Le concept de Notre Grande Puissance, CG VI,4* (Fribourg: Éditions Universitaires; Göttingen: Vandenhoeck & Ruprecht, 1982). For discussions of its use of the OT, see Krause, "Aussagen," 451; Bethge, "Geschichtstraditionen," 97–98; and Filoramo and Gianotto, "L'interpretazione gnostica," 60.

59. Bethge, "Geschichtstraditionen," 97, crediting H.-M. Schenke.

60. Cf. Bethge's discussion of the various Gnostic interpretations of Noah and the flood, in "Geschichtstraditionen," 94–98.

say, is there a Gnostic use of the Old Testament that is not at the same time "Christian" in some recognizable sense? The Mandaean material already briefly cited suggests that there is.[61]

"Rewritten Scripture": The *Apocryphon of John* and Related Literature

The *Apocryphon of John* (NHC II,1; III,1; IV,1; BG,2)[62] is, in its present form, a Gnostic apocalypse in which the risen Christ transmits revelation of "mysteries" to his disciple John concerning "what is, and what was, and what will come to pass" (II 2,16–18; cf. 1,1–2).[63] It is one of the most important of the Gnostic texts that have come down to us, for it contains a Gnostic myth that probably served as the basis for the myth developed by the great Gnostic teacher Valentinus and further elaborated by his disciples, especially Ptolemaeus.[64]

Not long after the publication of the Berlin Gnostic Codex in 1955, Søren Giversen published a valuable article on the use of the Old Testament (especially Genesis 1–7) in the *Apocryphon of John*.[65] Using the BG version, Giversen first distinguishes four forms that the use of the Old Testament takes in the text:

1. actual quotations, with introductory formulas (e.g., "the prophet said");

2. quotations without introductory formulas;

---

61. See the earlier discussion of *Treat. Seth*.

62. Several editions of one or more of the versions of *Ap. John* have been published, but the synoptic edition of all four versions, Waldstein-Wisse, *Apocryphon,* is now standard. The English translation in *NHLE* (by F. Wisse) renders the "long recension" in NHC II. See also Layton, *Gnostic Scriptures,* 23–51. There is an English translation of the BG version ("short recension"), together with the parallel material in Irenaeus, *Haer.* 1.29, in Foerster, *Gnosis,* 1:105–20. The translation used here is that of Waldstein-Wisse, *Apocryphon.* See also my analysis of *Ap. John* in chapter 7 of this book.

63. For a genre study of Gnostic apocalypses, see F. Fallon, "Gnostic Apocalypses," in Collins, *Apocalypse,* 123–58, esp. 130–31 (on *Ap. John*).

64. See esp. G. Quispel, "Valentinian Gnosis and the Apocryphon of John," in Layton, *Rediscovery,* 1:118–27.

65. S. Giversen, "The Apocryphon of John and Genesis," *StTh* 17 (1963): 60–76; published originally in Danish in 1957. For a valuable analysis of *Orig. World* (NHC II,5 and XIII,2) along the same lines, see O. Wintermute, "A Study of Gnostic Exegesis of the Old Testament," in *The Use of the Old Testament in the New and Other Essays: Studies in Honour of William Franklin Stinespring,* ed. J. E. Efird (Durham, N.C.: Duke University Press, 1972), 241–70.

3. expressions and phrases clearly derived from the biblical text, or sentences recounting events described in the scripture; and

4. use of key words that call for special (allegorical) interpretation.

Instances of the first category also include direct refutation of what "Moses said." Among the examples cited by Giversen, the following illustrates the fourth category, the use of key words:

[Christ said,] "Then the Mother [Sophia] began 'to move to and fro' [ἐπιφέρεσθαι], when she became aware of her deficiency, because her consort had not agreed with her when she was blamed by her perfection." But I [John] said, "Christ, what [does it mean that] she 'moved to and fro' [ἐπιφέρεσθαι; cf. Gen 1:2 (LXX)]?" And he smiled and said, "Are you thinking that it is, as Moses said, 'above the waters' [Gen 1:2]? No, but she saw the wickedness and rebellion that would happen through her son [the Creator]. She repented."[66]

In discussing the question as to how the author of the *Apocryphon of John* interprets Genesis, Giversen states that the interpretation is "largely but not exclusively allegorical."[67] He rightly qualifies this with reference to the basic Gnostic doctrines: phenomena in this world are only likenesses of realities in the world

---

66. BG 44,19–45,13. See Giversen's discussion, "Apocryphon of John," 64–65. Giversen (66–67) provides the following table of Genesis passages used in one way or another in *Ap. John:*

Genesis	Apocryphon of John (BG)
1:2	45,1.7.10.19
1:26	48,10–14
2:9	57,8–11
2:15–16; 3:23–24	56,1–10
2:17	57,12–13
2:21	58,17–18
2:21–22	59,18–19
2:24	60,7–11
3:16	61,11–12
3:23	61,19–62,1
4:25	63,12–14
6:1–4	74,1–5
6:6	72,12–14
6:17	72,14–17
7:7	73,5–6

Other passages in Genesis could be added to this list. See my later discussion of the "blasphemy of the Demiurge"; see also my discussion of the use of Gen 2:7 in *Ap. John*, in "Biblical Exegesis in Gnostic Literature," chap. 3 in Pearson, *Gnosticism*.
67. Giversen, "Apocryphon of John," 67.

of light; the Creator and his world are evil and inferior to the highest God and the world of light; and so on. The attitude taken toward the biblical text is mixed: What "Moses said" is sometimes flatly rejected, but sometimes the counterinterpretation is bolstered by a reference to another biblical passage (e.g., the citation of "the prophet" Isaiah at 59,1–5). In general, the use of Genesis often involves a "reverse" interpretation. What is presented in the *Apocryphon of John*, finally, does not involve a rejection of Genesis or a revision of its text, but "secret doctrine," that is, "true knowledge."[68]

Giversen's discussion is quite sound as far as it goes, that is, insofar as it takes account of the *Apocryphon of John* in its present form as a postresurrection revelation transmitted by Christ to John and, by extension, to Christian Gnostic readers. However, formal analysis of the text reveals that it is a composite product and contains editorial expansions of an earlier stratum of material. The effect of this redactional activity was to create a specifically Christian Gnostic text out of an earlier non-Christian Gnostic revelation. This was done by adding a framework according to which "Christ" provides revelation to John; by opening up the text at ten different points to create a dialogue between "Christ" and his interlocutor, John; and by adding a few easily recognizable glosses.[69] That such a procedure was actually carried out with Gnostic texts is indisputably proved in the case of two other Nag Hammadi writings, *Eugnostos the Blessed* (III,3 and V,1) and the *Sophia of Jesus Christ* (III,4 and BG,3).[70]

The putative urtext underlying the *Apocryphon of John* consists of theosophical revelation (the unknown highest God and the world of light), cosmogony (the fall of Sophia, the lower world, and the blasphemy of the Demiurge), and soteriology, in which the primal history in Genesis is retold with the use of other biblical and extrabiblical materials in such a way as to emphasize the saving role of Sophia in behalf of the Gnostic elect, the "race of

---

68. Ibid., 75–76.

69. See my discussion in chapter 7.

70. *Soph. Jes. Chr.* is a Christian Gnostic "revelation dialogue" constructed as such using *Eugnostos*, a non-Christian text, as its basic source. See esp. M. Krause, "Das literarische Verhältnis des Eugnostosbriefes zur Sophia Jesu Christi," in *Mullus: Festschrift für Theodor Klausner* (Münster: Westfalen, 1964), 215–23; D. Parrot, "Evidence of Religious Syncretism in Gnostic Texts from Nag Hammadi," in *Religious Syncretism in Antiquity: Essays in Conversation with Geo Widengren*, ed. B. Pearson (Missoula, Mont.: Scholars Press, 1975), 173–83; and Perkins, *Gnostic Dialogue*, 94–98.

Seth."[71] The closest analogies to this kind of text are found in the Jewish pseudepigraphical literature, specifically those writings that fall into the category of "rewritten scripture," such as portions of *1 Enoch, Jubilees,* the *Genesis Apocryphon* from Qumran, the Books of Adam and Eve, and the like.[72] The putative urtext of the *Apocryphon of John* is only one of a number of Gnostic texts that can be classified as "rewritten scripture."[73] Such texts, in my opinion, represent the earliest stage of Gnostic literary production and can be seen as a by-product of the history of Jewish literature. They are comparable, in their method of composition and in their use of biblical texts and extrabiblical traditions, to the Jewish Pseudepigrapha. The difference, of course, is in what is conveyed in the respective literatures. If, for example, the book of *Jubilees* is a rewriting of Genesis 1–Exodus 14 for the purpose of presenting an alternative sectarian halakah,[74] the urtext of the *Apocryphon of John* is a rewriting and expansion of Genesis 1–7 for the purpose of presenting an alternative sectarian *myth,* a myth that will reveal saving gnosis.[75] The use made of the biblical text in the respective cases is quite comparable both in method and in attitude. That is to say, the biblical text is not rejected out of hand; it is corrected and amplified by the composition of a superior version of the truth.

To be sure, there is an observable difference between the Gnostic texts and the Jewish Pseudepigrapha, even the most "nonconformist" or "sectarian" of them. This difference is so basic that it finally marks Gnosticism as a new religion altogether, one that has broken through even the widest definable boundaries of what constitutes "Judaism." The following passage from the *Apocryphon of John* exemplifies this breach:

---

71. *Ap. John* has rightly been included in the group of texts that belong to "Sethian" Gnosticism. On the Sethian form of Gnosticism, see esp. Schenke, "Das sethianische System"; Schenke, "Gnostic Sethianism"; and Pearson, "The Figure of Seth in Gnostic Literature," chap. 4 in Pearson, *Gnosticism*. See also Stroumsa, *Another Seed.*

72. See esp. G. W. E. Nickelsburg, "The Bible Rewritten and Expanded," in Stone, *Jewish Writings,* 89–156.

73. See Filoramo and Gianotto, "Interpretazione gnostica," 69–73, a valuable discussion with the heading "Reinterpretazione o rescrittura del racconto biblico." The following texts attributed to the "gruppo Sethiano" are discussed under that heading: *Ap. John; Hyp. Arch.* (NHC II,4); and *Orig. World* (NHC II,5 and XIII,2). See also Simonetti's extensive discussion of Gnostic reinterpretation of the opening passages in Genesis ("Note sull' interpretazione," 9:347–59; 10:103–26).

74. See Nickelsburg, "Bible Rewritten," 97–104.

75. On Gnosticism as a "mythological phenomenon," see, e.g., Stroumsa, *Another Seed,* 1–14; and H. Jonas, "The Gnostic Syndrome: Typology of Its Thought, Imagination, and Mood," in *Philosophical Essays,* 263–76, esp. 266–73.

And when he saw the creation which surrounds him and the multitude of angels around him which had come forth from him, he said to them, "I am a jealous God and there is no other God beside me." But by announcing this he indicated to the angels who attended to him that there exists another God, for if there were no other one, of whom would he be jealous? (NHC II 13,5–13).

This passage, treating the "blasphemy of the Demiurge," is an example of a Gnostic tradition found in a number of texts, and reflects the Gnostic end product of a discussion in Jewish circles concerning "two powers in heaven." The Gnostic conclusion to the debate effectively marks a "revolution" on the part of Jewish Gnostics against the biblical Creator and a radical alienation from his created order.[76] The text itself is artfully constructed as a rewriting (and reordering) of the biblical material in Genesis 1. The Gnostic author indicates that he knows that the "creation" (Gen 1:1) "seen" (Gen 1:4, 10, 12, 18, 21, 25) by the Creator is nothing "good"; rather, it is darkness and chaos (Gen 1:2), and the Creator himself is not only arrogant but also foolish, not understanding the import of his own vain pronouncements (Isa 45:21; 46:9; Exod 20:5).[77]

The blasphemy of the Demiurge is immediately followed in the *Apocryphon of John* by the statement quoted earlier concerning the "moving to and fro" (= "repentance") of "the mother" (= Sophia), a reinterpretation of Genesis 1:2. Following Sophia's repentance, a *bat qol* ("heavenly voice") comes from heaven with the announcement, "Man exists and the Son of Man" (14,14–15). With this revelation, we come to know the identity of the highest God whose existence (together with that of his "son," primal Adam) has been blasphemously denied by the Creator. The highest God is "Man" (cf. Gen 1:26–27).[78]

The material that follows in the text deals with the creation of earthly man, a composite being whose inner self is akin to "Man," the highest God. The Gnostic account of the creation of Adam

---

76. See esp. N. Dahl, "The Arrogant Archon and the Lewd Sophia: Jewish Traditions in Gnostic Revolt," in Layton, *Rediscovery,* 2:689–712.

77. One of the three names given to the Creator in *Ap. John* is Saklas (Aramaic for "fool"). The other names are Samael and Yaldabaoth; all three occur together in the text at II 11,16–18. On these names, see Pearson, "Jewish Haggadic Traditions," 47–49 (see n. 36); and B. Barc, "Samaèl-Saklas-Yaldabaôth: Recherche sur la genèse d'un myth gnostique," in Barc, *Colloque International,* 123–50.

78. See Schenke, *Der Gott "Mensch."*

was constructed with the use and reinterpretation of a number of Jewish exegetical traditions, some of which reflect the influence of contemporary Platonism.[79] The import of this Gnostic "rewritten scripture" is that the knowledge of God requisite to salvation is really knowledge of the awakened self within, a "man" whose kinship with "Man" makes him superior to the world and its Creator. That such a doctrine, so self-evidently alien to the biblical tradition (both Old and New Testaments), was read out of the Bible and given expression in the form of "rewritten scripture" is one of the fascinating curiosities of ancient Jewish history and the history of Hellenistic-Roman religions.

Although the *Apocryphon of John* is arguably the most important Gnostic text for the purposes of this discussion, there are others, too, that fit the category of "rewritten scripture." Some of these are closely related to the *Apocryphon of John* in structure and content: the *Hypostasis of the Archons* (NHC II,4); *On the Origin of the World* (NHC II,5 and XIII,2); and the system described by Irenaeus in *Adversus Haereses* 1.30.[80] Like the *Apocryphon of John,* these texts have undergone Christianizing redaction. The *Apocalypse of Adam* (NHC V,5) is an especially interesting example of rewritten scripture because of its relation to the Jewish Adam literature.[81] There is no discernible Christian content in the *Apocalypse of Adam.* The *Paraphrase of Shem* (NHC VII,1),[82] another non-Christian text, could conceivably be

---

79. See Pearson, "Biblical Exegesis" (see n. 66); and esp. R. van den Broek, "The Creation of Adam's Psychic Body in the Apocryphon of John," in *Studies,* 67–85.

80. For critical editions of *Hyp. Arch.,* see Layton, *Codex II;* and B. Barc, *L'Hypostase des Archontes: Traité gnostique sur l'origine de l'homme, du monde et des archontes (NH II,4)* (Québec: Université Laval, 1980). Barc posits several redactional stages in the text's composition, the most primitive of which is a product of Jewish Gnosticism.

The most recent editions of *Orig. World* are Layton, Codex II; and L. Painchaud, *L'Écrit sans titre: Traité sur l'Origine du Monde,* BCNH "Textes" 21 (Québec: Université Laval, 1995). See Wintermute, "Gnostic Exegesis" (see n. 65) for an analysis of that text's use of the OT.

Irenaeus does not label the system he describes, but scholarly tradition refers to it as "Ophite." For an English translation and discussion, see Foerster, *Gnosis,* 1:54–94. For a good discussion of that text's correlation of the biblical prophets with the various archontic powers (1.30.16–11), see F. Fallon, "The Prophets of the Old Testament and the Gnostics: A Note on Irenaeus, Adversus Haereses I.30.10–11," *VC* 32 (1978): 191–94. On the problem of "Ophite" Gnosticism in general, see J.-D. Kaestli, "L'interprétation du serpent de Genèse 3 dans quelques textes gnostiques et la question de la gnose 'ophite,'" in Ries, *Gnosticisme et monde hellénistique,* 116–30.

81. See my discussion in chapter 7.

82. See F. Wisse's edition of *Paraph. Shem* in Pearson, *Codex VII,* 15–127.

included in the category of rewritten scripture, though the divergences from the biblical text are greater in that writing. In addition, the Mandaean anthropogonic myths are clearly related to that of the *Apocryphon of John* and other Gnostic texts.[83] Unfortunately, limitations of space prevent us from taking up these materials for discussion here.

Conclusions

The earliest Gnostic literature was heavily indebted to the biblical text and to Jewish exegetical traditions. Though the Gnostics denigrated the biblical Creator by relegating him to an inferior position below a transcendent deity, they did not reject the Bible itself. On the contrary, they came to their radical theology and worldview in the very process of *interpreting* the scriptural text, the authoritative ("canonical") status of which was self-evident. Their earliest literature took the form of "rewritten scripture" and resembled, in that respect, some of the pseudepigraphical literature produced in sectarian Jewish circles. The Gnostic writings were mythological in character and relied heavily on the primal history of Genesis and on current Jewish interpretations thereof. Indeed, there is every reason to believe that the authors of the early Gnostic texts were disaffected Jewish intellectuals open to the various religious and philosophical currents of Hellenistic syncretism.

Early in the history of the Gnostic religion, the Christian mission exerted a profound influence on Gnostic thinking. And, conversely, Gnosticism came to play a prominent role in the early development of the Christian religion, particularly as Christianity moved away from its ethnic Jewish matrix and assumed a separate identity as a Hellenistic religion. The coalescence of Gnosticism and Christianity was expressed particularly in making Jesus Christ a Gnostic "savior" figure, that is, a revealer of gnosis. The literary manifestation of this trend first takes the form of editorial Christianization of originally non-Christian texts. This was accomplished by attributing the Gnostic myth to Jesus Christ and/or by making him the paradigm of Gnostic salvation. Eventually, a new Gnostic Christian literature was created.

The Bible (Old Testament) was part of the Christian heritage, as it was of the Gnostic heritage. But there was considerable variety

---

83. See esp. Kurt Rudolph, "Ein Grundtyp gnostischer Urmensch-Adam-Spekulation," in *Gnosis: Aufsätze,* 123–43; and Rudolph, "Coptica-Mandaica" (see n. 32).

in the way in which Gnostic Christians looked upon it. Three basic attitudes emerged: open rejection of the Old Testament; whole-hearted acceptance of it; and an intermediate position according to which the biblical text was inspired by the lower Creator or lesser powers but nevertheless contained "spiritual truth" to be ferreted out by means of a spiritual (allegorical) exegesis. Authorization for this procedure was found in revelation attributed to the Savior, Jesus Christ, and to various of his apostles.

As we have seen, the use and interpretation of the Bible among the various Gnostic groups in antiquity is characterized by a great deal of variety and complexity, thanks to the creative inventiveness of the different Gnostic teachers in their elaboration of Gnostic myth. Two of the tractates that have been discussed in this essay are taken up again in greater detail in the following chapter.

_____ *Chapter 7* _____

The Problem of
"Jewish Gnostic" Literature

The Problem

As is implied in the title of this chapter, to speak of "Jewish Gnostic" literature involves a much-disputed problem of considerable
proportions, bearing on the larger issue of the genesis and development of Gnosticism itself. This larger problem, as I would
pose it, is the historical relationship among three religions: Gnosticism, Judaism, and Christianity. To be sure, it can no longer be
doubted that Gnosticism, especially in its earliest forms, displays
a fundamental indebtedness to Jewish concepts and traditions.
The Nag Hammadi discovery has provided much new material
of relevance here. Nevertheless, the precise historical relationship
between Gnosticism and Judaism, and between Gnosticism and
Christianity, are still very controversial issues. Some scholars, the
present author included, have argued that Gnosticism originated
from within Judaism.[1] Other scholars contend that such a cir-
cumstance is improbable, if not impossible.[2] Still others adopt a

---

1. An early proponent of this view was M. Friedländer, *Der vorchristliche
jüdische Gnosticismus* (Göttingen: Vandenhoeck & Ruprecht, 1898; repr., Franbor-
ough: Gregg International, 1972). Cf. my essay "Friedländer Revisited: Alexandrian
Judaism and Gnostic Origins," chap. 1 in Pearson, *Gnosticism;* and, on various aspects of this issue, chaps. 2–9 in the same volume. See also K. Rudolph's discussion
in "Gnosis und Gnostizismus: Ein Forschungsbericht," *ThR* 34 (1969): 121–75,
181–231, 358–61; 36 (1971): 1–61, 89–124; 37 (1972): 289–360; and 38 (1973):
1–25; esp. 36: 89–119; cf. Rudolph, *Gnosis,* 27–82. Other relevant works are cited
subsequently in this chapter.
2. See, e.g., H. Jonas, "The Hymn of the Pearl: Case Study of a Symbol, and
the Claims for a Jewish Origin of Gnosticism," in *Philosophical Essays,* 277–90;
"The Gnostic Syndrome: Typology of Its Thought, Imagination, and Mood," in
Philosophical Essays, 263–76, esp. 274; and literature cited in chapter 6 of this
book, nn. 15–17. More recent studies in which the Jewish factor is minimized
are nevertheless more ambiguous on the question. See, e.g., E. Yamauchi, "Jewish

broader view of Gnosticism and speak of "gnostic" forms of various religions, such as Christianity or Islam.[3] A variant of this broader view would posit various forms of the Gnostic religion: Jewish, Christian, and pagan. According to this last-named view, one which I share, one can legitimately speak of Jewish Gnosticism[4] as well as Christian and other forms of Gnosticism. Such a Jewish Gnosticism should, of course, be differentiated from the kind of "Jewish Gnosticism" described by Gershom Scholem in one of his famous books;[5] that is more appropriately designated Jewish mysticism.[6]

Gnosticism should really be understood as a religion in its own right.[7] There are very good reasons for using such a designation as "the Gnostic religion" to clarify what is meant by "Gnosticism" or "gnosis," terms that have been used with a notable lack of precision in scholarly discourse.[8] This lack of precision is often due to the differences in approach to the subject based on the respective disciplines or methodologies of the researchers involved. For exam-

Gnosticism? The Prologue of John, Mandaean Parallels, and the Trimorphic Protennoia," in van den Broek-Vermaseren, *Studies-Quispel*, 467–97; I. Gruenwald, "Aspects of the Jewish-Gnostic Controversy," in Layton, *Rediscovery*, 2:713–23; and I. Gruenwald, "Jewish Merkavah Mysticism and Gnosticism," in *Studies in Jewish Mysticism: Proceedings of Regional Conferences Held at the University of California, Los Angeles, and McGill University in April 1978*, ed. J. Dan and F. Talmage (Cambridge: Association for Jewish Studies, 1981), 41–55. In the last-named article, e.g., Gruenwald takes issue with my contention that Gnosticism "originates *in a Jewish environment*" (44; italics his), yet eight pages later he expresses his agreement with K. Rudolph that "Gnosticism emerged from a Jewish matrix" (52)! See also his important books *Apocalyptic and Merkavah Mysticism* (Leiden: E. J. Brill, 1980) and *From Apocalypticism to Gnosticism: Studies in Apocalypticism, Merkavah Mysticism, and Gnosticism* (Frankfurt: Peter Lang, 1988).

3. See, e.g., A. Hultgård, in his foreword to the Swedish version of E. Pagels's *The Gnostic Gospels, De Gnostiska Evangelierna* (Stockholm: Wahlström & Widstrand, 1979); see also G. Widengren, *The Gnostic Attitude*, trans. B. A. Pearson (Santa Barbara, Calif.: Institute of Religious Studies, 1973).

4. See, e.g., M. Stone, *Scriptures, Sects, and Visions: A Profile of Judaism from Ezra to the Jewish Revolts* (Philadelphia: Fortress Press, 1980), 99–105.

5. G. Scholem, *Jewish Gnosticism, Merkabah Mysticism, and Talmudic Traditions* (New York: Jewish Theological Seminary, 1965).

6. See, e.g., Jonas, "Hymn of the Pearl," 288; Gruenwald, "Merkavah," 41–42; and Gruenwald, *Apocalyptic and Merkavah Mysticism*, esp. 110.

7. I have argued this point at some length elsewhere; see Pearson, "Gnosticism a Religion." The best full-length study of the Gnostic religion from the perspective of the history of religions is Rudolph, *Gnosis;* see also G. Filoramo, *A History of Gnosticism*, trans. A. Alcock (Oxford: Blackwell, 1990).

8. Witness the attempt at defining Gnosticism set forth at the Messina Colloquium on the Origins of Gnosticism, published in Bianchi, *Le origini*, xxvi–xxix. Cf. Rudolph's criticisms in "Gnosis: Ein Forschungsbericht," 36:13–22; and Rudolph, *Gnosis*, 56–57.

ple, a philosopher — Hans Jonas is the primary example here[9] —
would have an approach to the subject matter different from that
of a historian of early Christianity or a patristics scholar, such as
Bentley Layton.[10] A historian of religions — Kurt Rudolph is the
preeminent one in the field — would take yet another approach.[11]
I intend in my own work to approach the subject from the standpoint of the history of religions, and it is from that vantage point
that I make the claim that Gnosticism can best be understood
historically as a religion in its own right.

Getting back to the relationship between the Gnostic religion
and Judaism: when one begins to assess this relationship, one runs
into the difficulty that the former seems to be decidedly un-Jewish
in spirit, if not anti-Jewish,[12] especially in its earliest forms. The
Gnostic spirit is essentially anticosmic, whereas Judaism is the
clearest example in late antiquity of a religion that affirms the cosmos, with its doctrine of the one and only God, Creator of heaven
and earth.[13] Thus, it is the anticosmicism of the Gnostic religion,
especially its hostile stance vis-à-vis the Jewish Creator God, that
makes it appear "un-Jewish.[14] To speak of a "Jewish Gnosticism,"
therefore, would, at first glance, appear to imply a contradiction in

9. See essays cited in n. 2; Jonas, *Gnostic Religion;* and his magnum opus,
Gnosis und spätantiker Geist, vol. 1, *Die mythologische Gnosis,* and vol. 2, *Von
der Mythologie zur mystischen Philosophie,* FRLANT 51, 63, 159 (Göttingen:
Vandenhoeck & Ruprecht, 1934, 1954, 1993).

10. See Layton, "Prolegomena"; *Gnostic Scriptures.* See also A. H. B. Logan,
Gnostic Truth and Christian Heresy: A Study in the History of Gnosticism (Ed-
inburgh: T. &. T. Clark; Peabody, Mass.: Hendrickson, 1996). For a desperate
attempt to make "Gnosticism" disappear as a category, see M. A. Williams,
Rethinking "Gnosticism": An Argument for Dismantling a Dubious Category
(Princeton: Princeton University Press, 1996).

11. See n. 7; and the forty essays in Rudolph, *Gnosis: Aufsätze.* There are, of
course many other approaches as well. For an approach that combines actual religious commitment to Gnosticism and Jungian psychoanalytical theory, see S. A.
Hoeller, *The Gnostic Jung and the Seven Sermons to the Dead* (Wheaton, Ill.: Theosophical Publishing House, 1982). (Hoeller is bishop of the Ecclesia Gnostica in Los
Angeles, California.)

12. In the original version of this essay, I used the phrase "essentially anti-Jewish"
of the Gnostic religion, but I see now that Gnostic "anti-Judaism" has probably
been overestimated. For a necessary corrective, see R. M. Wilson, "Anti-Semitism in
Gnostic Writings," in *Anti-Semitism and Early Christianity: Issues of Polemic and
Faith,* ed. C. A. Evans and D. Hagner (Minneapolis: Fortress Press, 1993), 269–89.
Wilson concludes that an examination of the sources reveals that "real evidence for
an anti-Jewish animus is generally hard to come by." Gnostics did, of course, feel
superior to non-Gnostics, whether these were Jews or Christians.

13. These issues are treated with extraordinary insight by K.-W. Tröger, "The
Attitude of the Gnostic Religion towards Judaism as Viewed in a Variety of
Perspectives," in Barc, *Colloque International,* 86–98.

14. This important point is stressed by N. A. Dahl, "The Arrogant Archon and

terms. But history, especially religious history, is not the same thing as logic!

Thus, it is one of the curiosities of the religious history of late antiquity that certain Jewish intellectuals could, and arguably did, use the materials of their ancient religion — the Bible and various extrabiblical sources and traditions — in giving expression to a new, anticosmic religion of transcendental gnosis, "knowledge." Such a step would involve a fundamental religious protest against the older traditions, an apostasy from "normative Judaism" as it would later come to be defined, and the development of alternative traditions. Based on the evidence now at our disposal, it appears that this development took place among educated, literate people. That is to say, Gnosticism was, from the beginning, a religion that was given shape by, and transmitted in, literature. The production of written texts is one of the hallmarks of the Gnostic religion.

It is against this historical background (reconstructed, to be sure) that one can speak of Jewish Gnostic literature. This "Jewish Gnostic" literature can be so labeled because the Gnostic authors produced their texts by adopting and adapting the forms of the (non-Gnostic) Jewish literature of the Second Temple period (apocalypse, testament, scriptural commentary, midrash, and epistle).[15] The Gnostic documents were also frequently attributed pseudonymously to important patriarchs and other personages of the Bible (e.g., Adam, Seth, Enosh, Enoch, Shem, Ham, Moses, Abraham, Melchizedek, Solomon),[16] as was the case with so much of the Jewish pseudepigraphal and apocryphal literature of the period.

---

the Lewd Sophia: Jewish Traditions in Gnostic Revolt," in Layton, *Rediscovery,* 2:689–712.

15. For good treatments of Jewish literature of the Second Temple period, see G. W. E. Nickelsburg, *Jewish Literature between the Bible and the Mishnah* (Philadelphia: Fortress Press, 1981); and Stone, *Jewish Writings.*

16. Adam: see subsequent discussion. Seth: NHC III,2; VII,2 and 5; XI,1; plus numerous patristic and other references (see Pearson, "The Figure of Seth in Gnostic Literature," chap. 4 in Pearson, *Gnosticism*). Enosh: Cologne Mani Codex 48.16–60.12 (apocalypses of Adam, Seth, Enosh, Shem, and Enoch, perhaps not Gnostic). Enoch: Mani Codex; *Pistis Sophia* 99, 134. Shem: Mani Codex; NHC VII,1. Ham: Basilidians, according to Clem. Al., *Strom.* 6.6.53.5. Moses: *Orig. World* II,5 (102,8–9). Abraham: Sethians, according to Epiph., *Pan.* 39.5.1; Audians, according to Theodore bar Konai (on which see H.-C. Puech, "Fragments retrouvés de l'Apocalypse d'Allogène," in *En quête de la gnose* [Paris: Gallimard, 1978], 1:271–300, esp. 273). Melchizedek: NHC IX,1. Solomon: *Orig. World* II (107,3). Cf. also Norea, wife-sister of Seth: NHC IX,2; *Orig. World* II (102,10–11.24–25); and numerous patristic references, on which see "The Figure of Norea in Gnostic Literature," chap. 5 in Pearson, *Gnosticism.*

We must assume that the vast bulk of this Gnostic literature is irretrievably lost.

As it happens, it is the Christian forms of the Gnostic religion that are the best known, and whose materials and testimonies are the most abundant. Indeed, one can hardly speak of the problem of Jewish Gnostic literature without also addressing the problem of the relationship between Gnosticism and early Christianity. In that case, we have to do, in my view, with a clash of these two religions, one that looms very large in second-century C.E. religious history. More specifically, we have to do with two religions each of which is rooted in a third (Judaism) and one of which (Christianity) is threatened with being engulfed and swallowed up by the other (Gnosticism) in certain areas of the Mediterranean world. The importance of this for our special topic is that much (but not all) of the relevant Gnostic material now extant appears in Christian dress, that is, in "Christianized" versions.

I cannot take up the full range of the evidence for discussion here.[17] What I intend to do, instead, is to examine two examples of what I take to be Jewish Gnostic literature, look at them as Jewish Gnostic texts, and then examine their relationship to Christianity. One of the examples I have chosen is not in any sense a Christian document: the *Apocalypse of Adam* (NHC V,5). The other one, which I shall take up first, has undergone secondary Christianization: the *Apocryphon of John* (NHC II,1: III,1; IV,1; BG,2). These two texts having been examined, some general conclusions may then be extrapolated pertaining to Jewish Gnostic literature, on the one hand, and the relationship of Jewish Gnosticism to Christian forms of the Gnostic religion, on the other.

The *Apocryphon of John*

This document is extant in two basic recensions, a shorter one and a longer one.[18] Although there are some minor differences to be observed among all four versions, two of the versions are very fragmentary and can safely be ignored for our present purposes.[19]

---

17. See my article "Jewish Sources in Gnostic Literature," in Stone, *Jewish Writings*, 443–81.

18. For the texts of *Ap. John*, see Waldstein-Wisse, *Apocryphon*. The shorter recension is represented by BG,2 and NHC III,1; the longer by NHC II,1 and IV,1.

19. These are NHC III,1 and IV,1. I have used here the translation in Waldstein-Wisse, *Apocryphon*. That of II,1 is very similar to the translation by F. Wisse in *NHLE* (98–116). There is a translation of BG,2 by M. Krause and R. M. Wilson in Foerster, *Gnosis*, 1:105–20.

The *Apocryphon of John* is surely one of the most important of all Gnostic texts known, for it contains a basic Gnostic myth that was widely used and elaborated. For example, this myth probably served as the basis for the Gnostic mythology of the Christian Gnostic teacher Valentinus, and was further elaborated by Valentinus's disciples.[20] The *Apocryphon of John* is widely (and correctly) taken to be a key text of Sethian Gnosticism.[21] In its extant form, the *Apocryphon of John* is an apocalypse, containing a revelation given by the risen Christ to his disciple John.[22] Within the apocalypse frame at the beginning and end of the document, there are two main sections, a revelation discourse and a commentary on Genesis 1–7. The commentary has been editorially modified, rather clumsily, into a dialogue between Jesus and his interlocutor John. A number of sources seem to be reflected in the document as a whole, and considerable internal confusion is evident. The basic structure, nevertheless, is quite clear.

The following outline represents my analysis of the structure and content of the *Apocryphon of John*. I use as a basis the version in Codex II and show the corresponding sections in BG in parentheses:

Preamble and apocalyptic frame	1,1–2,26 (19,6–22,17)
I. Revelation discourse	2,26–13,13 (22,17–44,18)
A. Theosophy	
1. Negative theology; the unknown God	2,26–4,10 (22,17–26,6)
2. Heavenly world	4,10–9,24 (26,6–36,15)
B. Cosmogony	
1. Fall of Sophia	9,25–10,23 (36,15–39,4)
2. Cosmic world of darkness	10,23–13,5 (39,4–44,9)
3. Blasphemy of the Demiurge	13,5–13 (44,9–18)

20. See esp. G. Quispel, "Valentinian Gnosis and the Apocryphon of John," in Layton, *Rediscovery*, 1:118–27.
21. For groundbreaking studies of the Sethian Gnostic system, see H.-M. Schenke, "Das sethianische System" and "Gnostic Sethianism." See also Stroumsa's important monograph *Another Seed*; and J. Turner, "Sethian Gnosticism: A Literary History," in *Nag Hammadi, Gnosticism, and Early Christianity*, ed. C. W. Hedrick and R. Hodgson (Peabody, Mass.: Hendrickson, 1986), 55–86.
22. An especially useful discussion of the structure and form of *Ap. John* is that of A. Kragerud, "Apocryphon Johannis: En formanalyse," *NTT* 66 (1965): 15–38.

II. Dialogue: soteriology	13,13–31,25 (44,19–75,15)
A. Repentance of Sophia	13,13–14,13 (44,19–47,18)
B. Anthropogony[23]	14,13–21,16 (47,18–55,18)
C. Adam in Paradise	21,16–24,8 (55,18–62,3)
D. Seduction of Eve; Cain and Abel	24,8–34 (62,3–63,12)
E. Seth and his seed	24,35–25,16 (63,12–64,12)
F. Two spirits; classes of men	25,16–27,30 (64,12–71,2)
G. Production of Heimarmene, "Fate"	27,31–28,32 (71,2–72,12)
H. Noah and the flood	28,32–29,15 (72,12–73,18)
I. Angels and the daughters of men	29,16–30,11 (73,18–75,10)
J. Triple descent of Pronoia, "Foreknowledge"[24]	30,11–31,25 (75,10–13)
Apocalyptic frame and title	31,25–32,9 (75,14–77,5)

I have already stated my view that the *Apocryphon of John* is a document whose present form represents a secondary Christianization of previously non-Christian material.[25] Its literary structure suggests such a conclusion: when we remove from the *Apocryphon of John* the apocalyptic framework at the beginning and the end, together with the dialogue features involving the ten questions put to Christ by his interlocutor John, we are left with material in which nothing Christian remains, except for some easily removed glosses. The revelation discourse (section I in our outline), containing the theosophical and cosmogonical teaching, may originally

---

23. The longer recension has a lengthy section devoted to the work of 365 cosmic angels at 15,29–19,2. Cf. the reference to 360 angels in BG 50,8–51,1.

24. The hymn of the triple descent of Pronoia is absent from BG. On this hymn, see M. Waldstein, "The Providence Monologue in the *Apocryphon of John* and the Johannine Prologue," *JECS* 3 (1995): 369–402.

25. The classic example of such a Christianizing redaction of non-Christian material is *Soph. Jes. Chr.* (NHC III,4; BG,3) in relation to *Eugnostos* (NHC III,3; V,1). The latter is an "epistle" containing a discussion of the unknown God and the heavenly world, reflecting a sophisticated Gnostic exegesis of key texts in Genesis. It has no obvious Christian elements in it. *Soph. Jes. Chr.* is a composite document in which the text of *Eugnostos* has been taken over and opened up into a revelation dialogue between Christ and his disciples. See esp. M. Krause, "Das literarische Verhältnis des Eugnostosbriefes zur Sophia Jesu Christi: Zur Auseinandersetzung der Gnosis mit dem Christentum," in *Mullus: Festschrift Theodor Klausner*, ed. S. Stuiber and A. Hermann, JAC Ergänzungsband 1 (Münster: Aschendorff, 1964), 215–23; and D. Parrott, "Evidence of Religious Syncretism in Gnostic Texts from Nag Hammadi," in *Religious Syncretism in Antiquity: Essays in Conversation with Geo Widengren*, ed. B. Pearson (Missoula, Mont.: Scholars Press, 1975), 173–89.

have been a separate unit. Indeed, it is this material which is parallel to Irenaeus's description of the doctrine of the "Gnostics" (*Haer.* 1.29). Apparently, this is all that Irenaeus had; he certainly gives no indication that he is excerpting a section from a "secret book of John."[26] The dialogue (section II in our outline) consists essentially of a commentary on Genesis 1–7, expanded by means of questions A–C and J of the dialogue between Christ and John. The material treated in questions D–I on the destiny of the soul is extraneous material that has been interpolated into the commentary.[27]

As for the aforementioned Christianizing glosses, these vary in extent from one version to another. For example, the heavenly aeon Autogenes is identified by means of glosses with the pre-existent Christ in the first part of the revelation discourse; this identification is made initially in the BG version at 30,14–17, but it is absent from the parallel passage in Codex II (6,23–25). Sophia in Codex II is called "our sister Sophia" in the BG version.[28] Whereas the BG version has Epinoia, "Thought" (a manifestation of Sophia), teach Adam and Eve knowledge from the forbidden tree, in the other version it is Christ who does this.[29] Such examples could be multiplied, but the main point here is that the various versions of the *Apocryphon of John,* taken together, show that the Christian elements in it are altogether secondary.[30] We have to do essentially with a Jewish Gnostic body of literature, as can be seen from its content.

A survey of the content of the *Apocryphon of John* will show that its various sections, especially the basic myth, are based upon the Jewish Bible and Jewish traditions of biblical interpretation, as well as Jewish apocryphal writings. The Jewish traditions in question are not only those of Greek-speaking Diaspora Judaism but also some from Aramaic-speaking Palestinian Judaism.

The theology of the "unknown God" in the *Apocryphon of John* (I.A.1 in our outline) is based upon a Platonizing Jewish

---

26. Cf. H.-M. Schenke, "Nag Hammadi Studien I: Das literarische Problem des Apokryphon Johannis," *ZRGG* 14 (1962): 57–63; and Krause's discussion in Foerster, *Gnosis,* 1:100–103.

27. So according to Kragerud, "Apocryphon Johannis," 31, 34–35; cf. Krause in Foerster, *Gnosis,* 1:100–101. Krause suggests that this material was already in dialogue form before being woven together with the commentary material.

28. Cf. NHC II 9,25 and BG 36,16. Both versions, however, have "our sister Sophia" in a later passage: II 23,21 and BG 54,1 (restored in a lacuna).

29. Cf. BG 60,16–61,2 and II 23,26–28.

30. This has been shown conclusively by S. Arai, "Zur Christologie des Apokryphons des Johannes," *NTS* 15 (1969): 302–18. See also Perkins, *Gnostic Dialogue,* 91–92; and Schenke, "Gnostic Sethianism," 611.

theology of divine transcendence, such as is richly documented in first-century Judaism. To be sure, the Platonic ingredient here is important. As is well known, doctrines of divine transcendence were developing in Platonic schools of the period, and the *via negativa* of the sort found here in the *Apocryphon of John* could be accounted for without recourse to Judaism.[31] But, in my view, the Platonic elements have been mediated through Hellenistic Judaism. Philo of Alexandria provides numerous examples of the sort of Jewish-Platonic theology that I would posit as a theological background for the *Apocryphon of John*'s doctrine of divine transcendence. For example, in his treatise *On Dreams* (*Somn.* 167), Philo refers to God as "unnameable" (ἀκατονόμαστος), "ineffable" (ἄρρητος), and "incomprehensible" (ἀκατάληπτος).[32] All three of these terms are reflected in the Coptic text of a single passage in the *Apocryphon of John* (BG 24,2–6).

Josephus is also an interesting witness to a first-century C.E. Jewish theology of transcendence. According to him, Moses represents the biblical Creator as "One, uncreated, and immutable to all eternity; in beauty surpassing all mortal thought, made known to us by His power, although the nature of His real being passes knowledge" (*Ap.* 2.167).[33]

What the Gnostics do, of course, is split the transcendent God of the Bible into a supreme, ineffable being (I.A.1) and a lower Creator responsible for the material world (I.B). It is precisely this radical dualism that marks the decisive point in the development of

---

31. An extensive discussion of this material will appear in M. Waldstein, *The Apocryphon of John: A Curious Eddy in the Stream of Hellenistic Judaism* (forthcoming). Meanwhile, see Waldstein, "The Primal Triad in the Apocryphon of John," in *The Nag Hammadi Library after Fifty Years: Proceedings of the 1995 Society of Biblical Literature Commemoration*, ed. J. Turner and A. McGuire, NHMS 44 (Leiden: E. J. Brill, 1997), 154–87.

32. Cf. *Quod Deus* 62; *Quaest. in Exod.* 2.45; *Post.* 168–69. On the basis of such passages as these, H. Jonas has argued that Philo was really a Gnostic! See Jonas, *Gnosis und spätantiker Geist*, 2.1:70–121; and my discussion in "Philo and Gnosticism," *ANRW* II.21.1: *Hellenistisches Judentum in römischer Zeit: Philon* (1984), 295–342, esp. 303–9. Philo is more appropriately considered as standing within the tradition of Middle Platonism. See. e.g., J. Dillon, *The Middle Platonists: A Study of Platonism, 80 B.C. to A.D. 220* (London: Duckworth, 1977), 139–83.

33. Thackeray's translation in the LCL edition. Note especially the phrase ὁποῖος δὲ κατ᾽ οὐσίαν ἐστὶν ἄγνωστον. The term ἄγνωστος ("unknown"), as applied to the transcendent God, is widely regarded as a favorite term of the Gnostics. It does not occur in *Ap. John*, however. On "the Unknown God in Neoplatonism," see E. R. Dodds, *Proclus: The Elements of Theology*, 2d ed. (Oxford: Clarendon, 1963), appendix 1, 310–13.

a new religiosity, one that can hardly any longer be included within the boundaries of (normative) Judaism. The heavenly world as presented in the *Apocryphon of John* (I.A.2) is populated by a number of emanations from the supreme God; chief among them are the "Thought" (*ennoia*) of God, called "Barbelo," and her product "Autogenes" ("self-begotten"). Dependent upon the latter are the four "Luminaries" (Armozel, Oriel, Daveithai, and Eleleth). Heavenly prototypes of Adam and his son Seth are also given prominence. Although much of this is presumably based upon theological speculations of contemporary philosophy,[34] the key figures have their origin in Jewish biblical exegesis and incipient Jewish mysticism. The supreme God is given the esoteric name "Man," obviously read out of Genesis 1:26–27, and possibly Ezekiel 1:26 as well.[35] The figures of Autogenes and (Piger)Adamas may have been spun out of an earlier Jewish Gnostic Anthropos myth.[36] The esoteric name for the first divine emanation, "Barbelo," is probably based on a wordplay on the divine tetragrammaton.[37] The four luminaries have their biblical prototypes in the four angelic beings beneath the throne of God in Ezekiel's vision (Ezek 1:4–21).[38] The heavenly Adam and Seth are Platonic projections into the divine realm of the biblical patriarchs (Gen 5:1–3) and recall the Platonizing Jewish exegesis of the double creation story in Genesis 1 and 2 such as is found, for example, in Philo (*Op. Mund.* 66–135).[39] Adam and Seth also play key roles in the development of Gnostic *Heilsgeschichte*.[40]

The Gnostic figure of Sophia — her fall, repentance, and subsequent role in salvation history are central features of Gnostic

---

34. See, e.g., J. Whittaker, "Self-Generating Principles in Second-Century Gnostic Systems," in Layton, *Rediscovery*, 1:176–89.

35. See H.-M. Schenke's groundbreaking study *Der Gott "Mensch"*; and G. Quispel, "Ezekiel 1:26 in Jewish Mysticism and Gnosis," *VC* 34 (1980): 1–13.

36. R. van den Broek, "Autogenes and Adamas: The Mythological Structure of the Apocryphon of John," in van den Broek, *Studies*, 56–66.

37. *Barba'elo*, "in four, God." This etymology, first proposed by W. W. Harvey in his 1857 edition of Irenaeus (Cambridge, Cambridge University Press), 1:221 n. 2, but not widely accepted, has been more convincingly stated by M. Scopello, "Youel et Barbélo dans le traité de l'Allogène," in Barc, *Colloque International*, 374–82 and esp. 378–79.

38. See A. Böhlig, "Der jüdische Hintergrund in gnostischen Texten von Nag Hammadi," in *Mysterion und Wahrheit*, 80–101, esp. 84. See also the four archangels of *1 Enoch* 9–10, suggested by Stroumsa, *Another Seed*, 55. On the use of *1 Enoch* in *Ap. John*, see subsequent notes.

39. Cf. Pearson, "Philo and Gnosticism," 323–30.

40. These roles are especially important in *Apoc. Adam*; see subsequent discussion.

mythology (I.B.1; II.A–H in our outline) — is clearly derived from the Wisdom theology of Judaism. What is said of Sophia in the Gnostic sources cannot be understood without attention to her pre-history in Jewish tradition, even if (or because) the Gnostics turn much of this tradition upside down.[41]

The myth of the origin of the Gnostic Demiurge[42] as an "abortion" (BG 46,10) of Sophia (I.B.1; II.A) reflects a sophisticated reworking of the biblical traditions of the fall of Eve, the birth of Cain, and the fall of the "sons of God,"[43] together with extrabiblical Jewish traditions of interpretation. The use of the word "abortion" in this connection reflects a Hebrew wordplay documented in rabbinic aggadah.[44]

The description of the world of darkness (I.B.2), with its demonization of the seven planets and the twelve zodiacal signs, is based upon contemporary astrological speculation enriched by specifically Jewish lore.[45]

The tradition of the "blasphemy of the Demiurge" (B.3), found in a number of other Gnostic sources as well,[46] reflects the end product of a discussion in Judaism concerning "two powers in heaven," in which a number of biblical texts appear both in the background and in the foreground. Here in the *Apocryphon of John*, Exodus 20:5 and Isaiah 46:9 are combined. This tradition is a succinct reflection of the "revolution" on the part of Jewish Gnostics against the biblical Creator-Lawgiver.[47]

The anthropogony that follows the blasphemy of the Demiurge and the repentance of Sophia (II.B in our outline) is organized around several key texts in Genesis: 1:2; 1:26–27; 2:7; and 2:18. The Gnostic commentary is based upon Jewish traditions of exe-

---

41. See esp. G. MacRae, "The Jewish Background of the Gnostic Sophia Myth," *NovT* 12 (1970): 86–101; also K. Rudolph, "Sophia und Gnosis: Bemerkungen zum Problem 'Gnosis und Frühjudentum,'" in *Gnosis: Aufsätze*, 170–89.

42. On the names Yaldabaoth, Saklas, and Samael, as applied to the Demiurge, see Pearson, *Gnosticism*, 47–49; and B. Barc, "Samael-Saklas-Yaldabaôth: Recherche sur la genèse d'un mythe gnostique," in Barc, *Colloque International*, 123–50.

43. Gen 3:4–6; 4:1; 6:1. This is admirably treated in Stroumsa, *Another Seed*.

44. *Nepilim*, "fallen ones"; *nepalim*, "abortions"; see *Midr. Gen. Rab.* 26.7; and Stroumsa, *Another Seed*, 106; cf. 65–70. Dahl ("Arrogant Archon," 703 [see n. 14]) traces the concept of the Demiurge as an "abortion" to Jewish interpretations of Isa 14:19.

45. See esp. A. J. Welburn, "The Identity of the Archons in the 'Apocryphon Johannis,'" *VC* 32 (1978): 241–54.

46. See, e.g., *Hyp. Arch.* (NHC II,4); *Orig. World* (NHC II,5); *Gos. Eg.* (NHC III,2 and IV,2); and Irenaeus, *Haer.* 1.29–30.

47. See Dahl's seminal study "Arrogant Archon."

gesis, both Alexandrian and Palestinian. For example, one can see in the commentary both the Alexandrian Jewish tradition that God relegated the creation of man's mortal nature to the angels,[48] and the Palestinian tradition that God created man as a *golem* ("formless mass").[49] I have elsewhere treated these and other details in the text.[50]

The rest of the material in the second main section of the *Apocryphon of John* (except II.F and J)[51] continues an elaborate commentary on Genesis 1–7, much of which has parallels in other Gnostic texts.[52] Especially important is the section on the birth of Seth (II.E in our outline), built upon the key texts Genesis 4:25 and 5:3. Seth is regarded by the Gnostics as the spiritual "ancestor" and prototype of the Gnostic; indeed, his "seed" or "race" constitutes the totality of the Gnostic elect.[53] But here in the *Apocryphon of John,* in contrast to some other "Sethian" Gnostic texts, Seth (with his seed) assumes a passive role in salvation. That is, the notion of Seth as Savior does not seem to be explicit here. It is the Mother (Sophia in her various manifestations) who initiates salvation for the race of Seth, by sending down her "spirit" (25,2–16)[54]

The section corresponding to the account in Genesis 6:1–4 of the descent of the "sons of God" (II.I in our outline) is undoubtedly dependent upon *1 Enoch* 6–8, which itself is part of a commentary on Genesis 6:1–4.[55] It also shows influence from other Jewish apocryphal texts dealing with that crucial passage in Genesis 6,

48. See, e.g., Philo, *Fug.* 68–70; cf. Pl., *Ti.* 41A–42B.
49. See, e.g., *Midr. Gen. Rab.* 14.8; cf. Ps 139:16.
50. See my "Biblical Exegesis in Gnostic Literature," chap. 2 in Pearson, *Gnosticism;* and "Philo and Gnosticism," 330–38.
51. The hymn of the triple descent of Pronoia (II.J in the outline), absent from BG, may be regarded as a reinterpretation of, or alternative to, the triple appearance of the redeemer Seth in other Gnostic texts, such as *Apoc. Adam* and *Gos. Eg.* (see subsequent notes). The Pronoia hymn constitutes the basis for the structure and content of *Trim. Prot.* (NHC XIII,1). See J. Turner, "The Gnostic Threefold Path to Enlightenment: The Ascent of Mind and the Descent of Wisdom," *NovT* 22 (1980): 324–52, esp. 326–28. On II.F in the outline, see subsequent discussion.
52. See esp. *Hyp. Arch.* (NHC II,4), and B. Barc's edition, with introduction and commentary, *L'Hypostase des Archontes (NH II,4),* BCNH "Textes" 1 (Québec: Université Laval, 1981).
53. See my essay "The Figure of Seth in Gnostic Literature," chap. 4 in Pearson, *Gnosticism;* and Stroumsa, *Another Seed.*
54. Cf. Pearson, *Gnosticism,* 61. In *Hyp. Arch.,* it is Seth's sister-consort, Norea, who functions as Savior. See "The Figure of Norea in Gnostic Literature," chap. 5 in Pearson, *Gnosticism.*
55. See my article "*1 Enoch* in the *Apocryphon of John*," in *Texts and Contexts: Biblical Texts in Their Textual and Situational Contexts* (in honor of Lars

which in Second Temple Judaism was a locus classicus for the explanation of the origins of evil on earth.[56] For example, the *Apocryphon of John* has the angels assume the likenesses of the husbands of the daughters of men in order to accomplish their purpose. This detail is found in the *Testament of Reuben* 5:5–7, but not in *1 Enoch.*[57] The occurrence of the "counterfeit spirit" in this passage (BG 74,8)[58] also represents a deviation from *1 Enoch,* and ties this section with the passage on the "two spirits" and the classes of men found earlier (II.F). The editor who interpolated that passage into the *Apocryphon of John* may also be responsible for working the "counterfeit spirit" into the material taken from *1 Enoch.*

The interpolated passage on the two spirits and the classes of human beings has been referred to as a Jewish "catechism" in which the ultimate fate of the human soul is tied to the operation of two spirits: the "Spirit of life" and the "counterfeit spirit."[59] The resemblance of this doctrine to that of the Rule Scroll from Qumran (1QS iii,13–26) has also been noted, and it can hardly be doubted that it has been gnosticized here in the *Apocryphon of John.* "The immovable race" on whom the "Spirit of life" descends is, of course, the "race" of Gnostics. The interpolated passage now stands in the text of the *Apocryphon of John* as an anthropological excursus elaborating upon the previous section in the text dealing with Seth and his seed.[60]

In summary, it can cogently be argued that the basic content of the *Apocryphon of John* is Jewish Gnostic, in that its various elements have been drawn from Jewish traditions: the Bible, Jewish extracanonical literature, and Jewish traditions of biblical exegesis. Indeed, the Christian veneer that is applied in the text's final redaction turns out to be exceedingly thin.

Hartman), ed. D. Hellholm and T. Fornberg (Oslo: Scandinavian University Press, 1995), 355–67.

56. See esp. G. W. E. Nickelsburg, "Apocalyptic and Myth in *1 Enoch* 6–11," *JBL* 96 (1977): 383–405.

57. See Stroumsa, *Another Seed,* 37–38.

58. See A. Böhlig, "Zum Antimimon Pneuma in den koptisch-gnostischen Texten," in *Mysterion und Wahrheit,* 162–74. The other version has here "despicable spirit" (ⲡⲛⲁ ⲉϥϣⲏⲥ, II 29,24). The Coptic ⲉϥϣⲏⲥ probably reflects a misreading of ἀντίμιμον ("counterfeit") as ἄτιμον ("despicable").

59. See W.-D. Hauschild, *Gottes Geist und der Mensch: Studien zur frühchristlichen Pneumatologie* (Munich: Kaiser, 1972), 225–47.

60. So according to Kragerud, "Apocryphon Johannis," 35.

The *Apocalypse of Adam*

This document consists essentially of a testamentary revelation mediated by Adam to his son Seth, setting forth the subsequent history of the world and the salvation of the elect (i.e., the Gnostics). Its first editor, Alexander Böhlig, regarded this text as a document of pre-Christian Sethian Gnosticism, originating in a Jewish Gnostic baptismal sect in Palestine or Syria.[61] A subsequent editor, George MacRae, took special cognizance of the document's dependence upon Jewish apocalyptic traditions, and suggested that it represents a "transitional stage in an evolution from Jewish to gnostic apocalyptic."[62] To be sure, the Jewish-Gnostic background of the document has not gone unchallenged in recent scholarly discussions, and some scholars argue for a comparatively late date for the document.[63] In my view, however, it is still possible to regard the *Apocalypse of Adam* as an example of "Jewish Gnostic" literature, whatever its date.[64] This point will be elaborated in what follows.

A complicating factor in the discussion is the question of the literary history of the *Apocalypse of Adam*. Charles Hedrick has argued, for example, that the document as it now stands is the amalgamation of two distinct sources, edited with additions by a final redactor at around the end of the first century C.E. The starting point for this source analysis is the presence of what are taken to be two introductions and two conclusions. The first introduction (64,6–65,23 and 66,12–67,12) is assigned to source A, the second (65,24–66,12 and 67,12–21) to source B. The first conclusion (85,19–22a) is assigned to source A, and the second (85,22b–31) to the redactor.[65] These observations are more cogent than is the division of the main body of the text (i.e., the apocalypse proper) into sources and redaction, for Hedrick's analysis breaks up the

---

61. A. Böhlig and P. Labib, *Koptisch-gnostische Apokalypsen aus Codex V von Nag Hammadi im Koptischen Museum zu Alt Kairo* (Halle-Wittenberg: Wissenschaftliche Zeitschrift der Martin-Luther-Universität, 1963).

62. G. MacRae, "The Apocalypse of Adam, V,5:64,1–85,32," in D. Parrott, ed., *Nag Hammadi Codices V,2–5 and VI with Papyrus Berolinensis 8502,1 and 4*, NHS 11 (Leiden: E. J. Brill, 1979), 151–95 (quotation on 152); cf. C. W. Hedrick, *The Apocalypse of Adam: A Literary and Source Analysis*, SBLDS 46 (Chico, Calif.: Scholars Press, 1980), 85–87.

63. For discussion of the literature on *Apoc. Adam*, see Hedrick, *Apocalypse of Adam*, 9–17. Some more recent studies are cited in subsequent notes.

64. *Apoc. Adam* is the only Gnostic text included in the standard edition of OT Pseudepigrapha: *OTP*, 1:707–19.

65. See Hedrick, *Apocalypse of Adam*, esp. 21–28.

tripartite structure of the Gnostic history of salvation, organized around the three critical events of flood, fire, and end-time struggle. This structure is integral to the document as a whole.[66] An alternative way of understanding the obvious seams dividing up the two "introductions" would be to posit the redactional weaving together of materials that might have occurred previously in sequence — that is, to posit that the material in Hedrick's second introduction followed upon that of his first introduction. To be sure, such a suggestion implies the activity of an editor, who might also be responsible for additions to his source.

As an example of additional editorial activity, I would cite the passage concerning the thirteen kingdoms plus the "kingless generation" (77,18–83,4). I subscribe to the argument of those who see in this passage a later interpolation into the text,[67] presumably supplied by the document's final redactor. The second conclusion may also be assigned to the redactor, as Hedrick has suggested.

My understanding of the structure and content of the *Apocalypse of Adam* is set forth in the following outline:

Introduction 64,1–5

I. Setting: Adam's testamentary speech to Seth	64,5–67,21
A. Adam and Eve's experiences with their Creator	64,5–65,23
B. Adam's dream vision: three heavenly men	65,24–66,8
C. Adam and Eve's experiences (continued)	66,9–67,14
D. Adam's intention to transmit revelation to Seth	67,14–21
II. Revelation	67,22–85,18
A. End of Adam's generation[68]	67,22–28+
B. Flood, first deliverance	69,2–73,29

---

66. See P. Perkins, "Apocalypse of Adam: The Genre and Function of a Gnostic Apocalypse," *CBQ* 39 (1977): 382–95, esp. 387–89; but cf. Hedrick, *Apocalypse of Adam,* 31 and 48 n. 46.

67. MacRae, "Apocalypse of Adam," 152. For a contrary view, see Stroumsa, *Another Seed,* 82–103. Böhlig refers to this passage as an "excursus" (Böhlig and Labib, *Apokalypsen,* 87, 91–93, 109). Hedrick includes the passage in his source B yet sees it as originally a separate unit (*Apocalypse of Adam,* 115–19).

68. The death of Adam is implied in the phrase "after I have completed the times of this generation" (67,22–24). Noah is probably to be supplied in the lacuna in line 28. Cf. Hedrick's translation: "[then Noah], a servant [of God . . .] (*Apocalypse of Adam,* 233). Cf. also the translation by Krause and Wilson in Foerster, *Gnosis,* 2:17. P. 68 in the MS is blank.

Formally, the *Apocalypse of Adam* is both an "apocalypse" and a "testament." It is an apocalypse in that it contains a revelation given by heavenly informants to Adam, who mediates the revelation to his son Seth. It adheres closely to the "apocalypse" genre.[69] It is also a testament, with close formal connections with the Jewish testamentary literature, in that it is presented as a speech given by Adam to his son just before his death, "in the seven hundredth year" (64,4).[70]

The close parallels between the *Apocalypse of Adam* and the Jewish Adam literature, especially the *Life of Adam and Eve* and the *Apocalypse of Moses*, have often been noted.[71] George Nickelsburg, for example, posits the existence of an apocalyptic testament of Adam as a common source utilized by the *Apocalypse of Adam*

---

69. See F. Fallon, "The Gnostic Apocalypses," in Collins, *Apocalypse*, 123–58, esp. 126–27; and Perkins, "Genre and Function."

70. See MacRae, "Apocalypse of Adam," 152; Perkins, "Genre and Function," 384–86; and Hedrick, *Apocalypse of Adam*, 243. The figure of 700 follows the LXX of Gen 5:3, setting Adam's age at the birth of Seth at 230 rather than 130, as in the MT. Adam's death at the age of 930 years (Gen 5:4) would then account for the figure of 700. See also Joseph., *Ant.* 1.67, where the same figures are used.

71. See Perkins, "Genre and Function"; Pearson, *Gnosticism*, 71–73; and G. W. E. Nickelsburg, "Some Related Traditions in the *Apocalypse of Adam*, the Books of Adam and Eve, and *1 Enoch*," in Layton, *Rediscovery*, 2:515–39.

and *Adam and Eve.*[72] Another Adam book has also been brought into purview, namely, the Syriac *Testament of Adam.*[73] The prophetic section of this work (chap. 3) consists of a prophecy given by Adam to Seth of future catastrophes of flood and fire, and the coming of a savior who will deliver the elect posterity of Adam. G. J. Reinink has noted the close correspondences between the *Apocalypse of Adam* and the Syriac *Testament,* and has plausibly posited the existence of an early document upon which both are based.[74]

We should also take note here of the Adam apocalypses referred to in the Cologne Mani Codex. Indeed an Adam "apocalypse" is quoted in that important document, in which a radiant angel says to Adam, "I am Balsamos,[75] the greatest angel of light. Wherefore take and write these things which I reveal to you on most pure papyrus, incorruptible and insusceptible to worms" (49.3–10).[76]

---

72. Nickelsburg, "Related Traditions," esp. 537.

73. See S. Robinson, *The Testament of Adam: An Examination of the Syriac and Greek Traditions,* SBLDS 52 (Chico, Calif.: Scholars Press, 1981); cf. *OTP,* 1:989–95. Robinson has published the Syriac text, with English translations, of three recensions of this important work, with a very useful discussion of its place in the Adam cycle of traditions. Unfortunately, he omits any consideration of the apocalypses of Adam mentioned in the Mani Codex, on which see subsequent discussion.

74. G. J. Reinink, "Das Problem des Ursprungs des Testaments Adams," *OrChrA* 197 (1972): 387–99, esp. 397–98.

75. The name Balsamos is originally that of the Phoenician "Lord of Heaven" (*Ba'al Šamem*). Cf. *Beelsamen* in the *Phoenician History* of Philo of Byblos; see H. W. Attridge and R. A. Oden, eds., *Philo of Byblos: The Phoenician History,* CBQMS 9 (Washington: Catholic Biblical Association, 1981), 40–41, 81. Balsamos is the name of an angel in the Coptic *Apocalypse of Bartholomew* (rec. A) in a hymn sung by angels to Adam in Paradise. See A. Kropp, *Ausgewählte koptische Zaubertexte* (Brussels: Fondation Egyptologique Reine Elisabeth, 1930–31), 1:80. Balsamos's name is in a lacuna in the MS used by E. A. W. Budge, *Coptic Apocrypha in the Dialect of Upper Egypt* (London: British Museum, 1913); see pl. 23 and pp. 23 (transcription) and 198 (translation). See also C. D. G. Müller, *Die Engellehre der koptischen Kirche* (Wiesbaden: Harrassowitz, 1959), 310. "Balsamos" is also found in a list of names that the Basilidian Gnostics pretended to take from Hebrew sources, according to Jerome, *Ep.* 75.3. The other names mentioned by Jerome are Armazel, Barbelon, Abraxas, and Leusibora.

76. See R. Cameron and A. Dewey, *The Cologne Mani Codex (P. Colon. inv. nr. 4780) "Concerning the Origin of His Body,"* SBLTT 15 (Missoula, Mont.: Scholars Press, 1979). The text of pp. 1–72 of the codex was first published by A. Henrichs and L. Koenen, "Der Kölner Mani-Kodex (P. Colon. inv. nr. 4780)," *ZPE* 19 (1975): 1–85. See L. Koenen and C. Römer, *Der Kölner Mani-Kodex: Über das Werden seines Leibes,* Papyrologica Coloniensia 14 (Opladen: Westdeutscher Verlag, 1988), a critical edition of pp. 1–191 of the MS; and C. E. Römer, *Manis frühe Missionsreisen nach der Kölner Manibiographie,* Papyrologica Coloniensia 24 (Opladen: Westdeutscher Verlag, 1994), a text-critical commentary on pp. 121–92 of the MS.

The text goes on to say that this angel revealed many things and that Adam beheld angels and great powers. It also refers to other "writings" produced by Adam. The writings referred to may very well have been Jewish Adam books,[77] but the use of our Gnostic *Apocalypse of Adam* by Mani may perhaps be indicated in the following statement: "And he became mightier than all the powers and the angels of creation" (50.1–4).[78] Be that as it may, it can hardly be doubted that the *Apocalypse of Adam* is closely related to the Adam cycle of Jewish literature that goes back, at the latest, to the first century c.e. Josephus is acquainted with such literature and may be relying on an early testament of Adam when he tells of Adam's predictions of deluge and fire and of the erection of inscribed steles of stone and brick by the progeny of Seth for the purpose of preserving their lore.[79]

Of course, it also cannot be doubted that the *Apocalypse of Adam* is a *Gnostic* text from beginning to end. It therefore has a far different slant in its interpretation of the Adam-Seth traditions from that of the other Jewish and Christian Adam books. This is already evident in its first section, wherein Adam addresses Seth and gives him a biographical account of his and Eve's misadventures after their creation. A comparison with *Adam and Eve* is especially instructive. In *Adam and Eve* (chaps. 1–11), on the one hand, the two protoplasts have been banished from Paradise for their sin and are duly repentant. In the *Apocalypse of Adam,* on the other hand, Adam and Eve see themselves as naturally "higher than the god who had created us and the powers with him" (64,16–18). The Creator acts against Adam and Eve out of jealous wrath, in a manner quite reminiscent of the devil in *Adam and Eve* (chaps. 12–17), banished from heaven because of his refusal to worship the newly created Adam. The author of this material is therefore not only dependent upon early Jewish Adam traditions, but also critical of them, and applies a radically new perspective on biblical history in his use of the traditions.

---

77. So, e.g., according to A. Henrichs, "Literary Criticism of the Cologne Mani Codex," in Layton, *Rediscovery,* 2:724–33, esp. 725; and Stroumsa, *Another Seed,* 146.

78. Cf. *Apoc. Adam* 64,16–19. This would tell against the late-third-century date for *Apoc. Adam* proposed by W. Beltz, "Die Adamapokalypse aus Codex V von Nag Hammadi: Jüdische Bausteine in gnostischen Systemen' (Th.D. diss., Humboldt-Universität, 1970). See also S. T. Carrol, "The Apocalypse of Adam and Pre-Christian Gnosticism," *VC* 44 (1990): 263–79; Carrol dates *Apoc. Adam* as late as the fourth century.

79. See Joseph., *Ant.* 1.67–71; cf. II.E in our outline of *Apoc. Adam.*

This perspective is carried over into the revelation proper, which constitutes the bulk of the *Apocalypse of Adam* (section II in the outline). In form, this revelation is a "historical apocalypse" in which the salvation of the elect seed of Seth (the Gnostics) is the dominant concern. The three cataclysms from which the Gnostics are to be saved are the flood (II.B), a destruction by fire clearly identifiable in the text as the destruction of Sodom and Gomorrah (II.C; cf. Gen 19:24–25), and the final "day of death" (II.D). The elect are rescued from each catastrophe by the Savior, who is Seth.

An Iranian background has been posited for the tripartite structure of this historical apocalypse.[80] But it is not necessary to posit a direct Iranian influence on this material, since the Jewish sources provide an altogether adequate background.[81] The destructions by flood and fire are set forth in the Adamic traditions already referred to,[82] and there are (non-Gnostic) Jewish texts in which the destruction by fire is separated from the end-time with a third and last catastrophic judgment. The "Apocalypse of Weeks" in *1 Enoch* is an especially important example, inasmuch as that document might have influenced the Adam testament posited as the common source behind the *Apocalypse of Adam* and *Adam and Eve*.[83] The "Apocalypse of Weeks" has a threefold scheme of judgments: flood, fire, and final judgment.[84] Moreover, the association of the fiery judgment with the destruction of Sodom and Gomorrah occurs not only in Gnostic texts[85] but even in Philo.[86]

To be sure, our Gnostic author has a slant on these traditions that would have been abhorrent to Philo or other non-Gnostic Jewish writers. The essential point here, therefore, is that the *Apocalypse of Adam* is, from beginning to end, a Gnostic text in which the numerous Jewish traditions it inherits, including the genre itself (apocalyptic testament), are thoroughly reinterpreted in the interests of a higher gnosis. With consummate irony our author

---

80. See A. Böhlig, "Jüdisches und Iranisches in der Adamapokalypse des Codex V von Nag Hammadi," in Böhlig, *Mysterion und Wahrheit*, 149–61; cf. C. Colpe, "Sethian and Zoroastrian Ages of the World," in Layton, *Rediscovery,* 2:540–52.

81. See esp. Perkins, "Genre and Function," 387–89; and Stroumsa, *Another Seed*, 103–13.

82. See *Adam and Eve* 49.2–50.2; Joseph., *Ant.* 1.68–70; and *Test. Adam* (Syriac) 3.5.

83. Nickelsburg, "Related Traditions," 535–37.

84. See *1 Enoch* 93.4, 8; 91.11–15. The judgment by fire (93.8) is interpreted as the burning of the Temple.

85. See *Gos. Eg.* III 60,9–18; and *Paraph. Shem* VII 28,34–29,33.

86. See Philo, *Vit. Mos.* 2.53–58, 263; *Abr.* 1. See also Stroumsa, *Another Seed*, 106.

sets forth the "real truth" concerning the heavenly origin of the spiritual "seed of Seth" (the Gnostics) and the utter folly of servitude to the Creator.[87] It is a *Jewish* Gnostic document in the sense that its genre and materials are derived from Jewish sources and could have been written only by someone thoroughly acquainted with biblical and extrabiblical Jewish traditions. Yet in its intentionality it is quite un-Jewish in the extreme, if not anti-Jewish,[88] a product of the Gnostic revolt against the biblical Creator and his ordinances. (The biblical Creator is distinguished, of course, from the transcendent God, who is the higher manifestation of the biblical God.)[89]

In our discussion of the *Apocryphon of John*, we were able to distinguish its essential features from the thin Christian veneer that was secondarily applied to it. The *Apocalypse of Adam* lacks such Christianizing features. The revelation is mediated not by Christ but by Adam. The Savior (the "Illuminator") is not Jesus Christ but Seth, who appears in various manifestations for the salvation of his seed.[90] To be sure, some scholars have thought they could find traces of Christian influence in the *Apocalypse of Adam*, particularly in the passage treating the final appearance of the Illuminator.[91] But this passage and its context can be interpreted without recourse to the New Testament or Christian tradition, for it adheres to a pre-Christian Jewish literary pattern based on biblical traditions. The pattern in question deals with the persecution and subsequent exaltation of the righteous man, and has been convincingly delineated by George Nickelsburg, with special reference to Wisdom 1–6 and other intertestamental Jewish litera-

---

87. See Perkins, "Genre and Function," for a perceptive discussion of the Gnostic irony in *Apoc. Adam*.

88. See n. 12.

89. See the preceding discussion on the "splitting" of the biblical deity in Gnosticism.

90. "The imperishable illuminators who came from the holy seed: Yesseus, Mazareus, Yessedekeus" (85,28–31) may represent "the three avatars of Seth at each of his comings," according to Stroumsa (*Another Seed*, 102). The names are therefore mystical names of Seth. The last one, Yessedekeus, could have been modeled on the name Ἰωσεδέκ in Jer 23:8 (LXX).

91. These scholars note especially the sentence "Then they will punish the flesh of the man upon whom the holy spirit has come" (77,16–18). See E. Yamauchi, *Pre-Christian Gnosticism: A Survey of the Proposed Evidences* (Grand Rapids, Mich.: Eerdmans, 1973), 107–15, esp. 110; and G. M. Shellrude, "The Apocalypse of Adam: Evidence for a Christian-Gnostic Provenance," in Krause, *Gnosis and Gnosticism*, 82–91, esp. 85–87.

ture.[92] This pattern is fully represented in the *Apocalypse of Adam;* it will also be noticed that it is disturbed by the interpolation on the competing views about the Illuminator (II.D.3 in our outline):[93]

1. Earthly persecution
   a. Signs and wonders of the Illuminator   77,1–3
   b. Conspiracy against him   77,4–15
   c. Punishment of the Illuminator   77,16–18
2. Exaltation, judgment
   a. Peoples acknowledge their sin   83,4–84,3
   b. Condemnation of the peoples   84,4–28
   c. Exaltation of the elect   85,1–18

The author of the *Apocalypse of Adam* has taken over a well-established Jewish pattern, rooted especially in Isaiah 52–53 and developed fully in Wisdom 1–6, in setting forth his prophecy concerning the final coming of the Illuminator. This pattern is especially apposite, for it corresponds to the "history" of the seed of Seth in the first two catastrophes of flood and fire: threatened with destruction, they are rescued by heavenly intervention. In the final catastrophe, a manifestation of Seth himself suffers with his seed, and with them achieves final victory and vindication. All of this is fully intelligible without any reference at all to Jesus Christ or Christian history.

The references to baptism in the *Apocalypse of Adam* have also been interpreted in relation to Christianity. Glen M. Shellrude, accepting the arguments of those who see in the *Apocalypse of Adam* a polemic against baptism,[94] sees in such passages as 83,4–8; 84,4–26; and 85,22–26 a polemic against orthodox Christianity and its baptismal practice. The Gnostics' opponents, according to Shellrude, claim the same redeemer as the Gnostic community, and baptism is associated with their acceptance of the redeemer, who

---

92. G. W. E. Nickelsburg, *Resurrection, Immortality, and Eternal Life in Inter-testamental Judaism* (Cambridge: Harvard University Press, 1972), 48–111.

93. See the earlier discussion of the literary history of *Apoc. Adam.* The pattern set forth here has also been noted with reference to *Apoc. Adam* by Perkins, "Genre and Function," 390–91. See also Nickelsburg, "Related Traditions," 537–38.

94. See, e.g., F. Morard, "L'Apocalypse d'Adam de Nag Hammadi: Un essai d'interprétation," in Krause, *Gnosis and Gnosticism,* 35–42; and F. Morard, "L'Apocalypse d'Adam du Codex V de Nag Hammadi et sa polémique anti-baptismale," *RevScRel* 51 (1977): 214–33. Cf. Hedrick, *Apocalypse of Adam,* esp. 192–215, on the redactor of *Apoc. Adam.*

can be only Christ.[95] But the spiritualization of "holy baptism" in the *Apocalypse of Adam* (85,25) does not imply a rejection of water baptism. And the main passage (84,4–10), which has been taken as implying a rejection of baptism, has more recently been seen to show just the opposite.[96] The Gnostics of the *Apocalypse of Adam* were, in fact, a baptismal sect, analogous to the Mandaeans,[97] and there is no reference to Christian baptism, either orthodox or heretical, anywhere in the text.

Is the *Apocalypse of Adam*, therefore, a "pre-Christian" Jewish Gnostic text? Here we must take up briefly the argument of Gedalyahu G. Stroumsa based upon the excursus on the competing views about the Illuminator (II.D.3 in our outline), which he refers to as "the Hymn of the Child."[98] Thirteen "kingdoms" are listed in this passage, each with a different interpretation of the Illuminator and each ending with the clause "and thus he came to the water."[99] Stroumsa argues that the first twelve "kingdoms," to which the Savior comes in various forms, represent the twelve tribes of Israel, whereas the thirteenth kingdom represents the Christian church. The reference to the "word" (*logos*) that is said to have "received a mandate there" (82,13–15) is taken to reflect the Logos doctrine of early Christianity. The Gnostic community, by contrast, is represented by the "generation without a king over it," those who alone have true knowledge concerning the identity of the Savior (i.e., the heavenly Seth) and who alone constitute the "seed" who "receive his [the Savior's] name upon the water" (82,19–20; 83,4–6). The *Apocalypse of Adam*, therefore, represents a strain of

---

95. Shellrude, "Apocalypse of Adam," 88–90.

96. "Micheu and Michar and Mnesinous, who are over the holy baptism and the living water," are positive, not negative, figures. See MacRae, "Apocalypse of Adam," 191; Schenke, "Gnostic Sethianism," 598, 603; A. Böhlig's remark in the seminar discussion printed in Layton, *Rediscovery*, 2:557–58; and esp. J.-M. Sevrin, *Le dossier baptismal séthien: Études sur la sacramentaire gnostique*, BCNH "Études" 2 (Québec: Université Laval, 1986), 144–81.

97. See Böhlig-Labib, *Apokalypsen*, 94–95. For an excellent summary of the evidence on ancient baptismal sects, see K. Rudolph, "Antike Baptisten: Zu den Überlieferungen über frühjüdische and -christliche Taufsekten," in Rudolph, *Gnosis: Aufsätze*, 569–606; on the Mandaeans in this connection, see 592–95.

98. Stroumsa, *Another Seed*, 88–103.

99. A number of interesting studies have been done on the religious background of the various "kingdoms." See, e.g., Böhlig, "Jüdisches und Iranisches," 154–61 (see n. 80); Beltz, "Adamapokalypse," 135–75 (see n. 78); A. J. Welburn, "Iranian Prophetology and the Birth of the Messiah: The Apocalypse of Adam," *ANRW* II.25.6: 4752–94. The "coming to the water" is probably a reference to the descent of the Savior in each case, rather than to baptism. See Hedrick, *Apocalypse of Adam*, 145–47.

Sethian Gnosticism resistant and in reaction to the Christianizing of Sethian gnosis.[100]

It seems to me that Stroumsa's interpretation of the first twelve "kingdoms" as referring to Israel is forced. Indeed, the first twelve kingdoms may better be seen as elaborating on the "twelve kingdoms" of Ham and Japheth referred to earlier in the text (73,26–27). The thirteenth would then presumably refer to the Shemites, and the "mandate" or "ordinance" (ⲧⲱϣ, 82,15) could be taken as referring to the Law. However, if Stroumsa is correct in his interpretation of the thirteenth kingdom, the *Apocalypse of Adam,* far from being a "pre-Christian" Gnostic text, is rather one in which the original themes of Sethian gnosis, based on Jewish traditions, are retained against a tendency on the part of Gnostic opponents to see in Jesus Christ the true incarnation of the Gnostic Savior. The *Gospel of the Egyptians,* with which the *Apocalypse of Adam* shares much material in common,[101] represents that other side of Sethian gnosis, as does the *Apocryphon of John.*

It is, therefore, unimportant for our discussion whether or not the *Apocalypse of Adam* is chronologically a "pre-Christian" text, inasmuch as it represents a very early type of Gnosticism in which Jewish components are central and in which no Christian influence occurs. Even if the *Apocalypse of Adam* were chronologically late, it would represent a form of Jewish Gnosticism that resisted the kind of Christianization that we have noted in the *Apocryphon of John.* Its possible relationships with Mandaean and Manichaean forms of the Gnostic religion deserve further investigation.[102]

Conclusions

The two documents chosen for special consideration here are intended to exemplify the "problem" of how to delineate a seemingly anomalous phenomenon, namely, "Jewish Gnostic" literature. It has been argued, in effect, that Gnostic texts can be identified as "Jewish" on the basis of their use of biblical and Jewish traditions, specifically traditions that are arguably not mediated through a "Christian" Gnosticism. The *Apocryphon of John,* on the one hand, shows how such a Jewish Gnostic text, or collection of texts, could become Christianized in its final form. The *Apocalypse of*

---

100. See Stroumsa, *Another Seed,* 94–103.
101. See MacRae, "Apocalypse of Adam," 152.
102. See Beltz, "Adamapokalypse"; and Böhlig, "Jüdisches und Iranisches."

Adam, on the other hand, shows how a Jewish Gnostic text could retain its essential features without taking on a Christian cast. To be sure, these are only two examples, albeit important ones; others (e.g., the *Hypostasis of the Archons* and the *Paraphrase of Shem*)[103] could have been chosen to make the same point. In the documents that we have chosen for examination here, we have seen how biblical and other Jewish texts and traditions have been radically reinterpreted in the service of a higher gnosis that denigrates the Creator and his world and overthrows the centrality of the Law. The "building blocks" of this new gnosis, as expressed in literature, are Jewish; yet the interpretation can be seen to be essentially "un-Jewish" in the extreme, if by "Judaism" we mean (at least) devotion to one God, the Creator, his Law, and his people.[104] This new gnosis quickly assumed Christian forms, as is illustrated by the *Apocryphon of John,* wherein Jesus Christ is finally assigned the role of the revealer of gnosis that had earlier in the text's history been associated with Sophia in her various manifestations. Thus, although there seems to be a necessary relationship between Gnosticism (at least in its earliest forms) and Judaism, there is no such necessary relationship between Gnosticism and Christianity. Nor is there a single trajectory running from Jewish to Christian forms of the Gnostic religion.

The early Gnostics utilized and created a great number of books and had access to exegetical and other Jewish traditions that were in oral circulation. What we have available now, as the result of chance discoveries, is undoubtedly only the "tip of the iceberg." In the material at our disposal, we can see how specifically Jewish literature (especially the Bible), Jewish exegetical and theological traditions, and Jewish literary genres were utilized to express a drastic reorientation of values and perceived religious truth.

An important question inevitably arises from this evidence: Who were the people who created these writings, and for whom did they write? Here, unfortunately, we are faced with a lack of external evidence and the concomitant necessity of applying our imagination to the texts themselves in order to extrapolate some answers.[105] In-

---

103. See esp. Barc's *L'Hypostase;* and F. Wisse, "The Redeemer Figure in the Paraphrase of Shem," *NovT* 12 (1970): 130–40.

104. We should recall, though, that "normative Judaism" did not begin to emerge until the end of the first century C.E., in connection with the post-Temple reorganization at Jamnia.

105. Contrast the case of the Dead Sea Scrolls: We have not only the scrolls themselves but massive evidence for the community that utilized them, as a result of

timate familiarity with specifically Jewish forms and traditions, an awareness of popular philosophy and pagan lore, a highly sophisticated and creative hermeneutic approach, a sensitivity to profound questions of human existence — such are the chief characteristics of the early Gnostic literature. We can readily posit as authors and avid readers of the Gnostic materials Jewish intellectuals who, estranged from the "mainstream" of their own culture and dissatisfied with traditional answers, adopted a revolutionary stance vis-à-vis their religious traditions, not by rejecting them altogether but by applying to them a new interpretation. These people were *religious* intellectuals,[106] not secularized apostates such as those Jews with whom Philo was well acquainted in Alexandria.[107] In reinterpreting their Jewish religious traditions, however, they burst the bonds of Judaism and created a new religion.[108] We are thus presented with the anomaly of Jews who finally intended to be "no longer Jews."[109]

---

the excavations at Khirbet Qumran. The only "external" evidence we have for the Gnostics is the polemic of the heresiologists. *Caveat lector!*

106. I would posit *groups* of Gnostics, perhaps at first still formally attached to the synagogue but developing their own religious life. Aspects of this religious life can be extrapolated from the documents, to some extent. Note, e.g., the references to baptism in *Apoc. Adam. Ap. John* contains material that could have been used in catechesis.

107. See Philo, *Virt.* 182; *Conf.* 2–3. Philo's own nephew, the notorious Tiberius Alexander, is one of the most famous examples of a Jewish apostate in antiquity.

108. Cf. our discussion at the beginning of this essay. In its Manichaean form, Gnosticism became a world religion, one that persisted in China into the seventeenth century. See K. Rudolph, "Gnosis — Weltreligion oder Sekte?" in Rudolph, *Gnosis: Aufsätze*, 53–65.

109. Irenaeus reports of the Basilidian Gnostics: "They say they are no longer Jews, but not yet Christians" (*Haer.* 1.24.6).

Chapter 8

Eusebius and Gnosticism

The topic of this chapter devoted to the great fourth-century bishop and church historian involves some basic methodological problems that need to be addressed at the outset. Consider, for example, how Eusebius might respond, were it possible for us to press him with the inquiry, if we should ask him what he thought of Gnosticism and what impact this "-ism" had on the early history of the church. He would, no doubt, respond with a blank stare, followed, perhaps, by a hesitant query, "What do you mean?"

Of course, we think we know what we mean by the term "Gnosticism" (though each of us might have a different definition of it), and we might even claim to know how Eusebius ought to respond to our hypothetical question. The fact remains, however, that the term "Gnosticism" is a relatively modern coinage,[1] and its use by modern writers has been sufficiently imprecise as to prompt a committee of scholars, on the occasion of an international conference on "the origins of Gnosticism," held at Messina, Italy, in 1966, to come up with a definition that could be agreed upon by the conference participants.[2] The Messina definition made a deliberate distinction between "gnosis," broadly conceived, and a more narrowly defined "Gnosticism," a distinction that has itself been subject to criticism.[3] Meanwhile, a "minimalist" reaction has set in, resulting in an even narrower definition according to which the ancient use of the Greek word *gnostikos,* as applied to a person or a group, becomes the key heuristic device for deciding the boundaries of that religious movement in antiquity which can be called "Gnostic" and to which the modern coinage "Gnosticism" might

---

1. "Gnosticism" was coined in the seventeenth century. See Layton, "Prolegomena," 348–49.
2. See Bianchi, *Le origini,* xxvi–xxix (English version).
3. See Rudolph, *Gnosis,* 57.

arguably be applicable.[4] I doubt whether Eusebius himself would be satisfied with these modern discussions.

Without claiming to solve these problems, I shall state in what follows what I mean by the term "Gnosticism." Then, after a brief discussion of Eusebius's use of the term *gnostikos,* I shall discuss Eusebius's treatment of those ancient teachers and groups that are encompassed by my own definition of Gnosticism. Others will have to judge whether or not this strategy is successful.

Gnosticism: The Gnostic Religion

Gnosticism, although the term itself is not attested in antiquity, can be viewed as analogous to such other "-isms" as *Ioudaismos* ("Judaism," 2 Macc 2:21), *Christianismos* ("Christianity," Ign., *Magn.* 10.1, 3; *Phld.* 6.1; *Rom.* 3.3), and the like.[5] "Mandaeism" is a semantic equivalent, in that both "Mandaeism" and "Gnosticism" are based on words meaning "knowledge."[6] In other words, "Gnosticism" (as I use the term here) refers to a distinct religious movement or cluster of movements attested in history. That is to say, one can speak of "the Gnostic religion" as a discrete historical phenomenon distinct from, even if closely related to, Judaism and Christianity.[7]

One can isolate the following essential features of this religion, as these are revealed to us in the available primary sources: (1) Adherents of Gnosticism regard *gnosis* (rather than faith, observance of law, etc.) as requisite to salvation. Saving "knowledge" involves a revelation as to the true nature both of the human self and of God; for the Gnostic, indeed, self-knowledge *is* knowledge of God. (2) Gnosticism has a characteristic *theology,* according to which there is a transcendent supreme God beyond the god or powers responsible for the world in which we live. (3) There is in Gnosticism a *cosmology* that entails a dualist stance, according to which the cosmos, having been created by an inferior power, is a dark

---

4. See M. Smith, "The History of the Term Gnostikos," in Layton, *Rediscovery,* 2:796–807; Layton, "Prolegomena"; cf. Layton, *Gnostic Scriptures,* esp. 5–21.

5. This discussion is based on part of the introduction to Pearson, *Gnosticism.* See also my article "Gnosticism a Religion."

6. *Manda* < *mad(d)a* (Mandaic [E. Aramaic]) = *gnosis* (Greek). On the word *manda,* see R. Macuch, *Zur Sprache und Literatur der Mandäer* (Berlin: de Gruyter, 1976), 6–7. On the Mandaeans, see esp. Rudolph, *Gnosis,* 343–66, and literature cited therein.

7. For the terminology, see Jonas, *Gnostic Religion.*

prison in which human souls are held captive. (4) Gnostic *anthropology* views the essential human being as constituted by an inner self, a divine spark that originated in the transcendent divine world and that can, through gnosis, be released from the cosmic prison and return to its heavenly origin. The human body is part of the cosmic prison from which essential "man" must be redeemed. The notion of release from the cosmic prison entails (5) an *eschatology* that, in its simplest form, assigns salvation to those with gnosis, and ultimate annihilation to the cosmos and its minions.

Ancient Gnosticism, though highly individualistic, involved (6) *social*, (7) *ritual*, and (8) *ethical* dimensions, as well as (9) an *experiential* dimension that included joy in the possession of gnosis, on the one hand, and alienation from the cosmic order and those beings attached to it, on the other. But what holds everything together in the Gnostic religion is (10) *myth*. Mythopoesis is a characteristic feature of Gnosticism, for it is myth that gives verbal and literary expression to all that gnosis entails. There was, among the ancient Gnostics, great variation in the telling of myths; and each Gnostic teacher would create new elements to be added to the received tradition. Thus, Gnostic myths could become more and more complicated as they developed.

The ten essential features of Gnosticism I have just enumerated certainly qualify it as a "religion."[8] But what makes this religion so hard to define is, finally, (11) its *parasitic* character, particularly as to its relationship to Judaism and Christianity. One might well ask, based on my discussion of the constitutive features of Gnosticism, what this religion has to do with Judaism, or with Christianity, at all. My own answer, based on study of such ancient primary sources as the Nag Hammadi corpus,[9] is that the Gnostic religion grew out of, and away from, Judaism and became, early in its development, intricately involved with Christianity. Its relationship to Judaism can best be seen in its mythology, the basic building blocks of which constitute a revolutionary borrowing and

---

8. See N. Smart's discussion of the seven dimensions of a "religion" — ritual, experiential, mythic, doctrinal, ethical, social, and material — in *The World's Religions: Old Traditions and Modern Transformations* (Cambridge: Cambridge University Press, 1989), 10–21. Cf. my discussion in chapter 1 of this book.

9. For complete bibliographical information on the Nag Hammadi codices and Gnosticism (except Manichaeism and Mandaeism) since 1948, see D. Scholer, *Nag Hammadi Bibliography, 1948–1969*, NHS 1 (Leiden: E. J. Brill, 1971); and *Nag Hammadi Bibliography 1970–1994*, NHMS 32 (Leiden: E. J. Brill, 1997), annually updated subsequently as "Bibliographia Gnostica: Supplementum" in the journal *Novum Testamentum*.

reinterpretation of Jewish scriptures and traditions.[10] Its relationship to Christianity can best be seen in its soteriology: in Christian Gnosticism (or Gnostic Christianity) it is Jesus Christ who plays the role of the heavenly revealer of gnosis (i.e., the Savior). It is to Jesus Christ that the Gnostic myth comes to be attributed in "Christianized" Gnostic texts, such as the *Apocryphon of John* and similar texts now available in the Nag Hammadi corpus.[11] In non-Christian Gnostic texts, other figures (Seth, Manda de hayye, Hermes Trismegistus, etc.) play the role of Savior-Revealer.

It is precisely the "parasitic" character of Gnosticism that has caused difficulty for its interpreters, both ancient and modern. Ancient Christian writers, Eusebius among them, regarded the Gnostics simply as Christian heretics. Even some modern interpreters, flying in the face of the primary evidence now available to scholarship, continue to maintain the older view of the patristic heresiologists, that Gnosticism originated as a Christian heresy.[12] Eusebius, at least, cannot be blamed for his views on this issue, for, as we shall see, he was lacking in firsthand knowledge of the Gnostics and their literature. Ignorance is his excuse.

Eusebius's Use of the Term γνωστικός

I have already referred to the tendency on the part of some modern scholars to restrict the use of the term "Gnostic" to those individuals or groups whom the ancient sources refer to as *gnostikoi* (γνωστικοί, "knowledgeable ones," i.e., those in possession of or capable of saving gnosis).[13] Applying this criterion to Eusebius, we come up with meager results indeed.

In Eusebius's *Ecclesiastical History,* the word γνωστικός appears only twice.[14] At 4.7.9, Eusebius refers to Carpocrates as "the father of another heresy which was called that of the Gnostics."[15]

10. See Pearson, *Gnosticism;* and chapters 6 and 7 in this book.

11. See, e.g., chapter 7 of this book.

12. See esp. S. Pétrement, *Le Dieu séparé: Les origines du gnosticisme* (Paris: Cerf, 1984); and my review "Early Christianity and Gnosticism: A Review Essay," *RStR* 13 (1987): 1–8. An unrevised English version of Pétrement is also available: *A Separate God: The Christian Origins of Gnosticism,* trans. C. Harrison (San Francisco: HarperSanFrancisco, 1990). See also A. H. B. Logan, *Gnostic Truth and Christian Heresy: A Study in the History of Gnosticism* (Edinburgh: T. & T. Clark; Peabody, Mass.: Hendrickson, 1996).

13. See n. 4.

14. Smith, "History of the Term Gnostikos," did not extend his study of the term to include Eusebius.

15. All translations of passages from Eusebius, *Hist. Eccl.,* quoted in this article

At 6.13.1, in the context of Eusebius's discussion of Clement of Alexandria, the word γνωστικός appears as part of the full title of Clement's *Stromateis* ("Titus Flavius Clement's *Stromateis* of Gnostic Memoirs according to the True Philosophy"). Here, of course, the word is not used of a person or group. Thus, on the basis of the evidence in the *History*, we might conclude that the only "Gnostics" that existed in history were those heretics associated with Carpocrates of Alexandria, despite the fact that some modern scholars, including Morton Smith and Bentley Layton, tend to deny that the religion of Carpocrates can appropriately be labeled "Gnostic."[16]

The evidence in Eusebius becomes somewhat more complicated, however, when we take into account his early *Chronicle*. That work, whose Greek original is unfortunately lost, includes as one of the items listed under the sixteenth year of Emperor Hadrian's reign (132 C.E.) the following information: "Basilides the heresiarch was living in Alexandria; from him derive the Gnostics."[17] This is the only mention in Eusebius's *Chronicle* of any "Gnostics,"[18] if, indeed, the terminology is that of Eusebius at all.[19]

The word *gnostikos* occurs three times in Eusebius's *Praeparatio Evangelica*. In book 7, which is devoted to the theology of the Hebrews,[20] Eusebius discusses the symbolism of the name of the antediluvian patriarch Enosh (Gen 4:26), "man" (Heb. *'enoš*). Eusebius says at 7.8.5, "Nor do they [the Hebrews] deem it appropriate to regard and to call any other person 'true man' [ἀληθῆ . . . ἄνθρωπον] than the one who has achieved knowledge of

are those of K. Lake (books 1–5) and J. E. L. Oulton (books 6–10) in the LCL edition.

16. See M. Smith, *Clement of Alexandria and a Secret Gospel of Mark* (Cambridge: Harvard University Press, 1973), 267–78; and Layton, *Gnostic Scriptures*, 199. For additional discussion of Carpocrates, see further discussion.

17. "Basilides haeresiarches in Alexandria commoratur"; R. Helm, ed., *Die Chronik des Hieronymus*, in *Eusebius Werke* 7:7, rev. ed., GCS 47 (Berlin: Akademie-Verlag, 1956), 201. (Jerome's Latin *Chron.* uses Eusebius's as a basis.) Cf. the Armenian version (A. Schoene, ed. and trans., *Eusebi Chronicorum canonum quae supersunt* [Dublin-Zurich: Weidman, 1967], 1:168): "Basilides haeresiarcha his temporibus apparuit" (Basilides the heresiarch appeared at this time).

18. So according to R. M. Grant, *Eusebius as Church Historian* (Oxford: Clarendon, 1980), 9.

19. The word *gnostici* appears in Jerome's Latin version, but not in Schoene's translation of the Armenian version; see n. 17. For additional discussion of Basilides, see subsequent discussion.

20. See the excellent introduction and notes by G. Schroeder in the SC edition of Eusebius, *Praeparatio Evangelica*, SC 215 (Paris: Cerf, 1975).

God and piety [θεοῦ γνώσεως καὶ εὐσεβείας], the one who is truly
knowledgeable as well as pious [τὸν ἀληθῶς γνωστικὸν ὁμοῦ καὶ
εὐσεβῆ]."[21] Further on, at 7.8.9, Eusebius says that Enosh is regarded by the Hebrews as the first truly God-loving man, because
it was he who first "hoped to call upon the name of the Lord God"
(Gen 4:26 [LXX]). The example of Enosh shows that "the rational
aspect of the soul is both knowledgeable and cognizant of piety
vis-à-vis the Deity [τὸ κατὰ ψυχὴν...λογικὸν ὄντως...καὶ γνωστικὸν καὶ τῆς περὶ τὸ θεῖον εὐσεβείας]." Here Enosh is presented
as the symbol of the γνωστικός man, and of the soul's rational el-
ement, which is also γνωστικόν. Eusebius's remarks here are based
essentially on Philo of Alexandria's discussion of Enosh (Det. 138–
40).[22] Philo, however, does not use the term γνωστικός.[23] I would
suggest that the use of this term by Eusebius reflects the influence
of Clement of Alexandria, who uses the term frequently for those
who have achieved the highest ideals of Christian piety.[24]

One other use of γνωστικός occurs in book 11 of the Praeparatio, in the context of an argument that the best of Greek
philosophy (Platonism) is dependent upon that of the Hebrews.
At 11.6.31, Eusebius interprets the names "Jacob" and "Israel,"
and says of the latter: " 'Israel' [means] 'seeing God'; such would
be the knowledgeable and contemplative mind in man ['Ισραὴλ δὲ
ὁρῶν θεόν, ὁποῖος ἂν εἴη ὁ γνωστικὸς καὶ θεωρητικὸς ἐν ἀνθρώπῳ
νοῦς]." Here again, one can detect the obvious influence of Philo.
The (false) etymology of the name "Israel" ("man seeing God")
is ubiquitous in Philo, as is the allegorical interpretation of the
name as meaning the higher "mind" in man.[25] The use of the term
γνωστικός here, as in the other cases in the Praeparatio, can best
be understood against the background of the influence of Clement.

One question remains to be considered here: Why, if Eusebius
does not shrink from using the term γνωστικός in the Praeparatio,
is he so sparing in his use of it in the History? Given the influence

---

21. This and other passages quoted from Praep. Evang. are my translation, based
on the SC edition.
22. See Schroeder's introduction (62–64), and notes to the text (176–81; see
n. 20). Schroeder makes no mention of the use of the term γνωστικός.
23. Smith refers to one dubious passage in Philo (Op. Mund. 154); see "History
of the Term Gnostikos," 799. He defines the term γνωστικός as "leading to knowledge, resulting in knowledge, capable of knowing, cognizant of," and traces its use
back to Plato and the Platonic-Pythagorean tradition (799–800).
24. See esp. book 7 of Clem. Al., Strom. On the difference in Clement between "true" knowledge and "false" (heretical) knowledge, see A. Mehat, "'Vrai' et
'fousse' gnose d'après Clément d'Alexandrie," in Layton, Rediscovery, 1:426–33.
25. For references, see the index of names in vol. 10 of the LCL edition (333–35).

of Clement that we posited for his usage in the *Praeparatio,* we might also expect him to elaborate on the meaning of the term γνωστικός in the title of Clement's *Stromateis* (6.13.1) and on its place in Clement's thought, particularly because he makes much of Clement at various points in his *History*[26] and is likely dependent on Clement at numerous places where the latter is not mentioned.[27] Unfortunately, I have no good answer to this question.

Whatever the answer might be, we can see that (1) Eusebius is capable of using the term γνωστικός in a positive sense, under the influence of Clement; and (2) the one occurrence of the term "the Gnostics" in the *History* refers to a specific heresy, i.e., that supposedly engendered by Carpocrates.[28]

Were we to adopt the "minimalist" position referred to earlier, we should have to conclude our investigation of Eusebius and Gnosticism here. I prefer another approach. We can achieve more satisfactory results if we choose another rubric for our discussion, namely, what Eusebius refers to in his *History* as "falsely called Knowledge."

Eusebius and "Falsely Called Knowledge"

In the prefatory material found in book 1 of the *History,*[29] Eusebius sets forth five basic kinds of subject matter, or "themes," that govern the composition of his work: apostolic succession, key events and persons, heresies, the fate of the Jews, and persecutions mounted by pagans against Christians.[30] The third theme is presented as "the names, the number and the age of those who, driven by the desire of innovation to an extremity of error, have heralded themselves as the introducers of Knowledge falsely so-called [ψευδωνύμου γνώσεως], ravaging the flock of Christ unsparingly like grim wolves" (1.1.1). It is interesting that Eusebius, in this preface, uses "falsely called Knowledge" as the paradigm of heresy in general. Indeed, he does not use the term "heresy" here at all.

---

26. See, e.g., 3.23.5–19; 5.11.1–5; 6.13.1–14.7.

27. See Grant, *Eusebius,* 28–30, 38, 40, and passim.

28. Clement never refers to the Carpocratians as "Gnostics." He does refer to one group of "Gnostic" heretics, the followers of a certain Prodicus, who "falsely call themselves Gnostics" (*Strom.* 3.30). On Prodicus, see H. Chadwick, *Alexandrian Christianity,* LCC (Philadelphia: Westminster, 1954), 30.

29. This preface was added to *Hist. Eccl.* after the basic material in books 1–7 was composed. See the penetrating discussion in Grant, *Eusebius,* 33–44.

30. These five "themes" provide the basis for the organization of the material in chapters 6–10 of Grant's *Eusebius* (114–25).

Appearing here as well are other key terms to refer to heresy: "innovation" (νεωτεροποιία) and "error" (πλάνη).[31]

Eusebius's use in his preface of "falsely called Knowledge" as a paradigm of heresy is probably inspired by the title of Irenaeus's treatise *Against Heresies,* which Eusebius quotes in full at 5.7.1: "Refutation and Overthrow of Knowledge Falsely So-Called." (Elsewhere, he uses the more common title of Irenaeus's work, *Against Heresies.*)[32] Of course, the ultimate source of the term "falsely called Knowledge" (ψευδώνυμος γνῶσις) is 1 Timothy 6:20 in the New Testament, a passage that can safely be regarded as directed against an incipient Gnosticism.

Eusebius next uses the term "falsely called Knowledge" at 3.32.7. In the preceding context (3.32.1–6), he has cited Hegesippus as the source of information on the martyrdom of Symeon (or Simon), son of Clopas, second bishop of Jerusalem after James, and a cousin of Jesus and James. According to Hegesippus, Symeon was denounced to the authorities "by the sects" (ὑπὸ τῶν αἱρέσεων) during the reign of Emperor Trajan (98–117). We then read the following:

> Besides this the same writer, explaining the events of these times adds that until then the church remained a pure and uncorrupted virgin, for those who attempted to corrupt the healthful rule of the Savior's teaching, if they existed at all, lurked in obscure darkness. But when the sacred band of the Apostles and the generation of those to whom it had been vouchsafed to hear with their own ears the divine wisdom had reached the several ends of their lives, then the federation of godless error took its beginning through the deceit of false teachers who, seeing that none of the Apostles still remained, barefacedly tried against the preaching of the truth the counter-proclamation of "knowledge falsely so-called." (*Hist. Eccl.* 3.32.7–8)

---

31. The term "innovation" (νεωτεροποιία) connotes an attitude of revolt against the established order in other historical writers, such as Thucydides and Josephus. See ibid., 84. "Error" (πλάνη) is a recurrent theme in Eusebius's *Hist. Eccl.* and represents virtually a personal, demonic force at work in the world. See Glenn F. Chesnut, *The First Christian Histories,* 2d ed. (Macon, Ga.: Mercer University Press, 1986), 105. In n. 31, Chesnut compares the figure of *Planē* in *Gos. Truth* (NHC I 17,14–18,38).

32. Πρὸς τὰς αἱρέσεις in Eus., *Hist. Eccl.* 2.13.5; 3.18.2; 3.28.6; 4.11.2; 4.18.9; 4.29.1; 5.5.9. Irenaeus, of course, treated other heresies in addition to those that can appropriately be included under the designation "falsely called Knowledge." See n. 77 for Eusebius's treatment of non-Gnostic heretics.

The direct sequel to this discussion of heresy is found in chapter 7 of book 4, to which we shall return. The passage just quoted, with its typically "orthodox" notion of the origins of heresy in the church,[33] poses an interesting question: Does Eusebius's source, Hegesippus, use the term "falsely called Knowledge," or has it been introduced by Eusebius himself at this point? (Eusebius is evidently not quoting Hegesippus here; he is paraphrasing him.) And who are the sectarians referred to by Hegesippus in the preceding context, that is, those who were implicated in the martyrdom of Symeon? The latter question is easily answered: they were not Christian "heretics," but representatives of one or more of "the seven sects among the people" elsewhere discussed by Hegesippus (*Hist. Eccl.* 2.23.8; 4.22.7); that is to say, they were Jews.[34] For Hegesippus, and for Eusebius who follows him, Christian "heresy" could take hold only with the passing of the apostles and their hearers (including Symeon: 3.32.4). "Falsely called Knowledge" is the cover term for this earliest expression of Christian "heresy," a term that could very well have been used already by Hegesippus.[35]

Yet Eusebius is compelled by his other sources, and by his own requirements of adhering (roughly) to chronological order in the arrangement of his material, to deal with a "heresy" that existed already in the days of the apostles. Indeed, the first use in his *History* of the Greek word *hairēsis* with the meaning "heresy" occurs in connection with Simon Magus at 2.1.10, where he is treating the events recorded in the New Testament in Acts 8 (2.1.8–13).[36] Eusebius mentions the "feigned" conversion of Simon Magus and refers to him as "the progenitor" of "those who continue his most unclean heresy to the present day." They "attach themselves to

33. See Bauer, *Orthodoxy and Heresy,* xxiii–xxiv.

34. See subsequent discussion of "the seven heresies... among the people."

35. In that case, Hegesippus may have inspired Irenaeus to use the term in his treatise *Against Heresies.* On Hegesippus's lost *Hypomnemata,* see esp. N. Hyldahl, "Hegesipps Hypomnemata," in *StTh* 14 (1960): 70–113. Cf. E. J. Goodspeed and R. M. Grant, *A History of Early Christian Literature* (Chicago: University of Chicago Press, 1966), 123–25; and Grant, *Eusebius,* 38, 40, 67–70, 86.

36. Eusebius uses the word αἵρεσις in a variety of ways in *Hist. Eccl.* The first occurrence refers to the "sect" of Judas the Galilean (1.5.3). The last two occurrences refer to the "most holy Catholic religion" (10.5.21–22, quoting from an imperial letter of Constantine)! An analogous use refers to the various schools of philosophy (6.18.3). The word can also mean, simply, "choice" (8.4.3; 8.10.10; 10.4.57; 10.5.4). It appears that the last occurrence of the word with the meaning "heresy" is found in Eusebius's discussion of the Manichaeans (7.31.1–2). The word is most widely used in this sense in books 2–7 of *Hist. Eccl.*

the Church like a pestilential and scurfy disease and ravage to the utmost all whom they are able to inoculate with the deadly and terrible poison hidden in them. Most of these, however, have already been driven out."

What is said here of Simon's progeny seems to apply to heretics in general, rather than to a specific group of Simonians. We note here, too, the absence of the use of the term "falsely called Knowledge," but later on in the *History* (4.7.3), Simon is appropriately subsumed under that catchall designation. Nothing is said here of Simon's teaching; Eusebius reports only that Simon's magical power led his victims to refer to him as "the Great Power of God" (2.1.11; cf. Acts 8:10).

Eusebius continues his discussion of Simon at 2.13, where he quotes extensively from Justin Martyr's account of Simon's Samaritan origins, his activities in Rome, and his consort Helena (13.3–4; cf. Justin, *Apol.* 1.26.1–3). Eusebius then refers to Irenaeus's report, remarking that "we have received from the tradition that Simon was the first author of all heresy" (2.13.5). After considerable vituperation ("frenzy and madness," "baseness and unspeakable conduct," etc.), Eusebius concludes his report with the information that Simon was successfully opposed by the apostles: "Wherefore no conspiracy, either of Simon, or of any other of those who arose at that time, succeeded in those Apostolic days" (2.14.3). Simon met his end in Rome when "the great and mighty Peter," "like a noble captain of God," came to Rome with the light of the gospel (2.14.6). "Thus," concludes Eusebius, "when the divine word made its home among them the power of Simon was extinguished and perished immediately, together with the fellow himself" (2.15.1). Eusebius does not report the manner of Simon's death, but he was probably aware of one or more of the accounts that circulated in the early church.[37]

In Eusebius's account of Simon thus far, there is no mention of "falsely called Knowledge." Simon is, to be sure, the arch-heretic, but Eusebius, for all of his vilification of Simon, does not inform his readers of the nature of Simon's "heresy."

Eusebius puts off to chapter 26 of book 3 his discussion of Simon's "successor," Menander. In so doing, he interrupts the narrative in both of his sources, Irenaeus (*Haer.* 1.23.5) and Justin Martyr (*Apol.* 1.26.4), interspersing here (2.15–3.25) material on the doings of the apostles and the canonical writings. At the end

---

37. See, e.g., the *Acts of Peter* (*Act. Verc.*) 32.

of 3.25, he refers to "writings which are put forward by heretics under the name of the apostles containing gospels such as those of Peter, and Thomas, and Matthias, and some others besides, or Acts such as those of Andrew and John and the other apostles" (3.25.6). Eusebius adds that such writings, as "forgeries of heretics" (3.25.7), have been avoided by anyone "who belonged to the succession of the orthodox" (3.25.6). They have obviously been avoided by Eusebius himself.

At this point, Eusebius returns to his previous discussion: "Let us now continue the narrative. Menander succeeded Simon Magus and showed himself as a weapon of the devil's power not inferior to his predecessor" (3.26.1). We note the use of the language of "succession" here — Eusebius follows Irenaeus's usage — for heresy is thus put forward as a diabolical counter to the true apostolic succession of the orthodox church. Eusebius, following his sources Irenaeus and Justin, mentions Menander's Samaritan origins, his sorcery, his claim to be the Savior sent from above, his baptismal ritual, and his eventual move to Antioch. But then Eusebius adds a remark that goes beyond what is contained in his sources: "It was assuredly at the instigation of the devil that the name of Christian was adopted by such sorcerers" (3.26.4). Eusebius erroneously attaches the label "Christian" to Menander and Simon, when, in fact, there is nothing in the extant evidence to suggest that either was, or claimed to be, a Christian. Both Simon and Menander, according to the available evidence, claimed for themselves the salvific role that is assigned to Jesus Christ by Christians, whether "heretical" or "orthodox." Yet it is clear that both Simon and Menander belong to the history of Gnosticism, in its pre-Christian phase.[38]

Of course, Eusebius was in no position to appreciate such historical distinctions, given the limitations of his sources, his lack of primary evidence, and his obviously deficient approach to writing history. Thus, it may be only a coincidence that he finally situates both Simon and Menander within the group of teachers expressly named under the heading "the leaders of Knowledge, falsely so-called" (4.7). This is noteworthy when we also observe that some

38. The "Gnostic" character of Simon's religion has sometimes been disputed, unjustifiably in my view. See esp. Rudolph, *Gnosis*, 294–98; and "Simon — Magus oder Gnosticus?" *ThR* 42 (1977), 279–359. See also G. Lüdemann, "The Acts of the Apostles and the Beginnings of Simonian Gnosis," *NTS* 33 (1987): 420–26. On Menander, see Rudolph, *Gnosis*, 298.

other heretics are omitted from that group: the Ebionites (discussed in 3.27), Cerinthus (3.28), and the Nicolaitans (3.29).[39]

The term "falsely called Knowledge" occurs in book 4 only in Eusebius's table of contents for that book, chapter 7: "Who were the leaders of Knowledge, falsely so-called, at that time," that is, in the time of Emperor Hadrian (117–138). The discussion in this chapter picks up the theme that was enunciated at 3.32.8 (discussed earlier) but was interrupted there with material dealing with subjects other than heresy. Eusebius takes up the earlier discussion in the following way:

> Like brilliant lamps the churches were now shining throughout the world, and faith in our Saviour and Lord Jesus Christ was flourishing among all mankind, when the devil who hates what is good, as the enemy of truth, ever most hostile to man's salvation, turned all his devices against the church. (4.7.1)

The devil's tools were, of course, "sorcerers and deceivers," who undertook to lead the faithful to destruction (4.7.2):

> Thus from Menander, whom we have already mentioned as the successor of Simon, there proceeded a certain snake-like power with two mouths and a double head, and established the leaders of two heresies, Saturninus, an Antiochian by race, and Basilides of Alexandria. The first established schools of impious heresy in Syria, the latter in Egypt. Irenaeus makes it plain that Saturninus uttered for the most part the same falsehoods as Menander, but Basilides, under the pretext of secret doctrine, stretched fancy infinitely far, fabricating monstrous myths for his impious heresy. (4.7.3–4)

Eusebius refrains from quoting Irenaeus's accounts of Saturninus (or Satornilos; *Haer.* 1.24.1–2) and Basilides (1.24.3–7); so a reader would learn virtually nothing from Eusebius as to the nature

39. It is interesting that Eusebius omits from his account of Cerinthus and the Nicolaitans those details in the sources available to him that might hint of a "Gnostic" connection. The Ebionites were obviously not Gnostics. Cerinthus, for Eusebius, was nothing more than a crass millennialist. The Nicolaitans, according to Eusebius, were a libertine group who falsely traced their behavior to the deacon Nicolaus (Acts 6:5). Eusebius relies on Gaius of Rome and Dionysius of Alexandria for his account of Cerinthus, and on Clement of Alexandria for his account of the Nicolaitans. See Iren., *Haer.* 1.26, for Cerinthus (26.1), Ebionites (26.2), and Nicolaitans (26.3); and Foerster, *Gnosis,* 34–36 (on Cerinthus) and 315–17 (on Nicolaus and the Nicolaitans).

of the teachings or mythological systems of these two heretics.[40] And if he had paid sufficient attention to Irenaeus's account, he would have noticed a crucial distinction between Menander and Saturninus: Saturninus was a *Christian* heretic (Gnostic), unlike Menander, in that he assigned the role of Savior to Jesus Christ. Eusebius does, however, provide valuable information on an orthodox writer who produced an extensive refutation of Basilides, Agrippa Castor (otherwise unknown). From Agrippa Castor, Eusebius derives the information that Basilides produced twenty-four books on the gospel (commentaries), that he had prophets named Bar Cabbas and Bar Coph and others, and that he counseled people to eat meat sacrificed to idols and to deny the faith in the face of persecution (4.7.7).

Eusebius next mentions Carpocrates, in the aforementioned passage that contains the only reference to γνωστικοί in the *History:* "Irenaeus also writes that Carpocrates was a contemporary of these [Saturninus and Basilides], the father of another heresy which was called that of the Gnostics" (4.7.9). Eusebius is misreading his source here, for Irenaeus does *not* connect Carpocrates with the sect that he specifically identifies as "Gnostics."[41] Eusebius goes on to report that it is the shocking obscenities perpetrated by the Carpocratian heretics, inspired by the devil, that have provided the occasion for unbelieving pagans to hurl calumnies on "the whole race of Christians" (4.7.10). Fortunately, in time, Christian teaching was vindicated, reports Eusebius (4.7.12–14). Of course, Eusebius tells us nothing about the specific doctrines of the Carpocratians.[42]

Strangely enough, Eusebius makes no mention in this chapter of the most important Christian Gnostic in the history of the church, Valentinus, whose teachings and influence provided the impetus for Irenaeus's great work *Against Heresies*. Valentinus comes in for an off-handed comment in Eusebius's report on the episcopacy of Hyginus: "Irenaeus ... states ... that in the time of Hyginus, the aforementioned bishop of Rome [138–141], Valentinus, the founder of a special heresy, and Cerdo, the founder of the Marcionite error, were both famous in Rome" (4.10.1; cf. Iren., *Haer.*

---

40. On Basilides, see esp. Foerster, *Gnosis,* 1:59–83; and Layton, *Gnostic Scriptures,* 417–43.

41. See subsequent discussion and n. 44.

42. On Carpocrates and the Carpocratians, see esp. Foerster, *Gnosis,* 1:36–40; and Smith, *Clement of Alexandria,* 266–78, 295–350 (see n. 16).

3.3.3). Eusebius elaborates somewhat in the following chapter, quoting Irenaeus:

> "Valentinus came to Rome in the time of Hyginus, but he flourished under Pius, and remained until Anicetus, and Cerdo, who before the time of Marcion, in the days of Hyginus, the ninth bishop, had come to the church and confessed, went on in the same way, sometimes teaching heresy, sometimes confessing again, and sometimes convicted by his evil teaching and separated from the assembly of the brethren." (*Hist. Eccl.* 4.11.1 = Iren., *Haer.* 3.4.3)

It is interesting that Eusebius leaves off quoting Irenaeus precisely here, for the passage in Irenaeus continues as follows: "Marcion, then, succeeding him [Cerdo], flourished under Anicetus, who held the tenth place of the episcopate. But the rest, who are called Gnostics, take rise from Menander, Simon's disciple, as I have shown" (*Haer.* 3.4.3).[43] The "Gnostics" referred to by Irenaeus were a distinct group of heretics whose teachings are presented at length in book 1 of Irenaeus's *Adversus Haereses* (1.29).[44] According to Irenaeus, the teachings of Valentinus were essentially an adaptation and revision of those of the "Gnostics" (*Haer.* 1.11.1; cf. 1.31.3). Eusebius passes over such information in silence, choosing to leave his readers virtually in the dark regarding the nature and substance of Valentinus's teachings[45] and, for that matter, the teachings of Irenaeus's "Gnostics." He reports only that Valentinus's system was a "bottomless pit" full of errors and wickedness (4.11.3). He does provide an excerpt from Irenaeus on the "foul mysteries" of the Valentinian Marcus (4.11.4–5; cf. Iren., *Haer.* 1.13.1; 1.21.3).[46] And, later on, Eusebius informs his readers that Justin Martyr's pupil Tatian fell into heresy, establishing his own doctrine and "telling stories of invisible Aeons, like the followers of Valentinus" (4.29.3), an assertion that is not borne out

---

43. ANF translation.
44. *Haer.* 1.29 corresponds to part of *Ap. John* (NHC II,1; III,1; IV,1; BG,2). On this correspondence, see esp. Foerster, *Gnosis*, 1:100–20; cf. Layton, *Gnostic Scriptures*, 163–69. For a synopsis of all four Coptic versions of *Ap. John*, with Irenaeus's report, see Waldstein-Wisse, *Apocryphon*.
45. On Valentinus and Valentinianism, see esp. Layton, *Gnostic Scriptures*, 219–353; and *Rediscovery*, vol. 1.
46. On the Marcosians, see esp. Foerster, *Gnosis*, 1:194–221.

by any available evidence.[47] As for Cerdo, we get from Eusebius some additional information:

> Moreover, in the first book he [Irenaeus] makes the following statement about Cerdo: "A certain Cerdo had come originally from the circle of Simon and settled in Rome in the time of Hyginus. . . . He taught that the God preached by the Law and the Prophets was not the father of our Lord Jesus Christ, for the one was known, the other unknown [ἀγνῶτα], the one was righteous and the other good. Marcion of Pontus succeeded him and increased the school, blaspheming unblushingly. (*Hist. Eccl.* 4.11.2; cf. Iren., *Haer.* 1.27.1)[48]

Eusebius has nothing more of substance to report concerning the second-century Gnostic heresies. For him, they cease to have any relevance beyond the history of their own time, at least until the appearance of Mani, who is said to have dredged up "long-extinct, godless heresies" and infected the world with a new version of "falsely called Knowledge" (7.31.2). Eusebius does grant the continuation of Valentinian influence until the time of Origen,[49] but only to report the conversion to ecclesiastical orthodoxy of one Ambrose, a former Valentinian, converted by the teachings of the great Alexandrian teacher (6.18.1).[50]

Before turning finally to Eusebius's treatment of Manichaeism, I want to take up for brief discussion a passage in which the origins of the aforementioned heresies are treated, and which also happens to be Eusebius's last and most puzzling citation of Hegesippus: *History* 4.22. The context is a discussion of Hegesippus and the five

---

47. On Tatian, see M. Elze, *Tatian und seine Theologie* (Göttingen: Vandenhoeck & Ruprecht, 1960).

48. On Cerdo, see Foerster, *Gnosis,* 1:44. Marcion, although he was influenced by Gnosticism, cannot properly be included among the Gnostic heretics. His religion was centered not on gnosis but on faith. See esp. A. von Harnack, *Marcion: Das Evangelium vom fremden Gott* (repr., Darmstadt: Wissenschaftliche Buchgesellschaft, 1960); and R. J. Hoffmann, *Marcion: On the Restitution of Christianity,* AAR Academy Series 46 (Chico, Calif.: Scholars Press, 1984). H. Jonas, however, regards Marcion as a Gnostic; see *Gnostic Religion,* 130–46.

49. The Valentinian heresy persisted into the eighth century. See K. Koschorke, "Patristische Materialen zur Spätgeschichte der valentinianischen Gnosis," in Krause, *Gnosis and Gnosticism,* 120–39. Eusebius himself reports in his later *Life of Constantine* that the emperor addressed a condemnatory letter "to the heretics," specifically "Novatians, Valentinians, Marcionites, Paulinians, and those called Cataphrygians" (*Vit. Const.* 3.64.1; my translation of the GCS edition).

50. Ambrose, apparently a very wealthy man, became Origen's patron (*Hist. Eccl.* 4.23.1–2). Another person who renounced the Valentinian heresy, according to Eusebius, was Bardesanes (Bar Deisan), but his subsequent views are adjudged to be less than orthodox (4.30.3).

books that he composed (the *Hypomnemata*) presumably in the time of Eleutherus (bishop of Rome 175–189; cf. 4.22.3). Eusebius brings up Hegesippus's discussion of the beginning of heresies and repeats Hegesippus's opinion that the church remained a pure "virgin," uncorrupted by heresies, until the time of Symeon, successor to James the Just (4.22.4). Our focal passage then follows, wherein Hegesippus is expressly quoted:

> " . . . but Thebouthis, because he had not been made bishop, begins its [the church's] corruption by the seven heresies, to which he belonged, among the people. Of these were Simon, whence the Simonians, and Cleobius, whence the Cleobians, and Dositheus, whence the Dositheans, and Gorthaeus, whence the Goratheni and the Masbothei. From these came the Menandrianists and the Marcianists and the Carpocratians and the Valentinians and the Basilidians and Saturnilians; each of these puts forward in its own peculiar way its own opinion, and from them come the false Christs and false prophets and false apostles who destroy the unity of the church by their poisonous doctrine against God and against his Christ." (*Hist. Eccl.* 4.22.5–6)

The same writer also described the sects that once existed among the Jews, as follows: " 'Now there were various opinions among the circumcision, among the children of Israel, against the tribe of Judah and the Messiah as follows: Essenes, Galileans, Hemerobaptists, Masbothei, Samaritans, Sadducees, and Pharisees' " (*Hist. Eccl.* 4.22.7). This passage is obviously garbled, but let us see if we can make some sense of it. We have noted, in another passage already discussed (3.32.7–8), Hegesippus's view that the church remained pure of heresy until the time of Symeon, successor to James. Now we read that a certain Thebouthis, otherwise unknown,[51] played a role in the introduction of heresy on the occasion of his being passed over for the episcopacy (of the Jerusalem church), presumably in favor of James's (and Jesus') cousin Symeon. Hegesippus says that this Thebouthis belonged to "the seven heresies . . . among the people," presumably meaning that he belonged to one of them ("Galileans"?). He may have been one of the Jewish sectarians implicated in the martyrdom of Symeon (3.32.6).

---

51. For the suggestion of a possible connection with the Thebouthis mentioned by Josephus (*BJ* 6.387), see Hyldahl, "Hegesipps Hypomnemata," 97 (see n. 35).

Hegesippus's reference to seven Jewish sects is only one of several such references in early Christian literature and reflects a widespread topos in ancient Christianity concerning pre-Christian Judaism: before the advent of Christ, the Jews were divided into seven sects.[52] We note that Hegesippus's list of the seven Jewish sects is the last of *three* lists of sects in this passage. The second list, beginning with "Menandrianists," consists of what the author regards as the first Christian heretics. What, then, of the first list, which is cited as the actual source of the Christian heresies and which, in turn, consists of groups derived from "the seven heresies... among the people"?[53] The answer, I believe, is this: the first list is meant to include specifically *Samaritan* sects, deriving from the Samaritans included in the list of seven.

For confirmation of this reading of the text, we can turn to Epiphanius's *Panarion against Heresies*.[54] Epiphanius's seven Jewish sects are sects 14–20: Sadducees, Scribes, Pharisees, Hemerobaptists, Nasaraeans, Ossaeans, and Herodians. Epiphanius treats four "Samaritan" sects, and we note that he (like Hegesippus) puts these before the Jewish ones. They are sects 10–13: Essenes, Sebuaeans, Gorothenes, and Dositheans. The lists are not exactly the same, of course, but the correspondences are striking enough between Hegesippus's first list of sects and Epiphanius's Samaritan group. They have in common "Baptists" (Masbothei

---

52. The lists are usually garbled, and to some extent fanciful, but they reflect the influence of Josephus (*Ant.* 18.11–25: Pharisees, Sadducees, Essenes, Galileans). The most important passages are Justin, *Dial.* 80.4; Ps.-Clement, *Homil.* 2.23; *Const. Ap.* 6.6; Epiph., *Haer.* 14–20 and 9–13 (see subsequent discussion); Ephraim Syrus, *Ev. Concord.*; and Philaster, *Haer.* 4–10. For discussion of the "pre-Christian heresies in Israel," see, in general, A. Hilgenfeld, *Ketzergeschichte des Urchristentums* (repr., Darmstadt: Wissenschaftliche Buchgesellschaft, 1963), 81–161. For an important discussion focusing on baptismal groups, see K. Rudolph, "Antike Baptisten: Zu den Überlieferungen über frühjüdische und -christliche Taufsekten," in *Gnosis: Aufsätze,* 569–606. For an important discussion of Hegesippus's treatment in Eus., *Hist. Eccl.* 4.22, see J. E. Fossum, *The Name of God and the Angel of the Lord: Samaritan and Jewish Concepts of Intermediation and the Origins of Gnosticism,* WUNT 36 (Tübingen: J. C. B. Mohr [Paul Siebeck], 1985), 20–22. The early Christian enumeration of seven sects is conservative! Rabbi Yohanan is credited with the observation that "the people of Israel did not go into exile before they had become twenty-four sects of heretics" (*y. Sanh.* 10.29c, as quoted by I. Gruenwald, "Aspects of the Jewish-Gnostic Controversy," in Layton, *Rediscovery,* 2:713–23, esp. 714).

53. Note the phrases ἀφ' ὧν and ἀπὸ τούτων (4.22.5) connecting the first list with the seven "sects" (= third list) and the second list with the first.

54. For a convenient translation of the first part of Epiphanius's *Panarion,* see F. Williams, trans., *The Panarion of Epiphanius of Salamis, Book I,* NHS 35 (Leiden: E. J. Brill, 1987).

= Sebuaeans),[55] Dositheans (a known Samaritan group),[56] and Gorothenes (otherwise unknown). As for Simon, mentioned in Hegesippus's list, his Samaritan origins are beyond doubt.[57] Cleobius, not well known, could also have been a Samaritan.[58]

This is not the place for an extensive discussion of the groups listed by Hegesippus and others.[59] For our purposes, it is enough to remark that, in quoting this passage from Hegesippus, Eusebius has quite unwittingly provided us with ancient evidence for the theory, now widely held by modern historians of Gnosticism, that Gnosticism arose independently of Christianity out of a Jewish-Samaritan milieu.[60]

We turn now to the last occurrence in Eusebius's *History* of the term "falsely called Knowledge," found in his discussion of Manichaeism in book 7. The text reads as follows:

> At that time[61] also the madman,[62] named after his devil-possessed heresy, was taking as his armour mental delusion; for the devil, that is Satan himself, the adversary of God, had put the man forward for the destruction of many. His very speech and manners proclaimed him a barbarian in mode of

---

55. Both names derive from the same Aramaic root, ṣbʿ (Rudolph, "Antike Baptisten," 576–77). Further identification of these "Baptists" is impossible, for the term — which refers simply to a characteristic ritual — could cover any number of groups known by other names, such as the Mandaeans. On baptismal rituals among the "Sethian" Gnostic groups, and their possible connections with Jewish baptismal groups, see J.-M. Sevrin, *Le dossier baptismal séthien: Études sur la sacramentaire gnostique*, BCNH "Études" 2 (Québec: Université Laval, 1986).

56. See esp. S. J. Isser, *The Dositheans*, SJLA 17 (Leiden: E. J. Brill, 1976); and Fossum, *Name of God*, 45–75.

57. The pseudo-Clementine literature links Simon and Dositheus together with John the Baptist (*Homil.* 2.22–25).

58. Cleobius is mentioned, together with Simon, in *3 Corinthians* (*Acts of Paul* 8.1.2). In the *Apostolic Constitutions* (6.8.1), Cleobius and Simon appear together as pupils of Dositheus.

59. See esp. Fossum's discussion in *Name of God*.

60. Cf. my earlier discussion.

61. In the time of Felix, bishop of Rome 269–274 (cf. 7.30.23), i.e., during the reign of Aurelian (270–275).

62. Eusebius employs a pun on the name Mani that was virtually universal in the Greek-speaking world among the detractors of Manichaeism: Μάνης (the Greek form of the Persian name) = μανείς ("madman"). On this and other puns on Mani's name, see S. N. C. Lieu, *Manichaeism in the Late Roman Empire and Medieval China: A Historical Survey* (Manchester: Manchester University Press, 1985), 104. Mani and his disciples also used an alternative name: Μανιχαῖος, based on the Syriac *Mani ḥayya* ("living Mani"), whence the adjective "Manichaean." See A. Böhlig and J. P. Asmussen, *Die Gnosis*, vol. 3, *Der Manichäismus*, 2d ed. (Zurich: Artemis, 1995), 325 n. 116.

life, and, being by nature devilish and insane, he suited his endeavors thereto and attempted to pose as Christ: at one time giving out that he was the Paraclete and the Holy Spirit himself, conceited fool that he was, as well as mad; at another time choosing, as Christ did, twelve disciples as associates in his new-fangled system. In short, he stitched together false and godless doctrines that he had collected from the countless, long-extinct, godless heresies, and infected our empire with, as it were, a deadly poison that came from the land of the Persians; and from him the profane name of Manichaean is still commonly on men's lips to this day. Such, then, was the foundation on which rested this knowledge which is falsely so-called, which sprang up at the time we have mentioned. (*Hist. Eccl.* 7.31.1–2)

Eusebius's brief account of the religion of Mani (216–276 or 277)[63] is based on his own limited knowledge of Manichaeism, which was very much alive in his own day. The only written source that can be identified behind Eusebius's remarks is a rescript against the Manichaeans published by Emperor Diocletian, probably in 301, which ordered that the leaders of the sect be burned, together with their scriptures.[64] The rescript describes the Manichaeans as "monstrosities among the race of the Persians" who have "made their way into our empire." Diocletian fears that they will "infect the modest and tranquil Roman people . . . with the damnable customs and the perverse laws of the Persians as with the poison of a malignant serpent."[65] This language is recognizable in Eusebius's treatment of Mani and Manichaeism.

Eusebius places the rise of Manichaeism during the episcopacy of Felix (bishop of Rome 269–274),[66] which accords well with the

---

63. On Mani and his religion, see esp. G. Widengren, *Mani and Manichaeism* (New York: Holt, Rinehart and Winston, 1965); Lieu, *Manichaeism;* and Rudolph, *Gnosis,* 326–42. The best anthology of Manichaean texts and testimonia is Böhlig and Asmussen, *Gnosis,* vol. 3. See also H.-J. Klimkeit, ed. and trans., *Gnosis on the Silk Road: Gnostic Texts from Central Asia* (San Francisco: HarperSanFrancisco, 1993).

64. On this rescript, see Lieu, *Manichaeism,* 91–95; cf. R. M. Grant, "Manichees and Christians in the Third and Early Fourth Centuries," in *Ex Orbe Religionum: Studia Geo Widengren,* vol. 1, ed. J. Bergman et al., SHR 21 (Leiden: E. J. Brill, 1972), 430–39, esp. 434 (where the rescript is dated 297).

65. See the translation in Lieu, *Manichaeism,* 91–92.

66. See n. 61. In his *Chronicle* (ed. Helm, 223 [see n. 17]), Eusebius dates the rise of Manichaeism to the year 280.

information that Epiphanius gives for the arrival of Manichaean missionaries at Eleutheropolis in Palestine (273 or 274).[67] Manichaean mission activity in Caesarea would have taken place at around the same time. This was actually part of a second wave of Manichaean activity in the Mediterranean lands, for Manichaean missionaries had already been sent westward to Egypt by the prophet himself sometime after 244.[68] Manichaeism had gained considerable strength in Egypt by the beginning of the fourth century.[69]

Eusebius's account presupposes that Manichaeism is some sort of Christian heresy, rather than the completely new religion that it actually was. Eusebius obviously knew little or nothing of Mani's life, and he was therefore ignorant of the connection between Mani and the Jewish-Christian Elchasaite sect in which the prophet had been raised and from which he withdrew to found his own religion.[70] (Eusebius treats the Elchasaite heresy at *Hist. Eccl.* 6.38.)

Eusebius's description of Mani's syncretistic approach (stripped of the invective in which it is couched) is essentially correct, though he is not fully appreciative of the role that Christian features, such as "Paraclete" and "twelve disciples," play in that syncretism.[71] His intuitive association of Manichaeism with groups falling under his category of "falsely called Knowledge" is also on the mark. What Eusebius could not know is that Gnosticism, in the form of Manichaeism, would ultimately emerge as a "world religion,"[72]

67. *Panarion* 66.1.1–2. See Grant, "Manichees," 432; and Lieu, *Manichaeism,* 68.
68. See Lieu, *Manichaeism,* 75.
69. See, e.g., G. G. Stroumsa, "The Manichaean Challenge to Egyptian Christianity," in Pearson-Goehring, *Roots,* 307–19.
70. Mani's early life in an Elchasaite community is attested in the Cologne Mani Codex, a Greek miniature book of the fifth century, which contains a partial biography of Mani. For the critical edition, see A. Henrichs, L. Koenen, and C. Römer, eds., *Der Kölner Mani-Kodex: Über das Wesen seines Leibes,* Papyrologia Coloniensia 14 (Opladen: Westdeutscher Verlag, 1988). For an English translation of the first ninety-nine pages of the MS, see R. Cameron and A. J. Dewey, *The Cologne Mani Codex (P. Colon. inv. nr. 4780) "Concerning the Origin of His Body,"* SBLTT 15, Early Christian Literature Series 3 (Missoula, Mont.: Scholars Press, 1979).
71. For Mani as "Paraclete" and "Spirit of Truth," see, e.g., *Kephalaia* 1.9.14 (Böhlig and Asmussen, *Gnosis,* 3:84). On his twelve disciples, see, e.g., August., *Haer.* 46 (Böhlig and Asmussen, *Gnosis,* 142).
72. See K. Rudolph, "Gnosis — Weltreligion oder Sekte?" in *Gnosis: Aufsätze,* 53–65.

one that would persist in far-off China until the seventeenth century.[73]

Conclusions

In the foregoing discussion, we have seen that Eusebius's treatment of those ancient teachers and groups that modern scholarship more or less appropriately includes under the category of "Gnosticism" (Simon Magus, Menander, Saturninus, Basilides, Carpocrates,[74] Valentinians,[75] Cerdo and Marcionites,[76] and Manichaeans) is fortuitously associated in the text of his *History* with the use of the catchall term "falsely called Knowledge." With the use of this term, Eusebius is clearly following the lead of his antiheretical predecessors, most notably Irenaeus. But, unlike Irenaeus, Eusebius obviously has no inkling of what this term really entails or how it came to be used in early Christian writings, that is, as a polemical counter to a religious claim to special "Knowledge" (gnosis) put forward by religious opponents. Eusebius is ignorant of the role that gnosis plays in the belief systems of those he attacks under his polemical rubric. Thus, it is almost coincidental that his discussion of Gnostic "heretics" is marked at all by this special rubric. Many other "heretics" and "heresies" occur in the *History*, of course, besides the Gnostic ones.[77]

As we have seen, Eusebius tells us little or nothing of the substance of the Gnostic heresies he so vigorously attacks. If we had only Eusebius to work with as our source of information on the various Gnostic groups in antiquity, we would be at a total loss as to what to make of them. We would know virtually nothing of their mythological systems or their basic beliefs and practices. Eusebius had obviously never read a single piece of Gnostic literature. If the church library at Caesarea ever contained any Gnostic books (which is doubtful), Eusebius would have taken pains to

---

73. See Lieu, *Manichaeism,* 220–64. Cf. the Mandaeans, who survive to this day in Iran and Iraq (with emigrant communities in the West as well); see n. 6.

74. See n. 16.

75. As we have seen, Eusebius does not expressly include Valentinus under his rubric "falsely called Knowledge." But Valentinians are associated with other Gnostic groups in Hegesippus's list, cited by Eusebius (*Hist. Eccl.* 4.22.5).

76. The "Marcianists" of 4.22.5. See n. 48.

77. Some of these have already been mentioned. Others include Hermogenes (4.23.1), "Encratites" (4.28.1), Severus (4.29.4), Montanus and Montanism (5.16–19), Artemon et al. (5.28), "Docetae" (6.12.6), Novatus (6.43), Sabellius (7.6), and Paul of Samosata (7.26–28).

avoid reading them. In this respect, the contrast with heresiologists such as Irenaeus, Hippolytus, Tertullian, and others is noteworthy.

Thus, as a historical source for Gnosticism, Eusebius is almost totally worthless. I say "almost" because Eusebius does provide us with information, otherwise lacking, on two important writers of the early church: Agrippa Castor and Hegesippus, both of whom had written about Gnostic heretics.[78] In short, one can summarize Eusebius's treatment of Gnosticism with the observation that, for him, representatives of "falsely called Knowledge" were "heretics" to be despised by all lovers of the Truth. Eusebius's treatment of "heretics" is crystal clear: he didn't know them, but he knew that he didn't like them.

---

78. See earlier discussion.

Chapter 9

Unity and Diversity in the Early Church as a Social Phenomenon

The Christian religion, with some one billion adherents, is a bewilderingly diverse phenomenon, as everyone knows. Yet Christian diversity exists in tension with an expressed ideal of unity at the very heart of the Christian tradition, a belief professed in numerous communities the world over in the words of the Nicene Creed: "one holy and apostolic church." It is often assumed that the diversity now evident in the churches after almost two thousand years of history is a factor of historical development, and that one can push backward in time to find the actual unity that is now only professed as an ideal. Historians of early Christianity have come to know better.

In what follows, I shall attempt to explore in a broad sketch the tension between unity and diversity in the early church, with special attention to social factors. We look first at "unity" as a theological ideal in the early church, then at "diversity" as a reality in the early church; finally, we consider a specific example, namely, the early history of the Egyptian church.

Unity: A Theological Ideal

From its beginning, the early church held the notion of "unity" as an important theological ideal. That God's people should be a unity was self-evident among the small groups of Jews who believed in Jesus at the beginning of the Christian church's history. That can be seen in the earliest Christian literature, namely, the letters of Paul. For Paul, it is "in Christ" that the "many" are constituted as "one" (Gal 3:28);[1] and to be "in Christ" is to be part of God's *ekklesia,* the "assembly" of God (which in the English-speaking world is rendered as "church"), a term that, when used with the qualifier "of the Lord," was used in Greek-speaking Judaism to refer to the people of Israel as a whole (e.g., in Deut 23:2).[2]

Paul's usage of the term ἐκκλησία is varied — he can use it both in the singular and in the plural — but I think his use of the singular is primary. When he tells us that he "persecuted the church of God" (1 Cor 15:9; Gal 1:13; Phil 3:6) before his conversion, he means that he took action against certain believers in Jesus as representatives of the group as a whole. (These references also imply, by the way, that the use of the term ἐκκλησία was not Paul's innovation but was already a feature of pre-Pauline Christianity [the Hebrew equivalent would be *qahal,* perhaps used among the earliest Semitic-speaking believers].) So Paul can use the singular ἐκκλησία in addressing "the church of God that is in Corinth" (1 Cor 1:2), and can go on to speak of the various leadership functions that "God has appointed in the church" (12:28, meaning the church as a whole, not only the one in Corinth). To be sure, Paul can also speak of the "churches" in Asia (1 Cor 16:19) or even "all the churches" (Rom 16:16, where he is referring more specifically to the ones of his own foundation). Even so, such usage means only that Paul can use the term for the whole to refer to one or more of its parts.

Paul's use of the metaphor of the "body" to express the church's unity is an important feature of his ecclesiology:

> For as in one body we have many members, and not all the members have the same function, so we, who are many, are one body in Christ, and individually we are members one of another. (Rom 12:4–5)

> For just as the body is one and has many members, and all the members of the body, though many, are one body, so it is with Christ. For in the one Spirit we were all baptized into one body — Jews or Greeks, slaves or free — and we were all made to drink of one Spirit. (1 Cor 12:12–13)

It is clear that Paul understands the notion of "oneness" in social terms. For him, the Spirit's activity in the church affects indi-

---

1. All quotations from the New Testament are taken from the NRSV.
2. See the article ἐκκλησία, by K. L. Schmidt, in *TDNT,* 3:501–36.

viduals and groups in various ways in the various congregations of which the one church consists. The unity of this church has important social consequences: "There is no longer Jew or Greek, there is no longer slave or free, there is no longer male and female; for all of you are one in Christ Jesus" (Gal 3:28).

That the church's unity also has theological consequences is also self-evident for Paul and his followers. Paul's praise of his Philippian congregation for "striving side by side with one mind for the faith of the gospel" (Phil 1:27) implies a doctrinal unity, adherence to a single norm, or "rule" (κανών, Gal 6:16). This is made explicit in the way in which the "body" metaphor is used in the deutero-Pauline letter to the Ephesians: "There is one body and one Spirit, just as you were called to the one hope of your calling, one Lord, one faith, one baptism, one God and Father of all, who is above all and through all and in all" (Eph 4:4–6).

This notion of social and theological unity was certainly not unique to Paul and Pauline Christianity. Other teachers in the early church had the same ideal, namely, that God's elect are one in belief and practice. The Johannine literature provides other well-known examples (John 11:52; 17:20–23). Paul is nevertheless the most interesting case, in my judgment, not only because he is the author of the earliest extant Christian literature, but also and especially because he was a radical and innovative teacher, in comparison with the others we know of in the early church.

An important feature of Paul's activity and pursuit of church unity was his notion of his own apostolic authority. One can see from his letters that Paul was very well aware that there existed in the church at large other points of view and other groups with beliefs that were at odds with his own, beliefs that were even introduced into some of his founded communities. He warned his adherents that they must remain true to his gospel; otherwise they would be in spiritual danger (2 Cor 10–13; Gal). Yet Paul did all that he could to maintain his own and his congregations' place in the unity of the larger church. His last fateful visit to Jerusalem in connection with his collection project is a vivid example of this.

Paul's collection project is probably one of the most important aspects of his career as a Christian apostle.[3] It shows him as a master fund-raiser with considerable organizational skill. We first hear

---

3. See esp. D. Georgi, *Die Geschichte der Kollekte des Paulus für Jerusalem,* *ThF* 38 (Hamburg: Herbert Reich Evangelischer Verlag, 1965); and K. F. Nickle, *The Collection: A Study in Paul's Strategy,* SBT 48 (London: SCM Press, 1966).

about this in Galatians 2:10, in the context of Paul's autobiographical report of his second visit to Jerusalem after his conversion, a visit that coincided with the "apostolic council" meeting reported in Acts 15. Paul claims that his apostleship to the gentiles received recognition from the Jerusalem church's leadership, expressed with "the right hand of fellowship" (Gal 2:9), whereas the mission to the Jews was put under the direction of Peter (2:7). There was the added provision that Paul and his coworkers were to "remember the poor" (2:10), which I take to be a self-designation of the Jerusalem church (= Heb. 'ebionim; cf. the later "Ebionites"). The way in which this was carried out in Paul's congregations can be seen in 1 Corinthians 16:1–4, referring to collections of money "on the first day of every week," and to the selection of delegates to accompany Paul on his visit to Jerusalem with the money. More extensive directions are given as the project proceeds in the two letters that make up 2 Corinthians 8 and 9.[4] Paul's last extant word on that subject, or any other, is found in Romans 15, where he tells of his plans to visit Rome on his way to Spain after he has been to Jerusalem with the collection (vv. 23–29). Paul asks the recipients of his letter to pray for his safety in Jerusalem, "and that my ministry to Jerusalem may be acceptable to the saints" (v. 31). Such prayers as were offered went unanswered: Paul barely escaped with his life from Jerusalem (Acts 21:27–23:35), and did so only under guard as a Roman prisoner. As for the collection, one might infer from a critical reading of Acts 21 that Paul's collection was not accepted by the Jerusalem church, led by James.[5]

Whatever the success or failure of the project, what is of importance here is Paul's intent. For Paul, his project was an important symbol of the unity of the church at large, whether ethnic Jews or gentiles.[6] Despite his strained relationships with the church leadership in Jerusalem, the need for him to express his connectedness with believers in Jerusalem was paramount. And the important symbolic function served by the "mother church" in Jerusalem is part of the picture. This is expressed in his last extant words on the collection:

---

4. See H. D. Betz, 2 Corinthians 8 and 9: A Commentary on Two Administrative Letters of the Apostle Paul, Hermeneia Series (Philadelphia: Fortress Press, 1985).

5. This has been argued convincingly by G. Lüdemann, Opposition to Paul in Jewish Christianity, trans. M. E. Boring (Minneapolis: Fortress Press, 1989). That the collection was gladly received is argued by Nickle, Collection, 70.

6. Nickle, Collection, 111–29.

Macedonia and Achaia have been pleased to share their re-
sources [κοινωνίαν τινὰ ποιήσασθαι] with the poor among
the saints at Jerusalem. They were pleased to do this, and
indeed they owe it to them [ὀφειλέται εἰσὶν αὐτῶν]; for if
the Gentiles have come to share [ἐκοινώνησαν] in their spiritual blessings, they ought [ὀφείλουσιν] also to be of service
[λειτουργῆσαι] to them in material things. (Rom 15:26–27)

This careful use of language on the part of Paul makes it clear
that believing gentiles are, in his view, "debtors" to the saints in
Jerusalem, certainly not because the Jerusalem people were instru-
ments in their conversion to the Christian gospel — that they owe
to Paul — but because the gospel and the church at large have their
origins in Jerusalem and its congregation. Jerusalem is a "sacred
center" not only to Jews (as the locus of the Temple) but even
to Paul, and, by extension, to his gentile converts. It is a divine
obligation laid upon the gentile converts of the messianic era to
bring their material treasures (Isa 60:5) as "liturgies" to the sacred
center, where the messianic era itself began.[7]

Moving on, we turn now to the beginning of the second century,
and Ignatius of Antioch. In his letters, the bishop of Antioch takes
up the Pauline notion of the church as the "body" of Christ, and
its function as an expression of the church's essential unity. I cite
two examples from his writings:

> ...truly nailed for us in the flesh under Pontius Pilate and
> Herod the tetrarch...that he might raise an ensign to the
> ages through his resurrection to his saints and believers
> whether among the Jews or among the Gentiles in the one
> body of his church. (*Smyrn.* 1.2)

> ...[the cross] through which by his suffering he calls you
> who are his members. The head, then, cannot be born
> apart without the members since God offers union, which is
> himself. (*Trall.* 11.2)[8]

We have already noted that Paul's own apostolic authority plays
a large role in his interpretation of the ideal of church unity. For Ig-

---

7. On "liturgies" in the Greco-Roman world, see chapter 10 in this book. On
the eschatological symbolism of Paul's collection project, see Nickle, *Collection*,
129–42. On the symbolic importance of Jerusalem in early Christianity, see R. L.
Wilken, *The Land Called Holy: Palestine in Christian History and Thought* (New
Haven: Yale University Press, 1992), 46–64.

8. The translations used here are those of W. R. Schoedel, *Ignatius of Antioch*,
Hermeneia Series (Philadelphia: Fortress Press, 1985).

natius, it is the bishop's role in the church's activity that is central. The church's unity requires unity with the bishop:

> Consequently it is right for you to run together with the purpose of the bishop, which you indeed do; for your worthily reputed presbytery, worthy of God, is attuned to the bishop like strings to a cithara; therefore, in your concord and harmonious love, Jesus Christ is sung. And may each of you remain joined in chorus, that being harmonious in concord, receiving God's variation in unity, you may sing with one voice through Jesus Christ to the Father, that he may both hear you and recognize you through what you do well, as members of his Son. It is profitable, then, for you to be in blameless unity that you may always participate also in God. (*Eph.* 4.1–2)

For Ignatius, unity as a theological ideal is tied to the bishop's authority, that is to say, to the office of bishop as such. Ignatius's own struggle against false teachers in the church, his struggle for the one and only Christian faith, is also tied to his role as bishop. According to him, where the bishop is there is also the universal church:

> You must all follow the bishop as Jesus Christ [followed] the Father, and [follow] the presbytery as the apostles; respect the deacons as the commandment of God. Let no one do anything apart from the bishop that has to do with the church. Let that be regarded as a valid eucharist which is held under the bishop or to whomever he entrusts it. Wherever the bishop appears, there let the congregation be; just as wherever Jesus Christ is, there is the whole church [καθολικὴ ἐκκλησία].[9] (*Smyrn.* 8.1–2)

Toward the end of the second century, Irenaeus of Lyons played an important role in the development of the Christian ideal of church unity. According to Irenaeus, the church's faith is one and the same over the whole world. The church has received from the apostles and their disciples its faith in God, Christ, and the Holy Spirit (*Haer.* 1.10.1). This faith the church has preserved as though all its members lived in one house (*Haer.* 1.10.2). To be sure, there are "heretics," but they are guilty of blasphemy against God and

---

9. This is the first occurrence in Christian literature of the term "catholic (i.e., universal) church."

do not belong at all to the church. The *true* church has one and the same faith throughout the world (*Haer.* 1.10.3).

Now, of course, come the important questions: How does one know that the church's faith is genuine or true? How can one distinguish between the true faith and the false? Who is it who decides? Irenaeus's answer to these questions is quite simple. He points to the tradition that the church has received from the apostles, and especially to the bishops, whom the apostles supposedly appointed for the preservation of the faith and genuineness of the church. That is to say, it is the office of the bishop that is the church's guarantee as to its faith and its genuineness.

Irenaeus claims that he can count up the bishops in the various churches, from the first ones appointed by the apostles right up to his own time (ca. 180). He does not do that; instead, he points at the Roman church, founded by Peter and Paul (*sic! Haer.* 3.3.2), which is the foremost of all. According to Irenaeus, all congregations must stand in harmony with that church. Irenaeus then presents a list of the bishops of Rome, from Linus to Eleutheros (*Haer.* 3.3.3). He goes on to insist that the "heretics" lack both bishops and the apostolic tradition. There were no "Valentinians" before Valentinus, no "Marcionites" before Marcion, and so on (*Haer.* 3.4.3).

Thus, according to Irenaeus, the true church is "one" wherever it is represented in the world. Its unity is grounded in the apostolic tradition that the office of bishop guarantees. That point of view remained dominant in the Christian religion almost everywhere up until the Protestant Reformation.

Diversity: A Reality from the Beginning

We have already noted the church fathers' view of the matter: there is no real diversity in the church. The (true) church has the same faith everywhere and at all times, a faith received from the apostles. "Heresy" is something that has developed in the period since the apostles. For Irenaeus, there are certain apostles who stand out in the tradition, apostles whose traditions are preserved in the church's writings, especially the four Gospels. These are Matthew, "among the Hebrews"; Peter, the authority behind the Gospel of Mark, Peter's "interpreter"; Paul, represented by the Gospel of Luke; and John (*Haer.* 3.1.1–2). Irenaeus thus provides evidence of a developing "New Testament" that preserves the Lord's sayings and the one apostolic faith. In this connection, I might mention that the heretic Marcion's "Gospel" and "Apostle" (Paul) must have played a role in the development of Irenaeus's list, and, for that matter, in the history of the New Testament canon in general.[10] However that may be, we have in Irenaeus the beginning of what eventually comes to be the church's "New Testament": the four Gospels (not more or less than four; *Haer.* 3.11), Paul's letters, and Luke's Acts of the Apostles.

But what is the reality that stands behind Irenaeus's list? New Testament scholars do not generally see much unity in the New Testament itself. Diversity is more to the point.[11] Of the four Gospels named by Irenaeus, each one has its own theology, its own way of presenting and interpreting Jesus' sayings, actions, and person. Paul, among the apostles, has a very radical stance vis-à-vis the Jewish Law and its role in the history of salvation. Paul sets himself against Peter (Gal 2:11), against "the Lord's brother" James (Gal 2:12; cf. 1:19), and against other Christian teachers. It is also clear, as a result of critical scholarly analysis, that all four Gospels are anonymous and do not at all go back to the "apostles" named by Irenaeus: Matthew, Peter (Gospel of Mark), Paul (Gospel of Luke), and John. One can note, instead, that each Gospel functions from the beginning as representative of a particular group's understanding of, and attitude toward, Jesus and the Jesus tradition. In the development of each tradition, a certain "apostolic" figure functions as the symbolic authority for the group. The matter becomes all the more complicated when we see that it is not possible to identify a single tradition that is tied to any particular apostolic figure. For example, Paul has his own "profile" in his authentic letters, but in the "deutero-Pauline" letters we see other profiles. The "Paul" of Colossians is not the same as the "Paul" of the "Pastoral" letters or of the Acts of the Apostles.

In modern scholarship, one often uses nowadays the term "trajectories" in connection with the development of various traditions and tradition complexes in early Christianity.[12] Paulinism, for example, develops in different trajectories that lead to heretics like Marcion, or Valentinus and other Gnostics; it also develops in an "orthodox" trajectory that leads to Irenaeus. And when we think

---

10. See H. von Campenhausen, *The Formation of the Christian Bible,* trans. J. A. Baker (Philadelphia: Fortress Press, 1972), 148–67.

11. See J. D. G. Dunn, *Unity and Diversity in the New Testament: An Inquiry into the Character of Earliest Christianity,* 2d ed. (London: SCM; Philadelphia: Trinity Press International, 1990).

12. See Robinson-Koester, *Trajectories.*

of Paulinism, we must not overlook the "anti-Paulinism" among the "Ebionites" and other Jewish-Christian groups (as expressed in the pseudo-Clementine writings, etc.).[13] In the case of the other apostolic figures, the matter is pretty much the same. John functions as an authority for Gnostics (as with *Ap. John,* etc.) and other heretics, but he is interpreted as "orthodox" by other groups and individuals, such as Irenaeus. Such is the case, too, with Peter, Judas Thomas, and even Jesus' brother James.[14]

We are thus driven to the conclusion that religious diversity was typical in the church from its very beginning. This diversity is clearly evident in the New Testament itself and in other early Christian writings. How, then, can one talk at all about an "orthodox" faith or a "heretical" belief?

Here we must bring in an important figure in contemporary scholarship: Walter Bauer. He wrote his famous *Rechtgläubigkeit und Ketzerei im ältesten Christentum* in the 1930s, but this work has become prominent as a result of its translation into English.[15] In it, Bauer subjected to critical analysis a key notion found in Irenaeus and the other church fathers regarding "orthodoxy" and "heresy," namely, that "heresy" is always a later development in the church, brought about as a result of the devil's activity.[16] Bauer noted that this idea is historically without foundation, and argued that in fact the opposite was often the case, namely, that "heresy" preceded "orthodoxy." He analyzed the available source material for the church's history in various geographical areas, from the beginning until the end of the second century and later, and discovered that in certain areas, that which was later called "heresy" was the earliest and strongest form of the Christian faith. Orthodoxy, which eventually prevailed over these earlier traditions, came as a result of the influence of the Roman church and its involvement in the affairs of churches elsewhere. The geographical areas investigated by Bauer were Edessa and Mesopotamia, Egypt, western Syria (Antioch), Asia Minor, Greece, and Rome.

Since Bauer's work appeared, other scholars have taken up these

---

13. See Lüdemann, *Opposition to Paul.*
14. Peter as a Gnostic: *Apoc. Pet.* (NHC VII,3) (see chapter 5 in this book); as "orthodox": 1–2 Peter in the NT; as a Jewish Christian: pseudo-Clementines. Judas Thomas as ascetic or "Gnostic": *Gos. Thom.* (NHC II,2), *Book of Thomas* (NHC II,7); as "orthodox": Epistle of Jude in the NT. James as a Jewish Christian: pseudo-Clementines; as a Gnostic: *1 Apoc. Jas.* (NHC V,3), *2 Apoc. Jas.* (NHC V,4); as "orthodox": Epistle of James in the NT. Other examples could easily be provided.
15. See Bauer, *Orthodoxy and Heresy.*
16. See our discussion of Eusebius in chapter 8.

issues for further discussion. Bauer's thesis has been accepted in
many quarters, although criticized in some.[17] One of the most
prominent of these scholars, Helmut Koester, accepts much of
Bauer's thesis but has come up with some important new results,
especially in the case of Edessa and Osroëne, with his examination
of the Judas Thomas tradition.[18]

Early Christian Diversity in Egypt

In the case of Egypt, by which is meant mainly Alexandria for
the earliest period, Bauer's thesis seems convincing to most critical
scholars. Egypt poses a big problem for church historians, because
adequate sources are lacking for the earliest history of the Egyptian
church. Bauer begins his discussion of Egypt with this observation:
sources must have existed. Why have they not been preserved? Answer: because the earliest Christians in Alexandria were heretics
("Gnostics"). Bauer refers to the names of the people who seem to
represent the earliest forms of Christianity in Egypt: Basilides and
his son Isidore, Carpocrates, Valentinus — all heretics, all Gnostics.
Bauer regards as historically groundless the legend of the Alexandrian church's founding by the evangelist Mark; the earliest witness
to this legend is Eusebius (fourth century). And the names of the
bishops in Alexandria who are reported by Eusebius to have succeeded Mark (*Hist. Eccl.* 2.16) are ciphers, "a mere echo and a puff
of smoke."[19] It is not until the time of the Alexandrian bishop Demetrius (189–232) that the orthodox form of Christianity began
to take hold.

The British papyrologist Colin Roberts has a completely different view of the matter, which he presents in his book *Manuscript,
Society, and Belief in Early Christian Egypt.*[20] Roberts bases his
work on the earliest Christian literary papyri and comes up with a
reconstruction of the earliest forms of Christianity in Egypt completely different from that of Bauer. To be sure, manuscripts are
lacking from the first century, but from the second there are some
extant: ten "biblical," six of (parts of) the Old Testament, four of

---

17. On Bauer's analysis of early Christianity in Asia Minor, see T. A. Robinson, *The Bauer Thesis Examined: The Geography of Heresy in the Early Church*
(Lewiston, N.Y.: Mellen, 1988).
18. H. Koester, "*Gnomai Diaphoroi:* The Origin and Nature of Diversification
in the History of Early Christianity," in Robinson-Koester, *Trajectories,* 114–57.
19. Bauer, *Orthodoxy and Heresy,* 45.
20. C. Roberts, *Manuscript, Society, and Belief in Early Christian Egypt* (London: Oxford University Press, 1979).

the New Testament (Matthew, Luke, John, Titus). The four extra-biblical manuscripts are the Egerton fragments, *Hermas,* P.Ox. 1 (= *Gos. Thom.*), and a fragment of Irenaeus's treatise *Adversus Haereses.* All are codices except for *Hermas* and Irenaeus. Roberts remarks that not a single "Gnostic" manuscript has been found from that period (unless *Gos. Thom.* be counted as "Gnostic"). There is therefore no indication at all from this evidence that Gnosticism was the earliest form of Christianity in Egypt.

Roberts presents some strong arguments that the use of the so-called *nomina sacra* in early manuscripts (abbreviations of "sacred names" marked with a supralinear stroke) was a Christian innovation. He argues similarly for the replacement of the roll by the codex. Of the (fifteen or so) *nomina sacra* that were used in early Christian manuscripts, not a single one is Gnostic.[21] Roberts thinks the earliest Christians in Alexandria emigrated there from Jerusalem; the church in Alexandria would have existed as part of the Jewish community there.

Who is right, Bauer or Roberts? I have taken up this issue in a number of my own studies,[22] and I tend to think that Roberts's reconstruction is more plausible, even if some further nuances are required. Indeed, his basic position can be bolstered with reference to the literary sources we have from early Christian Egypt, both non-Gnostic and Gnostic.

If we take a look at the early noncanonical gospels presumably composed in Egypt, we have at least the *Gospel of the Hebrews* and the *Gospel of the Egyptians,* as well as perhaps the Egerton fragments and the *Secret Gospel of Mark.*[23] Bauer tried to label the first two "Gnostic," but the fragments we have do not contain anything particularly "Gnostic." The *Gospel of the Hebrews*[24] contains Semitic (i.e., Jewish Christian) Christian traditions and

---

21. The most common *nomina sacra* are I̅C̅ (*Iesous*), X̅C̅ (*Christos*), K̅C̅ (*kyrios*, "Lord"), and Θ̅C̅ (*theos,* "God").

22. See my "Earliest Christianity in Egypt: Some Observations," in Pearson-Goehring, *Roots,* 132–59; "Christians and Jews in First-Century Alexandria," in *Christians among Jews and Gentiles: Essays in Honor of Krister Stendahl,* ed. G. W. E. Nickelsburg and G. MacRae (Philadelphia: Fortress Press, 1986; = *HTR* 79 [1984 (1986)]); "Gnosticism in Early Egyptian Christianity," chap. 13 in Pearson, *Gnosticism* (194–213); "Pre-Valentinian Gnosticism in Alexandria," in Pearson, *Future,* 455–66; and "Christianity in Egypt," *ABD,* 1:954–60.

23. For translations, see R. Cameron, *The Other Gospels: Non-Canonical Gospel Texts* (Philadelphia: Westminster, 1982), 83–86, 49–52, 72–75, and 67–71; also *NTApoc,* 1:172–78, 209–15; 96–99; 106–9.

24. Frag. 1 (from Pseudo-Cyril of Jerusalem) certainly does not belong to this gospel, as has been conclusively demonstrated by R. van den Broek, "Der Bericht

seems to reflect an early Christian group that held Jesus' brother James in high regard. The *Gospel of the Egyptians* also probably has a Jewish Christian background and is marked by a strongly ascetic tendency. Both gospels have material that is shared with the *Gospel of Thomas*. The Egerton gospel may have been brought into Egypt from elsewhere (Syria?), but perhaps was composed in Egypt. In any case, there is no trace of anything "Gnostic" in the fragments that we have. The same can be said of the *Secret Gospel of Mark*, which was unknown to Bauer. Assuming that the *Letter to Theodore* is an authentic writing of Clement, the *Secret Gospel of Mark* quoted in the letter belongs in a liturgical context in the Alexandrian church.[25]

The *Epistle of Barnabas*[26] is a writing that Bauer also attempted to label "Gnostic." In this case, since we have the entire text at our disposal, we can easily see that Bauer's position can hardly be sustained. *Barnabas* reflects a Christian group, presumably resident in Alexandria, that is stamped by apocalyptic fervor, a group that also interpreted the Old Testament in a particular way. Another Alexandrian writing that can be mentioned here is the *Kerygma Petri*, an apologetic writing that we have only in fragments quoted by Clement of Alexandria.[27]

All of these writings belong to the first quarter of the second century (*Gos. Heb.* possibly earlier), that is to say, in a period before the great arch-heretics named by Bauer were active. These writings, in fact, show that Christianity in Egypt comprised *several* different groups, each with its own set of Christian traditions. It may be only a coincidence that we do not know the names of the persons who functioned as leaders of these various groups. We can also surmise that the gospels and epistles that eventually came to be canonical were also used by at least some of these groups. This can be concluded on the basis of Roberts's discussion of the early Christian literary manuscripts. To be sure, Gnostics were no doubt also present in Egypt (Alexandria) from an early time, even if we do not have early evidence for them. Here we must underscore an important point: Bauer's only proof for an early Gnosticism in

des koptischen Kyrillos von Jerusalem über das Hebräerevangelium," in van den Broek, *Studies*, 142–56.

25. See M. Smith, *Clement of Alexandria and a Secret Gospel of Mark* (Cambridge: Harvard University Press, 1973); cf. H. Merkel's discussion in *NTApoc*, 1:106–9.

26. For a good English translation, with commentary, see R. H. Kraft, *Barnabas and the Didache*, Apostolic Fathers 4 (New York: Thomas Nelson & Sons, 1965).

27. See *NTApoc*, 2:34–41.

Egypt consists of the heresiological reports concerning Basilides, Carpocrates, and Valentinus; but these three were active in the time of Hadrian (117–138) or later.

Let us take a brief look at the fragments or testimonies that we have for these arch-heretics. What do we find?

First, Valentinus: Irenaeus reports that Valentinus adapted a "Gnostic" doctrine to a new system, one of his own (*Haer.* 1.11.1). In looking at the relevant sources, we can conclude that Valentinus took an early Gnostic myth (something like that of *Ap. John*) and "Christianized" it. In addition, Valentinus used in his own writings precisely those Christian texts that would eventually become canonical, especially Matthew and the Pauline epistles. This can be seen from a study of the fragments that we have from Valentinus's homilies, letters, and hymns.[28]

One can draw similar conclusions regarding the other two figures, Basilides and Carpocrates. We can see from Basilides's fragments[29] that he used Matthew and Mark, as well as Paul's epistles. As for Carpocrates, we have nothing left of his own writings, but according to Irenaeus's testimony (*Haer.* 1.25), he used Matthew, Mark, and some of Paul's epistles.

So where did these "heretics" get these Christian (New Testament) texts? The answer seems quite clear: from one or another non-Gnostic Christian congregation.

Such a conclusion can be supported even by the testimony of the "heretics" themselves. The Valentinians, for example, claim that they (i.e., those who are in possession of gnosis) are the "spiritual" Christians, whereas ordinary non-Gnostic Christians are only "psychics." The "spiritual" ones constitute a smaller elite group within the larger Christian community. There is even scriptural proof for this state of affairs in Jesus' own words: "Many are 'the called' [= the psychics] but few are 'chosen' [= the spirituals]" (Matt 22:14).[30] We see here clear evidence that the Gnostics looked upon themselves as a distinct minority among other Christians; the non-Gnostics were conceded to constitute the majority.

Thus, we have found proof from the Gnostic sources themselves that Bauer's thesis is largely wrong. The Gnostics were not the first Christians in Egypt, nor were they ever in a majority. The real situation was much more complicated than that.

---

28. For the fragments, see Layton, *Gnostic Scriptures*, 229–49.
29. In ibid., 417–44.
30. Quoted in Clem. Al., *Exc. Theod.* 58.1; cf. 56.2.

But Bauer's thesis is not completely wrong; there is some truth to his assertions. The great arch-heretics, Valentinus, Basilides, and Carpocrates, especially the first two, played a large role among Christian intellectuals in Alexandria. Both Valentinus and Basilides were educated in Greek philosophy, Valentinus primarily in Platonism and Basilides in Stoicism.[31] Greek philosophy occupied a prominent place in their theological writings. One can surmise that, at least from the early second century, there were schools in Alexandria where people could study various kinds of literature, including Christian literature. Indeed, it was among the Alexandrian Gnostics that the very first New Testament commentaries were produced (i.e., commentaries on texts that would eventually become part of the New Testament canon).

We do know of one famous Christian school in Alexandria, the so-called catechetical school, headed at one point by Clement of Alexandria. Concerning this school's earliest history we know nothing, though Clement's teacher Pantaenus is named in some sources as Clement's predecessor and a prominent leader of the school.[32] (Pantaenus was active during the time of Commodus, 180–192). Yet Pantaenus was not the school's founder. Who was? I would suggest that Pantaenus was the school's first "orthodox" leader (to use an anachronistic term), who probably brought the school into closer relationship with the Alexandrian bishop. It is quite possible that before Pantaenus, the school was headed by Gnostic teachers such as Isidore and, before him, Basilides. (Valentinus left Alexandria in mid-career and became active in Rome.)

There is yet another point at which Bauer's thesis can be sustained, namely, the important role played by Bishop Demetrius in the development of Christian "orthodoxy" in Alexandria. Demetrius probably gradually exercised more and more authority over the "catechetical school" and its faculty. About the bishops

---

31. For a recent full-scale study of the fragments of Valentinus, see C. Markschies, *Valentinus Gnosticus? Untersuchungen zur valentinianischen Gnosis mit einem Kommentar zu den Fragmenten Valentins,* SUNT 65 (Tübingen: Mohr-Siebeck, 1992). I do not agree with his arguments that Valentinus was not really a "Gnostic." For a recent full-scale study of the fragments of Basilides, see W. A. Löhr, *Basilides und seine Schule: Eine Studie zur Theologie- und Kirchengeschichte des zweiten Jahrhunderts,* WUNT 83 (Tübingen: Mohr-Siebeck, 1996).

32. See Eus., *Hist. Eccl.* 5.10–11. On the intellectual life of Alexandrian Christians, see R. M. Grant, "Theological Education at Alexandria," in Pearson-Goehring, *Roots,* 178–89. See also R. van den Broek, "The Christian 'School' of Alexandria in the Second and Third Centuries," in van den Broek, *Studies,* 197–205; A. van den Hoek, "The 'Catechetical' School of Early Christian Alexandria and Its Philonic Heritage," *HTR* 90 (1997), 59–87.

who preceded Demetrius we know, unfortunately, little or nothing, apart from the names given in the traditional bishop list. Whatever church leaders there were in Alexandria obviously did not make much of a mark on that church's early history.

Thus, we can conclude that in the time before Demetrius, diversity in doctrine and practice was the hallmark of Alexandrian Christianity. It would remain so, of course, for some time to come. But with Bishop Demetrius the ecclesiastical struggle for Christian unity began in earnest. This struggle affected even such an "unorthodox" teacher as Clement,[33] who eventually found himself involved in the struggle against diversity and "heresy" in the church, probably under pressure from the bishop. Here are Clement's own statements on the matter:

> We ought in no way to transgress the rule of the Church. Above all the confession which deals with the essential articles of faith is observed by us, but disregarded by the heretics. Those, then, are to be believed who hold firmly to the truth. (*Strom.* 7.15.90)

> The one Church, which they strive to break up into many sects, is bound up with the principle of Unity. We say, then, that the ancient and Catholic Church stands alone in essence and idea and principle and pre-eminence, gathering together, by the will of one God through the one Lord, into the unity of the one faith. (*Strom.* 7.17.107)[34]

The influence of Irenaeus can be detected in these statements, and we recall that the earliest fragments of Irenaeus's *Adversus Haereses* were found in Egypt and date to the time of Demetrius. In any case, it is clear that Clement took Demetrius's side in the struggle for the church's unity against all forms of heresy and schism.[35]

As to the other side of the struggle, we did not know very much until the discovery of the Nag Hammadi codices. But now we can gain some insights into that other side of the debate by reading the "heretics' " own writings. Two of these can be singled out

---

33. See esp. S. R. C. Lilla, *Clement of Alexandria: A Study in Christian Platonism and Gnosticism* (Oxford: Oxford University Press, 1971).

34. H. Chadwick, trans., *Alexandrian Christianity*, LCC (Philadelphia: Westminster, 1954).

35. For additional discussion of Clement, in another context, see chapter 10 of this book.

here: NHC XI,*3: The Testimony of Truth,* and NHC VII,*3: Apocalypse of Peter.*[36] Both are Gnostic texts. *The Testimony of Truth* is an "antiheretical" tract directed mainly against what can clearly be identified as ecclesiastical "orthodoxy."[37] The author takes his stand against water baptism, martyrdom, the doctrine of resurrection, and marriage and procreation. The *Apocalypse of Peter* contains a "docetic" christology and stringent warnings against opponents who can clearly be identified as "orthodox" Christians, people who use ecclesiastical titles such as "bishop" and "deacon" and claim spiritual authority for themselves (VII 79,21–27).[38] The Gnostic teachers who composed these tractates struggled hard for their convictions, but in the long run their struggle was in vain.

Gnosticism and other forms of heresy did, of course, persist in Egypt for a long time to come, being joined in the third century by Manichaeism.[39] The town of Lycopolis in Upper Egypt evidently became a center for varieties of Gnosticism and of Manichaeism as well. This is reflected in the Lycopolitan dialect of Coptic that is used in a number of the Nag Hammadi tractates and in the Manichaean Coptic manuscripts.[40] In the early fourth century, the monastic movement was expanding vigorously, both in Upper Egypt and in Lower Egypt outside Alexandria.[41] The Nag Hammadi codices, and the cartonnage found in their leather bindings, provide evidence that Gnostic books were being read and copied in the monasteries, in this case in those of the Pachomian *koinonia.*[42] There was, of course, a strong ascetic strain in Gnosticism,[43] and

---

36. *Testim. Truth* is found in Pearson, *Codices IX and X,* 101–203. *Apoc. Pet.* is in Pearson, *Codex VII,* 201–47. For excellent analyses of these two tractates, especially their antiecclesiastical polemic, see Koschorke, *Polemik der Gnostiker.*

37. See my essay "Anti-Heretical Warnings in Codex IX from Nag Hammadi," chap. 12 in Pearson, *Gnosticism.*

38. See chapter 5 in this book.

39. See, e.g., G. G. Stroumsa, "The Manichaean Challenge to Egyptian Christianity," in Pearson-Goehring, *Roots,* 307–19.

40. See B. Layton, "Coptic Language," in *IDBSup,* 174–79, esp. 176 ("Subachmimic"); and P. Nagel, "Lycopolitan (or Lyco-Diospolitan, or Subakhmimic)," in *The Coptic Encyclopedia* (New York: Macmillan, 1991), 8:151–59.

41. See J. E. Goehring, "The Origins of Monasticism," in *Eusebius, Christianity, and Judaism,* ed. H. W. Attridge and G. Hata (Detroit: Wayne State University Press, 1992), 235–55.

42. See F. Wisse, "Gnosticism and Early Monasticism in Egypt," in Aland, *Gnosis,* 431–40; A. Veilleux, "Monasticism and Gnosis in Egypt," in Pearson-Goehring, *Roots,* 271–306; and B. Pearson, "Nag Hammadi Codices," in *ABD,* 4:984–93.

43. Epiphanius of Salamis, however, claims to have encountered, in his youthful sojourn in Egypt (sometime between 330 and 340), Gnostic groups given to sexual license and other abominations. Women members of one such group, "lovely to look at," tried to seduce the young man, but he managed to escape their clutches.

that is probably the main reason that Gnostic literature could be read with appreciation by the desert ascetics in the monasteries.

The growth of monasticism in Egypt eventually resulted in rivalries between monks and bishops, with the ascetic monks suspicious of the more "worldly" bishops and other clergy in the town and village churches. Monasteries also vied with local churches for monetary support, thus increasing the tension. It was Athanasius (ca. 296–373), bishop of Alexandria, who, by incorporating into his own pastoral program much of the ascetic idealism of the monks, succeeded eventually in rallying the monasteries to his cause, thus creating a unified church in Egypt,[44] at least until the Council of Chalcedon (451) and its aftermath. By that time the Alexandrian bishop was engaged in a bitter controversy with the bishops of the other main sees, Rome, Constantinople, and Antioch, involving arguments over theological minutiae. The effects of that controversy linger into our own time.[45]

Conclusions

Unity and diversity: We have seen that religious diversity was characteristic of the church from the beginning, at the same time that unity functioned as a theological ideal. As we have also seen, the theological ideal could become a concrete reality in the church (more or less) only through the development of the office of the bishop in the church, with its attendant hierarchical sociopolitical structure. As a result of this structure, bishops and church leaders under their authority could decide what doctrines and practices would be "orthodox" and what would constitute "heresy." After Constantine, bishops could also call upon governmental authority to enforce their decisions. Thus, we can see that in religious settings, as in others, it is political power that creates history's winners.

Epiphanius goes on to report that he "lost no time reporting them to the bishops there, and finding out which ones were hidden in the church. [Thus] they were expelled from the city, about eighty persons, and the city was cleared of their tare-like, thorny growth." *Panarion* 26.17.9 (trans. F. Williams, *The Panarion of Epiphanius of Salamis, Book I (Sects 1–46)*, NHS 35 [Leiden: E. J. Brill, 1987]). Epiphanius does not say what city in Egypt he is referring to, but "the city" probably refers to Alexandria.

44. See D. Brakke's excellent monograph *Athanasius and the Politics of Asceticism*, Oxford Early Christian Studies (Oxford: Clarendon, 1995).

45. For a good survey of the entire history of Egyptian Christianity, especially useful for the periods after Chalcedon, see T. H. Partrick, *Traditional Egyptian Christianity: A History of the Coptic Orthodox Church* (Greensboro, N.C.: Fisher Park Press, 1996).

Chapter 10

Philanthropy
in the Greco-Roman World
and in Early Christianity

When Julian "the Apostate" became emperor in 360 C.E., he embarked on an ambitious program to reestablish the old "pagan" religion at the expense of the Christian religion, which had gained a firm foothold in the empire since the time of his uncle, Constantine. A major part of this effort involved the inculcation of a policy of "philanthropy" among the pagan priests, involving the establishment of charitable institutions to be run by the pagan temples and priesthoods. Despite his hatred of the "atheistic" religion of the "Galileans" (i.e., the Christians), he used the Christian practice of "philanthropy" as a model to be emulated by those who were charged with carrying out his new policy. In a letter to Arsecius, high priest of the province of Galatia, Julian wrote:

> Why do we not observe that it is their [the Christians'] benevolence [φιλανθρωπία] to strangers, their care for the graves of the dead and the pretended holiness of their lives that have done the most to increase atheism [i.e., Christianity]? ... In every city establish frequent hostels in order that strangers may profit from our benevolence [φιλανθρωπίας]; I do not mean for our own people only but for others also who are in need of money. (*Ep.* 22.429D–430C)[1]

In this passage, and in many other of Julian's writings, he uses the term "philanthropy." The Greek noun *philanthropia,* with its cognate adjective *philanthropos,* has a long and varied history of usage. Although Julian uses this term to describe the benevolent

---

1. Wright's translation in the LCL ed.

practices of the Christians that he wishes to establish under pagan auspices, it is certainly not the case that the Christians invented the term. Indeed, the word *philanthropia* was originally used in pagan religious contexts as a term for the love of the gods directed to humankind. Later, of course, Christians used the term, as Jews had done before them. What I want to do in this essay is to explore some of the relevant examples of how the term *philanthropia* and its cognates were used in pagan, Jewish, and Christian traditions, and to discuss some of the actual practices and social institutions that embodied *philanthropia*. As we explore the early Christian examples, we shall also come to see just how important the practice of Christian charity (*philanthropia*) was in the spread and eventual triumph of the Christian religion in the Roman Empire.

We begin at the beginning, with the world of the ancient Greeks.

Philanthropy in Greco-Roman Paganism

The earliest uses of the adjective *philanthropos* are found in Athenian drama, both tragedy and comedy, of the fifth century B.C.E. Aeschylus opens his famous tragedy *Prometheus Bound* with a speech put into the mouth of "Power" (Kratos) describing the Titan god Prometheus's fate and the reasons for it. Prometheus has been bound by Zeus to a rock for bestowing the gift of fire to mortals: "Such is his offense, wherefore he is bound to make requital to the gods, that so he may be lessoned to brook the sovereignty of Zeus and forbear his championship of men [φιλανθρώπου δὲ παύεσθαι τρόπου]" (lines 8–11).[2] Later, Hephaestus addresses Prometheus, telling him that this is what he gets as a reward for his "championship of men" (τοῦ φιλανθρώπου τρόπου, 1.28), more literally translated as "philanthropic manner."

A near-contemporary example of the use of *philanthropos* is provided by the comic poet Aristophanes in his *Peace*, produced during the Peloponnesian War in 421 B.C.E. The chorus addresses the god Hermes, "O most man-loving and most generous of the deities" (ὦ φιλανθρωπότατε καὶ μεγαλοδωρότατε δαιμόνων; 393–94).[3] This same Aristophanes is featured as one of the dinner companions in Plato's great dialogue the *Symposium*. In his speech Aristophanes refers to Eros (Love) as the "most man-loving of the gods" (θεῶν φιλανθρωπότατος; 189C; my translation).

---

2. Smyth's translation in the LCL ed.
3. My translation; B. Rogers (in the LCL ed.) translates loosely: "O God most gracious."

In book 4 of Plato's *Laws*, one of his last works (he died in 347 B.C.E.), Plato has an unnamed Athenian describe an earlier age of bliss for humankind, the age of Kronos (the father of Zeus in Greek mythology). Out of his great love for humanity, the god (ὁ θεὸς ἄρα ὡς φιλάνθρωπος; 4.713D) appointed daemons (semidivine beings) to rule over mankind rather than men, thus creating a state characterized by peace and justice. The idea of a "golden age" in the distant past was, of course, widespread in the ancient world.

From these examples, we can see that the Greeks, from the fifth and fourth centuries B.C.E. on, used the adjective *philanthropos* as an epithet of the gods, who were said to bestow gifts and other benefits upon humankind. The term could be used of individual gods or the gods in general, but gradually it came to be used in the superlative form and with the greatest frequency in relation to Asklepios, the god of healing and the patron of physicians. We shall return to the Asklepios cult presently.

Plato provides one of the first instances of the use of the noun *philanthropia* in one of his early dialogues, the *Euthyphro*,[4] in connection with the attitude of Socrates toward his fellow citizens. Socrates is quoted as saying to Euthyphro, "I fear that because of my love of men (ὑπὸ φιλανθρωπίας) they think that I not only pour myself out copiously to anyone and everyone without payment, but that I would even pay something myself, if anyone would listen to me" (3D).[5]

Socrates, of course, was an extraordinary man; and, in general, *philanthropia* was used at first only of extraordinary men, especially kings or emperors. Thus, Xenophon (d. ca. 357 B.C.E.), in his treatise on the education of Cyrus the Great of Persia, reports that "Cyrus was most handsome in person, most generous of heart [ψυχὴν δὲ φιλανθρωπότατος], most devoted to learning, and most ambitious, so that he endured all sorts of labour and faced all sorts of danger for the sake of praise" (*Cyr.* 1.2.1).[6] Isocrates, in his oration in praise of Evagoras, king of Cyprus (ca. 365 B.C.E.), says that this king "governed the city so reverently and humanely [θεοφιλῶς καὶ φιλανθρώπως] that visitors to the island did not so much envy

---

4. φιλανθρωπίη (Ionic form) is found in the *Precepts* ascribed to Hippocrates, but this work is probably a later compilation. The word is used in connection with advice to physicians to offer services for nothing to those unable to pay: "Where there is love of man [φιλανθρωπίη] there is also love of the art [φιλοτεχνίη]." *Praec.* 6; Jones's translation in the LCL ed.
    5. Fowler's translation in the LCL ed.
    6. Miller's translation in the LCL ed.

Evagoras his office as they did the citizens their government under him" (*Or.* 9.43).[7]

Another Athenian orator, the famous Demosthenes (d. 322 B.C.E.), used the terms *philanthropia* and *philanthropos* in a number of his speeches given in courts of law. In one example, against one Leptines, who had proposed a law in the Assembly abolishing special exemptions from "liturgies" (about which I will say more later) granted to benefactors of the state, Demosthenes includes in his summation that this is a case wherein "humanity [φιλανθρωπία] is arrayed against envy, justice against malice, and all that is good against all that is bane" (*Or.* 20.165).[8] In the other example that I shall cite here, Demosthenes, in defending his right to receive a golden crown for his benefactions to the state, applies the adjectives *philanthropos* and *philodoros* ("generous") to himself, on the grounds that he has given of his possessions for the public good (*Or.* 18.112).

The rhetorical usage of the term *philanthropia* influenced popular philosophical ethics, especially in the Stoicism of the empire. The lame Stoic preacher Epictetus cites as an ethical example the famous Cynic philosopher Diogenes, a true servant of Zeus who loved everyone and "was so gentle and kind-hearted (οὕτως ἥμερος ἦν καὶ φιλάνθρωπος) that he gladly took upon himself all those troubles and physical hardships for the sake of the common weal" (Arrian, *Epict. Diss.* 3.24.64).[9] In another sermon, Epictetus describes the attitude of the Cynic preachers, who are free from turmoil because they are not encumbered by material possessions: theirs is an attitude "both humane and noble" (καὶ φιλάνθρωπον καὶ γενναῖον; Arrian, *Epict. Diss.* 4.8.32), and it is actually the work of Zeus in them.

In these examples, we note that *philanthropia* is a human virtue, but the source of this virtue is God or the gods. This becomes a common theme in early imperial philosophy. Thus, Plutarch can say that God is "not only immortal and blessed but also humane and protective and beneficent" (φιλάνθρωπον καὶ κηδεμονικὸν καὶ ὠφέλιμον; *Com. not.* 32.1075E).[10] This usage, as we have seen, is consistent with the very earliest occurrences of the terms *philanthropia* and *philanthropos* in classical Greek.

---

7. Van Hook's translation in the LCL ed.
8. Vince's translation in the LCL ed.
9. Oldfather's translation in the LCL ed.
10. Cherniss's translation in the LCL ed.

However, there is another use of the root *philanthrop-* that needs to be mentioned here, the substantivized adjective, usually found in the neuter plural: τὰ φιλάνθρωπα (sg. τὸ φιλάνθρωπον). This term occurs mainly in documentary texts such as inscriptions and papyri from the third century B.C.E. on, and means something like "privileges," including privileges or concessions granted in return for monetary benefits offered to a city or state institution or to the operation of a private club or association.[11] It could also be used of the benefactions of people of means to these various institutions, or to persons of lower status. This usage reflects a very basic idea in ancient Greek society: reciprocity. Giving gifts was a two-way street, implying that donors would get something in return for their gifts, be it only the achievement of intangible "honor" or status in the eyes of the public, or something more tangible, such as a plaque or an inscribed stele recording the gift, or a dinner in the donor's honor. The gift itself would be called a *philanthropon*, and the honor or recognition bestowed in return likewise a *philanthropon*.[12] The motive, of course, was *philotimia* ("love of honor"), a term widely used in both inscriptions and literary works, and regarded as a positive virtue.

In the actual workings of a Greek city-state, the giving and receiving of *philanthropa* were voluntary in theory but often involuntary in practice, especially in the time of the empire. This brings up the institution of the "liturgy" (λειτουργία, lit. "work of/for the people"). This term is used for "public service" rendered by private citizens at their own expense. In classical Athens (fifth and fourth centuries B.C.E.), men of the wealthiest families were required to take turns, usually for a year at a time, in assuming the costs of one of many state functions. These liturgies paid the costs of religious temples and festivals, public works, ships for the navy, dramatic performances, and the like. This institution was a basic constituent of the administration of Greek cities (*poleis*) for many centuries, through the Hellenistic and imperial periods. Thus, what in our society would be funded either by government taxes or by voluntary donations would be funded by these "liturgies" virtually imposed on citizens of means.

In classical Athens, the benefit of honor and prestige that people got for their liturgies was usually thought to be adequate compen-

---

11. See citations in LSJ, p. 1932a.
12. See esp. A. R. Hands, *Charities and Social Aid in Greece and Rome* (Ithaca: Cornell University Press, 1968), 35–37.

sation. However, during the imperial period, the system of liturgies was expanded to result in the compulsion of public service from all levels of society. This is documented most fully in the case of Roman Egypt.[13] Especially in the troubled third century, the fiscal burdens imposed upon people in the cities and towns of Egypt in the form of liturgies and taxes became so great that flight was the last recourse. *Anachoresis,* "withdrawal," was a term often used in the case of flight from fiscal burdens. Perhaps some of the "anchorite" monks of Egypt had more than religious motivations for their retreat into the desert!

But back to philanthropy per se. There is considerable evidence for private and public benefactions in Greco-Roman society, including everything from the provision of food and oil for the needy, to the advancement of education and culture, to the promotion of health and hygiene. I cannot treat these in any detail here,[14] but I would like to cite as a special case the kind of philanthropic activity that was associated in the Greco-Roman world with the worship of the god Asklepios.

Asklepios was the Greek god of healing and the patron deity of physicians. His cult and his healing activities were centered in numerous temples devoted to him throughout the Greco-Roman world, the oldest and most famous being Epidauros in Greece. The healing done by the god was thought to take the form of nocturnal visitations to patients "lying in" a special room in the temple, a process called "incubation." The testimonies to Asklepios's healing, both literary and epigraphic, are numerous.[15] Alongside the direct intervention of the god was the medical treatment offered by physicians, whose patron Asklepios was.

The social position of Asklepios is of interest to us here.[16] The economic threat that disease posed to the lower classes was especially grave, and medical care was expensive. The god Asklepios was acclaimed as a god who gave help inexpensively, being satisfied with small thank-offerings. Indeed, he was praised for healing those unable to pay. In some instances, the god's nocturnal prescriptions would involve extended treatment in sanatoriums

---

13. See esp. N. Lewis, *Life in Egypt under Roman Rule* (Oxford: Clarendon, 1983), 177–84.

14. See esp. Hands, *Charities,* 89–145.

15. See the ancient testimonia assembled and evaluated by E. J. Edelstein and L. Edelstein in *Asclepius: A Collection and Interpretation of the Testimonies,* 2 vols. (Baltimore: Johns Hopkins Press, 1945; repr., New York: Arno Press, 1975).

16. See the discussion in ibid., 2:173–80.

attached to the temples. This treatment was offered free of charge to those without means to pay, with the result that Asklepios came to be generally regarded as the "most philanthropic" (φιλαν-θρωπότατος) of the gods.[17] It might be wondered why Asklepios's priests would put their facilities at the disposal of the needy; presumably, healings thus effected would bring fame to the god and his temples, resulting in the attraction of revenue from the more affluent.

In the Roman period, under the influence of Stoic philosophy, a more generous spirit was inculcated among the wealthy, and this was reinforced by the god Asklepios. An interesting example is provided by one of Asklepios's most famous devotees, the second-century orator Aelius Aristides. He was commanded by the god to distribute money to his fellow pilgrims during one of his sojourns in the god's temple (Or. 48.27). The editors of the ancient testimonia devoted to Asklepios summarize the philanthropic role played by the god in the following way: "In a world in which the poor were left to their fate by the state or by the communities at large, where laical medicine did not know of any special provisions for the needy, the asclepieia [Asklepios temples] and religious medicine were of the greatest importance for the medical welfare of the lower classes."[18]

Before leaving our discussion of the pagan evidence for philanthropy, I would like to take up briefly one aspect of Greco-Roman society that provides the greatest contrast to the Jewish and Christian cases that we shall be looking at next: attitudes toward wealth and poverty. Wealth, or at least adequate means, was generally regarded as a prerequisite for a virtuous life. Aristotle's remarks in his *Nichomachian Ethics* (fourth century B.C.E.) are typical. At the beginning of book 4, Aristotle discusses "liberality" (ἐλευθεριότης), a virtue that involves the observance of moderation ("the mean") in relation to wealth and its expenditure (4.1.1). The mean is that which lies between prodigality (ἀσωτία) and "meanness" (ἀνελευθερία; 4.1.2). Wealth is not only essential to life (4.1.5), it is essential to living a virtuous life (4.1.6–45), which involves the right use of wealth.[19] The famous dictum of Diogenes the Cynic,

---

17. See, e.g., Aelian, *N. A.* 9.33; and A. Aristides, *Or.* 39.5.
18. Edelstein and Edelstein, *Asclepius*, 2:178.
19. Another virtue involving wealth in *Eth. Nic.* is "Magnificence" (μεγα-λοπρέπεια; 4.2.1–22). An even greater virtue, for Aristotle, is magnanimity, "greatness of soul" (μεγαλοψυχία), which is concerned with honor (τιμή; 4.3.1–38).

"The love of money [is] the mother-city of all evils,"[20] represents an exception to the rule, in that the Cynic school advocated a kind of voluntary poverty as part of its countercultural stance. But even the Cynics did not hold up "poverty" as a virtue.

Poverty in the Greco-Roman world generally represented something to be avoided. Loss of wealth resulting in poverty was something to be feared, for this also meant a loss of status and a loss of a sense of self-worth. There were two main kinds of "poverty" in Greek usage, *penia* and *ptochia*. *Penia* was "poverty" or "need": a πένης was a "poor" person in the sense of one who was barely able to make a living. This, indeed, was the condition of the vast majority of the population of the ancient world, silent people whose voices are not represented in the literature that comes from the pens of those with the leisure and education to write for posterity. In fact, it included just about anybody who had to work with his hands to make a living. Manual labor was not respected in Greek society.

The other kind of poverty, *ptochia*, was much more severe.[21] A πτωχός was one who was utterly destitute, reduced to begging. And beggars were generally regarded with fear and loathing. Plato would banish beggars from his ideal state, on the grounds that they were likely to be thieves, pickpockets, temple robbers, or other criminal types (*Resp.* 8.552D). The Latin comic poet Plautus (third and second century B.C.E.) put it this way: "You do a beggar bad service by giving him food and drink" (*Trin.* 339).[22] Such a person was beyond the pity that would induce the well-to-do to help the penurious, that is, those with inadequate means. In short, beggars, the *ptochoi*, were usually outside the pale of Greco-Roman philanthropy.

Philanthropy in Ancient Judaism

As we consider first the use of the Greek word *philanthropia* in the Greek-speaking Judaism of the Greco-Roman Diaspora, we note that the term is used in much the same way as in the pa-

---

20. Diogenes Laertes 6.50, Hicks's translation in the LCL ed. Cf. 1 Tim 6:10 in the NT: "The love of money is the root of all evils" (RSV).
21. On these distinctions, see esp. G. Hamel, *Poverty and Charity in Roman Palestine, First Three Centuries C.E.* (Berkeley: University of California Press, 1990), 167–70.
22. Nixon's translation in the LCL ed. All of Plautus's Latin plays are presumably based on third-century B.C.E. Greek originals, now largely lost.

gan Greek literature. Thus, for example, the word is used of the benevolence shown by rulers to their subjects. In 3 Maccabees in the Greek Bible (the Septuagint), a text usually dated to the first century C.E., though it treats events supposed to have occurred in the third century B.C.E., King Ptolemy Philopator (Ptolemy IV) of Egypt is quoted in a letter addressed to his generals and soldiers, in which he claims to have treated his subject peoples "with great benevolence" (πολλῇ φιλανθρωπίᾳ; 3 Macc 3:15). In 2 Maccabees, the notorious Antiochus Epiphanes (Antiochus IV) is quoted in a letter to the Jews claiming that his policy has been to treat his subject people "moderately and kindly" (ἐπιεικῶς καὶ φιλανθρώπως; 2 Macc 9:27). Josephus can even use the term of the Romans (*Ant.* 12.124)!

In the Wisdom of Solomon (usually dated to the early first century C.E.), the personified divine Wisdom (Sophia) is said to be "a kindly spirit" (φιλάνθρωπον πνεῦμα; 1:6; cf. 7:23) who teaches the righteous to be "kind" (φιλάνθρωπον; 2:19). Thus, Sophia shares in God's own philanthropic nature and produces the same quality in God's people.

The best example of a discussion of *philanthropia* as a human virtue is found in the writings of Philo of Alexandria (first century C.E.), in his treatise *On the Virtues*. In that treatise, Philo takes up four virtues: courage (ἀνδρεία), humanity (φιλανθρωπία), repentance (μετάνοια), and nobility (εὐγένεια). His most extensive treatment is reserved for *philanthropia* (*Virt.* 51–174), which he says is the "sister and twin" of piety (εὐσέβεια). Philo finds illustrations of this virtue in the Law of Moses (the Torah), in regard to both the behavior of Moses himself (52–79) and the legislation that he gave to Israel. The *philanthropia* of the Mosaic Law is illustrated in its commandments against usury (Exod 22:25; Lev 25:36–37; Deut 23:19; see *Virt.* 82–87), on the payment of wages to the laborer (Lev 19:13; Deut 24:14–15; see *Virt.* 88), on improper seizure of debts (Deut 24:10–11; see *Virt.* 89), on the gleaning of crops by the poor (Lev 19:19; 23:22; see *Virt.* 90–94), on the first fruits for the priests (Deut 16:1–11; see *Virt.* 95), on the restoration of a stray animal to its owner (Deut 22:1; see *Virt.* 96), on sabbatical years (Exod 23:10–11; Lev 25:3ff.; see *Virt.* 97–98), and on the Jubilee year (Lev 25:8ff.; see *Virt.* 99). These laws were designed for Israelites in their relations with fellow Israelites. But equally humane laws are enjoined upon Israelites in their behavior toward strangers (Lev 19:33–34; see *Virt.* 102–4), sojourners (Deut 23; see *Virt.* 105–8), and even enemies (Deut

20:10ff.; 21:10–13; Exod 23:4–5; see *Virt.* 109–18). These examples show that the purpose of the Mosaic Law is to engender peace and brotherhood among people (119–20). Philo goes on to give examples of *philanthropia* in the laws regarding slaves (121–24), and even animals (125–47) and plants (148–59). In his concluding remarks on this virtue (161–74), Philo enumerates some of the vices for which *philanthropia* is an antidote.

Of course, the ultimate source of *philanthropia* is God, who is described as *philanthropos* in Greco-Jewish literature. Thus, Josephus, in his great work *The Antiquities of the Jews,* begins with an encomium on Moses, the lawgiver of the Jews, who has shown "that God possesses the very perfection of virtue"; Josephus then cites the "majesty of God and his love for man" (μεγαλειότητα τοῦ θεοῦ καὶ τὴν φιλανθρωπίαν; 1.23–24).[23]

These examples come, of course, from Jews who spoke Greek. There are no examples of the word φιλανθρωπία in the Greek translation of the Hebrew scriptures, for there is no exact equivalent in Hebrew. Thus, to get to the heart of what constitutes "philanthropy" in ancient Judaism, we must look first at the Hebrew scriptures, which are the source of both Jewish and Christian notions of philanthropy. In particular, we must look at what these scriptures tell us about the God of Israel.

Probably the best place to begin is with a well-known passage in the book of Exodus, chapter 34. Moses asks the LORD[24] to show him his glory, but God says, "You cannot see my face; for no one shall see me and live" (33:20).[25] Nevertheless, the LORD passes by him in a cloud and proclaims his name and attributes:

"The LORD, the LORD,
a God merciful and gracious [אל רחום וחנון],
slow to anger,
and abounding in steadfast love and faithfulness [חסד ואמת],
keeping steadfast love for the thousandth generation,
forgiving iniquity and transgression and sin,
yet by no means clearing the guilty,
but visiting the iniquity of the parents
upon the children

---

23. Thackeray's translation in the LCL ed.
24. The name of the God of Israel is Yahweh (יהוה), but the name when read aloud is pronounced "Adonai" (= "the Lord" or "my Lord").
25. All scripture quotations are from the NRSV, unless otherwise noted.

and the children's children,
to the third and the fourth generation." (Exod 34:6–7)

That is who the God of Israel is, and what he is like. But what
does he do, and what does he command? In numerous passages of
the Torah, God declares himself to be the protector of the poor and
the outsider, and commands his people to act accordingly:

> You shall not wrong or oppress a resident alien, for you were
> aliens in the land of Egypt. You shall not abuse any widow
> or orphan. If you do abuse them, when they cry out to me, I
> will surely heed their cry; my wrath will burn, and I will kill
> you with the sword. . . .
>   If you lend money to my people, to the poor among you,
> you shall not deal with them as a creditor; you shall not ex-
> act interest from them. If you take your neighbor's cloak in
> pawn, you shall restore it before the sun goes down; for it
> may be your neighbor's only clothing to use as cover; in what
> else shall that person sleep? And if your neighbor cries out to
> me, I will listen, for I am compassionate [כי־חנון אני]. (Exod
> 22:21–27 = MT 22:20–26)

> You shall not pervert the justice due to your poor in their
> lawsuits. Keep far from a false charge, and do not kill the
> innocent and those in the right, for I will not acquit the guilty.
> You shall take no bribe, for a bribe blinds the officials, and
> subverts the cause of those who are in the right.
>   You shall not oppress a resident alien; you know the heart
> of an alien, for you were aliens in the land of Egypt. (Exod
> 23:6–9)

> When you reap the harvest of your land, you shall not reap
> to the very edges of your field, or gather the gleanings of your
> harvest. You shall not strip your vineyard bare, or gather the
> fallen grapes of your vineyard; you shall leave them for the
> poor and the alien: I am the LORD your God. . . .
>   You shall not render an unjust judgment; you shall not be
> partial to the poor or defer to the great: with justice you shall
> judge your neighbor. . . .
>   . . . You shall not take vengeance or bear a grudge against
> any of your people, but you shall love your neighbor as
> yourself: I am the LORD. (Lev 19:9–18)

Every third year you shall bring out the full tithe of your produce for that year, and store it within your towns; the Levites, because they have no allotment or inheritance with you, as well as the resident aliens, the orphans, and the widows in your towns, may come and eat their fill so that the LORD your God may bless you in all the work that you undertake. (Deut 14:28–29)

If there is among you anyone in need, a member of your community in any of your towns within the land that the LORD your God is giving you, do not be hard-hearted or tight-fisted toward your needy neighbor.... Give liberally and be ungrudging when you do so, for on this account the LORD your God will bless you in all your work and in all that you undertake. Since there will never cease to be some in need on the earth, I therefore command you, "Open your hand to the poor and needy neighbor in your land." (Deut 15:7–11)

You shall not withhold the wages of poor and needy laborers, whether other Israelites or aliens who reside in your land in one of your towns. You shall pay them their wages daily before sunset, because they are poor and their livelihood depends on them; otherwise they might cry to the LORD against you, and you would incur guilt. (Deut 24:14–15)

Numerous other such texts could be cited as examples. It should be noted that the ones cited here, plus others, are also cited or alluded to by Philo of Alexandria in his discussion of *philanthropia*. What these texts illustrate most of all is that the God of Israel is the protector of the poor and the underdogs of society, and commands his people to be his agents in this regard. This is the heart and soul of Torah and the essential root of Jewish philanthropic work through the ages. And it is precisely in this that we note the stark contrast to the attitudes of the Greco-Roman world at large regarding poverty and the poor and the outcast of society. This is all the more striking when we also note that in two of the six instances where the English text reads "poor" in the passages here quoted, the Greek translation of the Hebrew text has a form of the adjective *ptochos*,[26] which (as we have noted) denotes the lowest level of destitution — beggary — in Greek texts of the larger Greco-Roman world.

---

26. Lev 19:10, rendering Heb. עני, and 19:15, rendering Heb. דל.

To be sure, ancient Israelite society did not always live up to the covenant obligations enshrined in the Torah. And so the prophets would preach against the breaches of covenant found in Israelite and Judean society, including its treatment of the poor. Thus, Amos, the earliest of the biblical prophets whose oracles are recorded in writing (eighth century B.C.E.), excoriates the leaders of the northern kingdom of Israel in thunderous tones:

> Thus says the LORD:
> For three transgressions of Israel,
>   and for four, I will not revoke the punishment;
> because they sell the righteous for silver,
>   and the needy for a pair of sandals —
> they who trample the head of the poor into the dust of the
>   earth,
>   and push the afflicted out of the way.
>   (Amos 2:6–7; cf. 4:1–3; 5:11–13; 8:4–6)

Somewhat later in the same century, Isaiah condemns the leaders of the southern kingdom of Judah in similar fashion:

> The LORD arises to argue his case;
>   he stands to judge the peoples.
> The LORD enters into judgment
>   with the elders and princes of his people:
> It is you who have devoured the vineyard;
>   the spoil of the poor is in your houses.
> What do you mean by crushing my people,
>   by grinding the face of the poor? says the LORD GOD of
>   hosts. (Isa 3:13–15; cf. 10:1–4).

Indeed, the special concern of the God of Israel for the poor runs like a thread through the entirety of the Hebrew Bible.

In the postbiblical Judaism of the Second Temple period and later, the provisions of the Torah for the poor were elaborated and expanded, especially among the scholars of the Pharisaic party. Their halakah, legal teaching, came to be codified toward the end of the second century in the Mishnah, to which was added further commentary resulting in the Jerusalem and Babylonian Talmuds. The relevant tractates of the Mishnah are three of the nine tractates in the first division, Zera'im ("Seeds"): Pe'a ("Gleanings," lit. "corner"), expanding on the commandments in Leviticus 19:9–10; 23:22; Deuteronomy 14:28–29; and 24:19–21; Shebi'it ("Seventh Year"), expanding on the commandments found

in Exodus 23:10–11; Leviticus 25:2–7, 20–2; and Deuteronomy
15:1–3; and *Ma'aserot* ("Tithes"), expanding on Numbers 18:21;
Leviticus 18:26; and Deuteronomy 14:22ff.; 14:28ff.; and 26:12.
An example of the sort of amplification and specification of the
commandments pertaining to "gleanings" follows:

> A poor man that is journeying from place to place should
> be given not less than one loaf worth a *pondion* [from wheat
> costing] one *sela* for four *seahs*. If he spends the night [in such
> a place] he should be given what is needful to support him
> for the night. If he stays over the Sabbath he should be given
> food enough for three meals. If a man has food enough for
> two meals he may not take aught from the [Paupers'] Dish,
> and if enough for fourteen meals he may not take aught from
> the [Poor] Fund. The [Poor] Fund is collected by two and
> distributed by three. (*m. Pe'a* 8.7)[27]

What is indicated in this passage is the transition from an agricultural context to a social context reflecting village and urban life
and a system of collection and distribution of food and other ne-
cessities. This involves a "Poor Fund," administered by officials of
local synagogues.[28] In other words, early Judaism had developed
an elaborate system of fund-raising and fund distribution whose
beneficiaries were mostly the poor and needy, not only the local
poor but also poor strangers.

Of course, Jews were also expected to give to the poor on an
individual basis, through almsgiving. The most frequent word used
for alms and almsgiving is *ṣedaqah,* which literally means "righteousness" or "justice." This usage implies a certain right on the
part of the poor, and an equivalent obligation on the part of the
well-to-do.[29]

The individual giving of alms and the use of the word *ṣedaqah*
in that connection is a relatively late development, reflected in postbiblical literature. Yeshu'a ben Sira (fl. early second century B.C.E.),
in his widely read but not canonical book of wisdom variously
called Ecclesiasticus or Sirach, says of almsgiving, "As water ex-

---

27. Translation in Herbert Danby, *The Mishnah* (Oxford: Oxford University
Press, 1933), 20.

28. See Hamel, *Poverty and Charity,* 218–19. See also G. F. Moore, *Judaism
in the First Centuries of the Christian Era: The Age of the Tannaim* (Cambridge:
Harvard University Press, 1927), 2:162–79.

29. Hamel, *Poverty and Charity,* 216. One of the five "pillars" of Islam is almsgiving (Arabic *zakat,* involving freewill offerings, *sadaqat*). This is obviously an
inheritance from Judaism.

tinguishes a blazing fire, so almsgiving [ἐλεημοσύνη][30] atones for sin" (3:30; cf. 7:10,32–36; 12:3–7; 14:13; 17:22; 18:15; 29:1–20; 35:4; 40:17).[31] Ben Sira elaborates on this theme in 4:1–10:34. Similarly, the author of the book of Tobit (third century B.C.E.) gives the following advice: "Almsgiving delivers from death and keeps you from going into the Darkness. Indeed, almsgiving, for all who practice it, is an excellent offering in the presence of the Most High" (4:10–11; cf. 12:8–9).

Almsgiving in early Jewish literature is often brought into connection with one of the supreme Jewish virtues, "deeds of lovingkindness" (*gemilut ḥasadim*):

> Almsgiving and deeds of lovingkindness are equal to all the commandments of the Law. Almsgiving is exercised toward the living, deeds of lovingkindness toward the living and the dead; almsgiving to the poor, deeds of lovingkindness to the poor and to the rich; almsgiving is done with a man's money, deeds of lovingkindness either with his money or personally. (*j. Pe'a* 15b–c; *t. Pe'a* 4.19; *Sukk.* 49b)[32]

Simeon the Just is quoted in *Pirke Aboth* ("The Sayings of the Fathers"), one of the tractates of the Mishnah: "By three things is the world sustained: by the Torah, by the divine service, and by deeds of lovingkindness."[33]

Before we leave this discussion of philanthropy in ancient Judaism, I want to mention one other feature that distinguishes Judaism from the other religions of the Greco-Roman world (except early Christianity): the high evaluation of poverty per se and the adoption of the vocabulary of poverty as a self-designation among certain Jews and Jewish groups in the Second Temple period. A prime example is provided by the Essenes, as documented particularly in the now famous Dead Sea Scrolls found in eleven caves above Khirbet Qumran.[34] The author of the Qumran

---

30. ἐλεημοσύνη, "alms" or "almsgiving," is the usual Greek translation of the Hebrew *ṣedaqah*.

31. Ben Sira wrote in Hebrew, and his book of wisdom was translated into Greek in Alexandria by his grandson. This translation is part of the Greek Bible, the Septuagint.

32. Qtd. in Moore, *Judaism*, 171–72.

33. Qtd. in I. Untermann's translation and commentary *Pirke Aboth: Sayings of the Fathers* (New York: Twayne Publishers, 1964), 31. Simeon the Just was high priest in the Jerusalem Temple ca. 200 B.C.E. After the destruction of the Temple, prayer takes the place of the "divine service" (sacrifices of the Temple cult) in Judaism.

34. For discussion, see Hamel, *Poverty and Charity*, 177–86.

Thanksgiving Hymns (1QH) repeatedly refers to himself and his community as "poor" or "the poor," and praises God for preserving both himself and his community from the hostile actions of enemies, who included the Jerusalem priestly establishment. Similarly, in the commentary on the book of Habakkuk (1QpHab), the prophet's description of violence in Habakkuk 2:17 is interpreted with reference to the hostile actions of the "wicked priest" against "the poor" (= the Qumran Essenes; 1QpHab xii 3,6,10). This adoption of the language of poverty as a self-designation at Qumran may have something to do with the way in which that community was organized, particularly with the obligation laid upon every member of the community to turn over all private property to the community's administration (1QS vi). Thus, the Qumran community is an interesting precursor to the monastic communities established by Christians in Egypt and elsewhere from the third century on.

This feature of Essene life was noted in antiquity by the writers who commented on the Essenes, one of whom was Philo of Alexandria. He says of the Essenes who dwelt in the villages (for whom the Qumran community was the source of leadership) that "they stand almost alone in the whole of mankind in that they have become moneyless and landless by deliberate action rather than by lack of good fortune" (*Quod omnis probus liber sit* 76).[35] Philo has more to say about a group closer to home, the Therapeutae, who lived on a strip of land between Lake Mareotis and the Mediterranean Sea, west of Alexandria. They were a Jewish group of persons who lived a kind of celibate monastic life, giving up their property and devoting themselves to the study of the scriptures, worship, and contemplation. An extensive description is provided by Philo in his treatise *On the Contemplative Life.*[36]

These, of course, are exceptional cases. The Jews generally did not despise wealth, and our sources provide abundant evidence of wealthy Jewish individuals (including Philo), families, and institutions. But what is especially noteworthy about Jewish religious laws and customs pertaining to wealth is their emphasis upon its proper use, grounded in the obligation of all Jews to reflect the mercy and "lovingkindness" (or "steadfast love," Heb. *ḥesed*) of God in their dealings with fellow human beings.

---

35. Colson's translation in the LCL ed.
36. The church historian Eusebius thought that Philo was describing the earliest Christians in Alexandria (*Hist. Eccl.* 2.17), but there is no foundation to this supposition.

Philanthropy in Early Christianity

It should be stressed at the start that the earliest religious bases for Christian philanthropy and attitudes toward wealth and poverty are the same as those for the Jews. The reason is simple: the earliest Christians were all Jews, and the church began its life as a Jewish sect that sprang up under the conviction that Jesus of Nazareth had been designated as Messiah by virtue of his having been raised from the dead by God after his execution on a Roman cross.[37] To be sure, the church rapidly extended itself outside the boundaries of the Holy Land, first into the scattered Jewish communities of the Diaspora, and soon incorporating gentiles into its "house churches." On the Jewish side, the destruction of the Jerusalem Temple eventually resulted in the consolidation of "normative" or "rabbinic" Judaism, based on traditions developed in the Pharisaic party. On the Christian side, the separation of the church, consisting of converted Jews and gentiles, from its Jewish matrix was hastened. The church became more and more acculturated to the surrounding Greco-Roman world as it lost its ethnic identification with Judaism and the legal protection that that entailed in Roman law. Roman law had encouraged Jews (and comparable ethnic groups) to conduct their lives and communities in accordance with their ancestral tradition. The Christians came to lack that ethnic identity, though they preserved it in symbolic terms by retaining the Jewish scriptures. (To be sure, these scriptures were interpreted in specifically Christian ways, and were also eventually supplemented by the "New Testament" canon.)

The earliest Christian writings we have are preserved in Greek, for the most part in what now constitutes the aforementioned New Testament canon.[38] The term *philanthropia* occurs twice in the New Testament: In the first instance, it characterizes the kindness shown by the inhabitants of Malta to Paul and his companions when they were shipwrecked on their way to Rome (Acts 28:2).[39] The other occurrence refers to the kindness of God in sending Jesus

---

37. See chapter 1 in this book.

38. Some noncanonical writings, e.g., *1 Clement* and *Didache,* are earlier than the later books of the NT, 1–2 Timothy, Titus, and 2 Peter. The NT canon itself is a fourth-century development. The earliest sacred scripture of the church was what came eventually to be referred to as the "Old Testament," i.e., the Hebrew Bible, specifically the expanded Greek version that eventually developed in the Jewish Diaspora.

39. The adverb φιλανθρώπως is used to characterize the behavior of the centurion of the Roman cohort guarding Paul on his journey (Acts 27:3).

Christ as Savior (Titus 3:4). In both cases, the term reflects usage we have already encountered in our discussion of pagan and Jewish cases. The term does not occur much in the earliest Christian literature, but it comes to be used much more beginning with Clement of Alexandria and Origen in the third century, being applied to God, Jesus Christ, and the conduct of Christians.[40]

Early Christian attitudes toward wealth and poverty are similar to the Jewish attitudes and are grounded in the traditional view of God as protector of the poor (discussed earlier). The teachings of Jesus of Nazareth can be said to represent an extreme, indeed radical, case. These teachings are embedded in the New Testament Gospels, though sometimes they are also reinterpreted by the respective evangelists.[41] Thus, in his famous "Beatitudes," Jesus is quoted as declaring, first of all, the blessedness of the poor. The Gospel of Luke probably contains the version that comes closest to Jesus' original pronouncements:

> Blessed are you who are poor,
> for yours is the kingdom of God.
> Blessed are you who are hungry now,
> for you will be filled.... (6:20b–21)[42]

These macarisms are balanced in Luke by pronouncements of "woe":

> But woe to you who are rich,
> for you have received your consolation.
> Woe to you who are full now,
> for you will be hungry.... (6:24–25b)

In the Matthean version, part of the "Sermon on the Mount" in Matthew, Jesus' radical sayings are somewhat "domesticated":

> Blessed are the poor in spirit,
> for theirs is the kingdom of heaven. (5:3)

> Blessed are those who hunger and thirst for righteousness,
> for they will be filled. (5:6)

---

40. See *TDNT*, 9:111–12. Clement was influenced heavily by Philo of Alexandria, and much of Philo's discussion of the virtue *philanthropia* is reflected in his *Stromateis*. See A. van den Hoek, *Clement of Alexandria and His Use of Philo in the Stromateis: An Early Christian Reshaping of a Jewish Model* (Leiden: E. J. Brill, 1988).

41. See chapter 2 in this book.

42. Cf. *Gos. Thom.*, saying 54: "Blessed are you poor, for yours is the kingdom of heaven" (my translation).

Matthew has "spiritualized" the beatitude on the poor to reflect a more general Jewish ideal of "poverty,"[43] and the beatitude on the hungry to refer to the spiritual "hunger" for righteousness. He has also omitted the woes on the rich.

Another example of Jesus' radical teaching on wealth and poverty is the famous saying about the camel and the needle's eye, found in all three synoptic Gospels (Luke 18:24–25 ‖ Mark 10:23–25 ‖ Matt 19:23–24). I quote the version in Luke: "'How hard it is for those who have wealth to enter the kingdom of God! Indeed, it is easier for a camel to go through the eye of a needle than for someone who is rich to enter the kingdom of God.'" Another example of what I take to be editorial "softening" is found in what follows that passage: "Those who heard it said, 'Then who can be saved?' He replied, 'What is impossible for mortals is possible for God'" (Luke 18:26–27).

Jesus' remark about the camel and the needle's eye follows immediately upon an episode involving a wealthy young man. This, too, is found in all three synoptic Gospels (Matt 19:16–22 ‖ Mark 10:17–22 ‖ Luke 18:18–23). The young man asks Jesus what he must do to inherit eternal life, and Jesus replies by quoting from the Ten Commandments. The young man says that he has kept all of them from his youth. Jesus' final word to him (in Luke's version) is a hard saying: "'There is still one thing lacking. Sell all that you own and distribute the money to the poor, and you will have treasure in heaven; then come, follow me'" (18:22). The young man then goes away, unable to meet the challenge. Jesus' challenge is summed up in another famous saying: "'No one can serve two masters; for either he will hate the one and love the other, or he will be devoted to the one and despise the other. You cannot serve God and mammon'" (Matt 6:24 ‖ Luke 16:13 [RSV]). Here the Aramaic word for "money" or "riches" is left untranslated in the Greek of the gospels, underscoring the effect of the saying: devotion to wealth is a form of idolatry.[44]

Jesus' attitude toward property is displayed in his own lifestyle. His own family background—he grew up in the home of a skilled artisan—was certainly not one of abject poverty; yet we meet him in the gospel tradition as an itinerant prophet of the kingdom of God, having no home or property of his own. He once said to a

---

43. "Poor in spirit" is a phrase that also occurs in the DSS, e.g., at 1QM xiv 7.
44. So according to M. Hengel, *Property and Riches in the Early Church: Aspects of a Social History of Early Christianity* (Philadelphia: Fortress Press, 1974), 24.

person who wanted to become a follower, "Foxes have holes, and birds of the air have nests; but the Son of Man has nowhere to lay his head" (Matt 8:20 ‖ Luke 9:58 ‖ *Gos. Thom.* 86).

His closest disciples seem to have adopted this stance. Peter is quoted at one point as saying, "We have left everything and followed you" (Matt 19:27 ‖ Luke 18:28: "We have left our homes … "). Jesus' reply assures him that anyone "who has left house or wife or brothers or parents or children, for the sake of the kingdom of God" will receive reward both "in this age, and in the age to come" (Luke 18:29–30 ‖ Matt 19:29 ‖ Mark 20:28–30). Matthew's and Mark's versions then add an oft-quoted saying: "Many who are first will be last, and the last will be first" (Matt 19:30 ‖ Mark 10:31).

What is the basis for this radical teaching? We have seen in the examples cited that it is bound up somehow with the "kingdom of God." Jesus taught that the absolute rule of God long awaited by the Jews was about to come, and he considered himself an agent in its arrival. In the face of the kingdom of God, property and even family become secondary. What is needed is turning, and the adoption of a way of life that comports with God's rule.

There are, to be sure, some apparent contradictions in the gospel accounts, for Jesus' condemnation of wealth did not prevent him from accepting the hospitality of the well-to-do. Indeed, as an itinerant charismatic prophet, he was dependent on people with homes and property.[45] The home of Peter in Capernaum seems to have been a kind of home base for his ministry, where he and his disciples could come back from time to time from their journeys. On one occasion there, Jesus is recorded as having healed Peter's mother-in-law of a fever (Mark 1:30ff.). Thus, the injunction to sell property and give to the poor cannot be taken as an absolute requirement for everyone, even in Jesus' own radical message. What is required is an attitude of detachment from wealth and attachment to God such as will result in the betterment of the lot of the poor as an anticipation of God's righteous rule, when the present unjust social roles will be reversed.

Jesus had proclaimed the imminent coming of the kingdom of God. What came instead was the church, constituted after Jesus' death and resurrection as an "assembly" (*ekklesia*) of "the Lord"

---

45. On the symbiosis of itinerant charismatics and their local support groups, see esp. G. Theissen, *Sociology of Early Palestinian Christianity* (Philadelphia: Fortress Press, 1978).

(Jesus), terminology adapted from a biblical term for the congregation of Israel.[46] It is within the early Christian groups that the sayings and deeds of Jesus were remembered and handed down, and eventually edited as written accounts. The "softenings" of Jesus' radical pronouncements that we have noted are part of this process.

In the case of the early church in Jerusalem, there are some notable parallels with features of the Qumran community (discussed earlier). The account in the book of Acts may, of course, be an idealization, but there is probably a historical kernel in it:

> All who believed were together and had all things in common; they would sell their possessions and goods and distribute the proceeds to all, as any had need. Day by day, as they spent much time together in the temple, they broke bread at home and ate their food with glad and generous hearts, praising God and having the goodwill of all the people. (2:44–47)

> Now the whole group of those who believed were of one heart and soul, and no one claimed private ownership of any possessions, but everything they owned was held in common. ... There was not a needy person among them, for as many as owned lands or houses sold them and brought the proceeds of what was sold. They laid it at the apostles' feet, and it was distributed to each as any had need. (4:32–35)

This system of commonality of goods administered by a council of twelve is reminiscent of the situation in the Qumran community. Acts records that the food distribution was extended to newcomers from the Greek-speaking synagogues in Jerusalem, who eventually had a council of seven who administered to their needs (6:1–6). It is the latter group, called the "Hellenists" (Greek-speakers), who fell under the suspicion of the Temple authorities and were forced to leave Jerusalem (Acts 8:1). A sizable contingent wound up in Antioch in Syria, where mission to the gentiles began and where the believers were first called "Christians" (Acts 11:19–26). The Aramaic-speaking "Hebrews" (Acts 6:1) remained in Jerusalem, under the leadership of Peter and the rest of the Twelve. Eventually, probably from the early 40s, the leadership of the Jerusalem church fell to Jesus' own brother, James ("Jacob").

---

46. *Ekklesia kyriou* = *Qehal YHWH*: Deut 23:2, etc.

How long the commonality of goods persisted in the Jerusalem church is hard to say (if, indeed, it actually existed). It probably would not have lasted long. There would have been an eschatological dimension to it, reminiscent of the eschatological preaching of Jesus. The earliest Christians expected the imminent return of Christ with the clouds of heaven, as exalted "Son of Man" (Dan 7:9–14). Such a belief is reflected in the gospel tradition, for example, at Matthew 16:28: " 'Truly I tell you, there are some standing here who will not taste death before they see the Son of Man coming in his kingdom.' " The parallel in Mark 9:1, which is a more original version of Jesus' pronouncement, has " 'until they see that the kingdom of God has come with power.' " The belief in the imminent return of Christ was taken over by the apostle Paul (1 Thess 4–5; 1 Cor 15, etc.) and was a guiding force in his own mission.

But let us return to the Jerusalem church for a moment: We are told of some economic pressures on it that may have resulted from an excess of liberality but were surely aggravated by a famine in Palestine in the days of Claudius (probably ca. 48 C.E.; Acts 11:28). The situation was alleviated by relief sent by the church in Antioch through its emissaries Barnabas and Saul (= Paul; Acts 11:29). Later, the apostle Paul, according to an agreement with James of Jerusalem, conducted a fund-raising campaign among the churches he founded in Asia Minor and Greece.[47] This campaign was meant for "the poor" in Jerusalem (Gal 2:10; cf. 1 Cor 16:1–4; 2 Cor 8–9; Rom 15:25–29). This term, "the poor," should probably be construed as a self-designation of the Jerusalem church (Heb. 'ebionim), which presents us with another interesting parallel to the Qumran community. That community, as we recall from our previous discussion, had adopted the same self-designation. This usage persisted into the fourth century and later among certain groups of Jewish Christians, as we can see in the use of the term "Ebionite" of their sects. Of course, by that time, the predominantly gentile church regarded those Jewish Christian groups as "heretics."[48]

It is not possible to treat here in detail the development of organized charity in the early church.[49] However, we can cite the Christian philosopher Aristides for a summary statement of the

---

47. See discussion in chapter 9 of this book.
48. On the Ebionites and other Jewish-Christian groups, see esp. A. F. J. Klijn, *Patristic Evidence for Jewish-Christian Sects* (Leiden: E. J. Brill, 1973).
49. See, e.g., Hengel, *Property and Riches*; and R. M. Grant, *Early Christianity and Society: Seven Studies* (New York: Harper & Row, 1977), esp. chap. 6, "The Organization of Alms" (124–45). For the Byzantine period, see D. J. Constantelos,

situation in the second century. In a defense of Christianity addressed to the emperor Hadrian (ca. 125), Aristides describes the social attitudes and practices of Christians as follows:

> They walk in all humility and kindness, and falsehood is not found among them, and they love one another: and from the widows they do not turn away, and they rescue the orphan from him who does him violence: he who has gives to him who has not, without grudging; and when they see a stranger, they bring him to their dwellings, and rejoice over him as over a true brother; for they do not call brothers those who are after the flesh, but those who are in the spirit and in God: but when one of their poor passes away from the world, and any of them sees him, then he provides for his burial according to his ability; and if they hear that any of their number is imprisoned or oppressed for the name of their Messiah, all of them provide for his needs, and if it is possible that he may be delivered, they deliver him. And if there is among them a man that is poor or needy, and they have not an abundance of necessaries, they fast two or three days that they may supply the needy with their necessary food. (*Apol.* 15)[50]

That this picture of philanthropy in second-century Christian communities is not overdrawn can easily be seen from the testimony of pagan detractors of Christianity of the same period. For example, Lucian of Samosata tells an entertaining story of a Cynic philosopher-charlatan, one Peregrinus "Proteus," whose wanderings brought him from Asia Minor to Palestine, where he became a leading member of a local Christian community before he finally moved on to other pursuits. When at one point Peregrinus was thrown into prison, his Christian supporters spared nothing in their efforts to help him:

> Indeed, people came even from the cities in Asia, sent by the Christians at their common expense, to succour and defend and encourage the hero. They show incredible speed whenever any such public action is taken; for in no time they lavish their all. So it was then in the case of Peregrinus; much money came to him from them by reason of his imprisonment, and

---

Byzantine Philanthropy and Social Welfare (New Brunswick: Rutgers University Press, 1968).

50. Aristides, *Apology*, trans. from the Syriac by J. R. Harris, Texts and Studies 1.1 (Cambridge: Cambridge University Press, 1891).

he procured not a little revenue from it. The poor wretches have convinced themselves, first and foremost, that they are going to be immortal and live for all time, in consequence of which they despise death and even willingly give themselves into custody, most of them. Furthermore, their first lawgiver persuaded them that they are all brothers of one another after they have transgressed once for all by denying the Greek gods and by worshipping that crucified sophist himself and living under his laws. Therefore they despise all things indiscriminately and consider them common property, receiving such doctrines traditionally without any definite evidence. So if any charlatan and trickster, able to profit by occasions, comes among them, he quickly acquires sudden wealth by imposing upon simple folk. (*Pereg.* 13)[51]

It is clear, of course, that the eschatologically oriented injunctions of Jesus of Nazareth could not be generally maintained in the church, though the rise of monasticism in the third century is at least partially rooted in that tradition.

An interesting example of how wealthy Christians could accommodate the injunctions of Christ to their own situation is presented in Clement of Alexandria's homily *The Rich Man's Salvation* (*Quis dives salvetur* [*QD*]).[52] Clement, whose Alexandrian church was one of the wealthiest in the empire, tackles the issue head-on by basing his sermon on the gospel text about the rich young man and Jesus, and the material that follows (Mark 10:17–31, discussed earlier). Clement begins by affirming the truth of the saying "What is impossible to men becomes possible to God" (cf. Mark 10:27; *QD* 2). A rich person should not, therefore, disqualify himself from salvation on the basis of his wealth, so long as he is a believer in the philanthropy (φιλανθρωπία) of God (*QD* 3). Clement then quotes the text in full (*QD* 4), which he follows immediately with the exhortation not to listen to the Savior's utterances "carnally," that is, not to take them literally, but to develop "the meaning hidden in them" (*QD* 5). Clement next goes on to develop the dominant theme. Riches are not to be thrown away; what must be banished should be banished from the soul, namely, improper notions about wealth (*QD* 11), for riches have the potential of benefiting our neighbors. Wealth in itself is not evil but can be used rightly or wrongly according to the decision and disposition of its

---

51. Harmon's translation in the LCL edition.
52. Butterworth's translation in the LCL ed.

owner (*QD* 14). The wealthy person who holds possessions and gifts of God for the sake of the brethren is truly the one blessed by the Lord as "poor in spirit" and as an inheritor of the kingdom of heaven (*QD* 16). These basic themes are further elaborated at considerable length in what follows in Clement's homily, with numerous citations and examples from scripture.

Similar arguments are found in the homily *On Riches,* attributed to Peter I, a bishop of Alexandria who lived about a century later than Clement.[53] He was bishop from 300 to 311 C.E. and was one of the last martyrs in the persecutions mounted against the Christians by Diocletian in 303. The homily consists of two main parts: an address to the rich on the proper use of wealth (pars. 14–54); and a smaller address to the poor, warning against envy of the rich and counseling a nonvengeful acceptance of their lot (pars. 55–69). Wealthy persons in the Old Testament are held up as examples of the benevolent use of wealth; these include Solomon, Job, Abraham, and David. Some of this homily's arguments and interpretations of scripture are reminiscent of those of Clement, and probably reflect some knowledge of that earlier Alexandrian work.

After Constantine's Edict of Milan in 313, which marks the beginning of the development of a Christian empire, the church's already highly developed system of aid to the needy was augmented by contributions from the state. Eventually, the entire administration of the state program of food distribution was given over to the churches and their ecclesiastical leaders.[54]

There was, to be sure, a pagan interlude in the history of the fourth-century empire after Constantine: the reign of Julian "the Apostate" (360–363), with whom we began this essay. As part of his attempt to revive paganism, Julian used the philanthropic practices of the despised Christians to shame the pagan priests into developing charitable institutions. His policies are reflected in letters that he addressed to these priests, in which he uses the word *philanthropia* quite frequently. A passage from Julian's letter to Arsecius, high priest of the province of Galatia, is quoted earlier,

---

53. The homily is preserved in Coptic, with what appear to be late expansions featuring material on the archangel Michael. For an introduction and translation, see B. A. Pearson and T. Vivian, *Two Coptic Homilies Attributed to St. Peter of Alexandria: On Riches, On the Epiphany* (Rome: CIM, 1993), 9–39 and 95–144. See also Pearson, "A Coptic Homily on Riches Attributed to St. Peter of Alexandria," *Studia Patristica* 26 (Louvain: Peeters, 1993), 296–307.

54. See Grant, *Early Christianity and Society,* 144f.

wherein he attempts to shame Arsecius and his colleagues with the example of the Christians.

Julian financed philanthropic endeavors with state allocations to the pagan temples and priesthoods. In addition, in a fragment of a letter to a priest, he even urged pagans to give private alms to the poor, and without regard to their virtue:

> We ought then to share our money with all men, but more generously with the good, and with the helpless and poor so as to suffice for their need. And I will assert, even though it be paradoxical to say so, that it would be a pious act to share our clothes and food even with the wicked. For it is to the humanity in a man that we give, and not to his moral character. Hence I think that even those who are shut up in prison have a right to the same sort of care, since this kind of philanthropy [φιλανθρωπία] will not hinder justice. (290D–291A [Wright])

As examples, he cited the Jews as well as the Christians: "It is disgraceful that, when no Jew ever has to beg, and the impious Galileans [Christians] support not only their own poor but ours as well, all men see that our people [pagans] lack aid from us" (*Ep.* 22.430D [Wright]) Thus, it is clear that Julian, for all his hatred of the Christian religion, had retained something valuable from his Christian upbringing. After his brief reign, the church was all the more empowered in various ways, including the state's support for churches and their charitable institutions. Under Theodosius (379–395) the systematic suppression of paganism began.

One effect of the Christianization of the empire was an increasing secularization of the church. This situation is reflected in the writings of the late-fourth- and early-fifth-century church fathers. The homilies of John Chrysostom (ca. 347–407, archbishop of Constantinople from 398) provide an interesting case in point, with which I conclude this discussion.[55] John bewailed the extravagance of the wealthy members of the church and their contempt for the poor. He was outraged by their excuses for not giving alms, especially their claim that almsgiving was the responsibility of the church's budget. And he found in that traditional Greek virtue *philotimia* ("love of honor," discussed earlier) a root cause of evil:

---

55. What follows is largely based on B. Layerle, "John Chrysostom on Almsgiving and the Use of Money," *HTR* 87 (1994): 29–47.

Riches lead those taken in by them into an honor which is the opposite of [real honor], but one painted over with colors so persuasive that they believe it is the same, although it is not really, even if it seems so to the eye. For while the lovely appearance of courtesans made up out of emollients and eye-liners is bereft of real beauty, it nevertheless makes an ugly and unsightly face appear beautiful and well-formed to those deceived by it, although it is not so in reality. In exactly this way riches force flattery to look like honor. (*Quod nemo se laedatur nisi a seipso* 9 [PG 52.470])[56]

John commended as an antidote to the attitudes of his wealthy flock the injunctions of Christ in the Gospels and the opportunities for salvation presented by the presence of poor folk in their midst. But one has to doubt that the "golden-mouthed" preacher had much success with his exhortations. Nor do such arguments have much force in most of the "mainline" churches of late-twentieth-century America.

Concluding Observations

In this survey of philanthropy in the Greco-Roman world and in early Christianity, we have traced the uses of the Greek term *philanthropia* and its cognates in the literatures and traditions of pagan Greece and Rome, ancient Judaism, and early Christianity. We have also considered some of the more important "philanthropic" institutions of these respective traditions. Our account culminated in the fourth-century Roman Empire, which saw the triumph of Christianity but also the ironies attendant upon that triumph.

This is not the place for an extended discussion of the factors that led to the Christian victory, but I do want to point out that a very important factor in the spread of Christianity and its eventual success in the empire was the Christian ideal and practice of philanthropy, involving networks of caring people who saw to the needs of the poor and the suffering in their midst, friends and strangers alike. Indeed, this point has convincingly been made in the important recent work by the sociologist Rodney Stark, *The Rise of Christianity*. The severe epidemics of the second and third centuries, as well as the social chaos rampant in the urban centers

---

56. Qtd. in ibid., 35–36.

of the Roman world, exposed the inherent weaknesses of paganism while also providing opportunity for Christianity to function very effectively as a social "revitalization movement." As Stark puts it,

> Christianity revitalized life in Greco-Roman cities by providing new norms and new kinds of social relationships able to cope with many urgent urban problems. To cities filled with the homeless and impoverished, Christianity offered charity as well as hope. To cities filled with newcomers and strangers, Christianity offered an immediate basis for attachments. To cities filled with orphans and widows, Christianity provided a new and expanded sense of family. To cities torn by violent ethnic strife, Christianity offered a new basis for social solidarity. And to cities faced with epidemics, fires, and earthquakes, Christianity offered effective nursing services.[57]

Stark argues that Christians constituted a majority of the population of the empire by the time of Constantine: "Constantine's conversion would better be seen as a response to the massive exponential wave in progress, not as its cause."[58] Julian must have understood that his program of revitalizing paganism could be carried out only by emulating the philanthropic ideals and practices of the Christians, ideals and practices that had led to the success of the Christian religion under Constantine. But Julian was promoting a cause that had already been lost.

The triumph of Christianity in the empire had its attendant ironies as well, illustrated in part by our discussion of John Chrysostom's exhortations to his Christian congregations. He was addressing people who were now part of a Christian imperial power structure, people who had begun to forget the very values that had led to the Christian religion's success. And that is a large part of the history of Christianity in the Western world into our own times.

---

57. R. Stark, *The Rise of Christianity: A Sociologist Reconsiders History* (Princeton: Princeton University Press, 1996), 161.
58. Ibid., 10.

perforce: by necessity
willy-nilly (whether desired or not)

_____ *Epilogue* _____

Some Personal Observations
on Scholarly Method

red herring: something that draws
attention from issue at hand

In this epilogue I want to comment on the various chapters of this
book in terms of the approach to the material that they reflect, or,
to put it another way, their "methodology." I want to make clear at
the outset, however, that methodology is not something that I concern myself with very much, at least not explicitly. Many scholars,
particularly in North America, have devoted entire careers to the
study of how other people study religion, to the point that there
is now a scholarly journal devoted to this fast-growing subfield of
religious studies.[1] To my mind, it is more interesting, and probably
more important, to study critically other people's religion(s) — or
even one's own — than to study at second hand how other people
study still other people's religion(s).[2]

Inasmuch as I indulged in some criticism of one of the books
of Wilfred Cantwell Smith (*The Meaning and End of Religion*) in
chapter 1, I want to express my basic agreement with something
else that he has written, namely, an article on methodology. At one
point in the article, he sets forth his view quite strongly, but with a
degree of (feigned?) modesty:

> Manifestly something is wrong when virtually all my friends,
> and many persons obviously much more intelligent than I,
> are stalwart methodologists, whereas I feel that methodol-
> ogy is the massive red herring of modern scholarship, the

_____

1. *Method and Theory in the Study of Religion*, published in Toronto.
2. On the juxtaposition of "religion" (singular) as a human phenomenon, and
the various "religions" (plural), i.e., concrete religious traditions, see my remarks in
chapter 1.

most significant obstacle to intellectual progress, and the chief distraction from rational understanding of the world.[3]

Smith goes on to argue that "academic method is what all scholars have in common, not what differentiates them," and that method is simply "preamble" and "subordinate" to the scholarly task at hand: "A good academic learns it [academic method], assimilates it, forgets it — in the sense that it is taken so much for granted that he moves on from there to the substance of his work. Ideally, he absorbs it to the point where he is unconscious of it, not self-conscious about it."[4]

It strikes me that there is much common sense in what Smith says, both in the remarks quoted here and in the rest of his essay. Why, then, this epilogue? I suppose the answer is partially to be found in the challenge of extrapolating and analyzing "methods" or approaches implicit in the writing of something that was not explicitly "methodological" at all, just in case there are people reading this book (perhaps my students) who are wondering where the author is coming from when he proffers this or that interpretation of his material. Perhaps a better way of putting it is to talk about "approaches" to our subject matter. In laying this out, I shall perforce bring in a little bit of autobiography, perhaps justifiable as I approach the "sunset" (or, more hopefully, the "late afternoon") of my career.

Returning now to chapter 1, it will be recalled that I took "a stand firmly against the theologian's claim" that Christianity is "not one of the religions of the world." I situated myself, rather, "squarely in the camp of the history of religions." Indeed, all of the chapters in this book (and, for that matter, all of my published work) have been written from the perspective of the history of religions. When I say "history of religions," I do not mean the "Chicago school" of the history of religions (Eliade & Co.); I mean that tradition of philologically based scholarship that has been carried out for more than a century and a half in continental Europe. In a sense, I can be regarded as an heir of the *Religionsgeschicht-*

classical scholarship / literary study

---

3. W. C. Smith, "Methodology and the Study of Religion: Some Misgivings," in *Methodological Issues in Religious Studies,* ed. R. D. Baird (Chico, Calif.: New Horizons Press, 1974), 1–25 (quotation on 2). The volume in which Smith's essay appears grew out of a symposium, "Methodology and World Religions," held at the University of Iowa in 1974. In addition to Smith, the other main participants were R. Baird, J. Neusner, and H. Penner.

4. Ibid., 3–4.

liche Schule ("history of religions school").[5] What that means, in
negative terms, is that I have never been a theologian, nor have I
ever published anything "theological" (at least not knowingly).

I hasten to add that I have nothing against theology or theologians — some of my friends are theologians — and theology
certainly has an important role to play in religious scholarship.
As I view the matter, theology is done, or ought to be done, in
the service of a particular faith community, or of the larger religion made up of faith communities. Lutheran theologians, for
example, have an important role to play in interpreting and com-
municating the Christian faith in ways that will illumine, buttress,
and (especially!) challenge the faith of the Lutheran faithful. I just
don't happen to be a theologian (though I do happen to be a Lutheran layman, which is why I used the Lutheran example). But if I
were a theologian, I would begin my work precisely as I have, and
then would take on the added responsibility of stating what it all
"means" to Christian believers in the present. The distinction between what any given text *meant* in its own historical context and
what it *means* to me, or what I think it ought to mean to Christian
believers, is the basis for responsible theology. This I learned from
one of my revered teachers, Krister Stendahl.[6]

I suppose I might have become a theologian; perhaps I would
have, had I done my teaching and scholarly research as a member of a theological faculty in a denominational seminary. As it
happens, I have spent my entire professional career in a university, most of it in a state university setting. It is from that vantage
point that I made my remarks in chapter 1 on the academic
study of Christianity in nontheological settings. Those remarks reflect very clearly the privilege that I enjoyed as a faculty member
of a department of religious studies in a state university setting
(the University of California at Santa Barbara). Moving from the
Department of Religion at Duke University (which at that time followed the "miniseminary" approach to the teaching of religion),
I was able to participate in developing a program of study that
implicitly eschewed the assumption of the superiority and unique-

| eschew | to avoid, to shun |

5. See K. Rudolph, "Early Christianity as a Religious-Historical Phenomenon,"
in Pearson, *Future,* 9–19.

6. K. Stendahl's article "Biblical Theology, Contemporary," published in *IDB,*
1:418–32, has become a classic statement. See also Stendahl, *Meanings: The Bible
as Document and as Guide* (Philadelphia: Fortress Press, 1984). Stendahl is professor emeritus at Harvard, former dean of the Harvard Divinity School, and bishop
emeritus of the Stockholm diocese of the (Lutheran) Church of Sweden.

ness of Christianity, a program in which Christianity was (and is) simply "one of the religions of the world." Over the years, in teaching my course on the origins of Christianity, I would often confess to my students my own Lutheran affiliation. In doing so, I would challenge them to confront me if they ever discerned any Lutheran bias in my presentation of the subject matter. No one ever did. However, some complained about my "un-Christian" approach.

In defining Christianity as "a religion" in chapter 1, I also had occasion to remark on the various "dimensions" of religion as these find expression in any given religion, with special reference to the work of my Santa Barbara colleague Ninian Smart. I did a similar thing in chapter 8, where I discussed the Gnostic religion.[7] Analyzing religious traditions, ancient or modern, in this fashion aids the comparative task. In that endeavor, we enter into that complement to the history of religions that is usually referred to as the "phenomenology"[8] or "morphology"[9] of religion. The challenge posed in chapter 1 was essentially to trace the historical process by which a new religion, Christianity, was generated out of an older one, Second Temple Judaism. Comparative phenomenology of religion is an aid to this sorting-out process.

A necessary component to the phenomenology of religion, and to the study of religion in general, is the need to "bracket" one's own faith stance (or unfaith stance), in my case to "bracket" my Lutheran identity, so as to view the ancient data pertinent to early Christianity (or any other religion) in their own historical contexts and to interpret the writings of ancient Christian authors on their own terms, in an unbiased fashion. Some scholars argue that this is impossible. Perhaps it is, but it is much better to *try* to achieve an unbiased, objective approach than it is to engage in deliberate hermeneutical jugglery. As to scholarly method, a prominent sociologist of religion speaks of "methodological atheism";[10] I might prefer "critical neutrality." The standard term in the phenomenol-

---

7. N. Smart's seven "dimensions" are utilized more consistently in Pearson, "Gnosticism a Religion."

8. See esp. "The Phenomenology of Religion," chap. 109 in G. van der Leeuw, *Religion in Essence and Manifestation: A Study in Phenomenology,* 2 vols. (New York: Harper & Row, 1963), 689.

9. N. Smart, *Dimensions of the Sacred: An Anatomy of the World's Beliefs* (Berkeley/Los Angeles: University of California Press, 1996), 1.

10. P. L. Berger, *The Sacred Canopy: Elements of a Sociological Theory of Religion* (Garden City, N.Y.: Doubleday, 1967), 100; cf. 180, where Berger distinguishes sociological theory from theology.

ogy of religion is *epoché*, "suspension of judgment."[11] I would add that a good historian of religions will complement his or her *epoché* with an attempt to deal empathetically with the data at hand. A scholar who thinks religion is just plain "bunk" has no more claim to be taken seriously than one who has a theological or ideological ax to grind.

To enlarge a bit on this last point, *epoché* and empathy are necessarily held in tension in the critical study of religion. Religion, as a universal human phenomenon with prehistoric roots,[12] comes to expression in bewilderingly different ways in human cultures. And religion (all religions, certainly including Christianity), has its "dark side" as well. As various cultures and religions intersect in the developing "globalization" that we see in our time, it is becoming increasingly more essential for people and governments to have some understanding of the religious dimensions of the cultural and nationalistic conflicts that surround us on all sides and that are so much a part of the daily world news. I would venture to suggest that U.S. governmental policies, at home and especially abroad, would be better formulated if specialists in the study of religion(s) were more involved in the process.[13]

But now back to the book, and chapter 2. Serious scholarship entails a great deal of hard work and many years of preparation. But that does not mean that scholarship cannot also be fun; indeed it can. And now I can say that the writing of the essay that constitutes chapter 2 in this volume was the most fun of anything I have ever written. That chapter also admittedly comes closest to doing what I say I don't usually do, namely, concern myself with

---

11. Van der Leeuw puts it this way in *Religion in Essence and Manifestation*: "The term *epoche* is a technical expression employed in current Phenomenology by Husserl and other philosophers. It implies that no judgment is expressed concerning the objective world, which is thus placed 'between brackets,' as it were. All phenomena, therefore, are considered solely as they are presented to the mind, without any further aspects such as their real existence, or their value, being taken into account; in this way the observer restricts himself to pure description systematically pursued, himself adopting the attitude of complete intellectual suspense, or of abstention from all judgment, regarding these controversial topics" (646 n. 1). The Greek word ἐποχή, with the meaning "suspension of judgment," was a key term in the ancient Skeptic school of Greek philosophy; see, e.g., Sext. Emp., *Pyr.* 1.10.

12. Some would argue that religion has sociobiological roots in the evolution of *homo sapiens sapiens*. See, e.g., W. Burkert, *The Creation of the Sacred: Tracks of Biology in Early Religions* (Cambridge: Harvard University Press, 1996).

13. A colleague of mine at Lund University in Sweden, a research professor of the history of religions specializing in Islam, has as part of his official duties to serve as a consultant in governmental policy matters involving Muslims and the Islamic religion.

"methodology," in this case with that reflected in the work of the Jesus Seminar. (It is also the only essay that I have ever written on Jesus and the Gospels, though I have taught the material my entire career.) Why was it so much fun? Perhaps because I took some naughty delight in poking holes in a hot-air balloon that was launched with such overweening arrogance.

The claims made in behalf of the "Jesus Seminar" in its "red-letter edition" of the Gospels are excessive, to say the very least. The "fellows" of the Jesus Seminar are presented as the only authentic spokespersons for "critical scholarship," ready to do battle against the "fundamentalists" as represented by the Southern Baptist Convention and other "conservative Christian groups." It is the Jesus Seminar that will save the American public from its biblical illiteracy and rescue it from "the radio and TV evangelists" who "indulge in platitudes and pieties." The Jesus Seminar will step into the "vacuum" caused by ignorance of "the assured results of critical scholarship," and will take the place of the "drugstore books and slick magazines" that "play on the fears and ignorance of the uninformed." The Jesus Seminar's founder now even offers "theses" on which to launch a revision of the Christian religion![14] As for people who oppose the Jesus Seminar and the hucksterism of its founder, they are people "who lack academic credentials"; or, if they have any, they are "elitists" who have "deplored the public face of the Seminar."[15]

In my critique of the work of the Jesus Seminar in chapter 2, I took no notice of the seminar's "public face," only the results of its work as published in its book. I adopted in my critique the same "principle of methodological skepticism" as the seminar claims to embrace, and I scrupulously avoided bringing into the picture any theological claims or considerations. I also ignored theologically based critiques of the Jesus Seminar.[16] I found that the seminar's claim to be acting "in accordance with the canons of historical inquiry"[17] was specious, at the very least. I found, indeed, that its project was ideologically driven. Especially with the ap-

Specious !: deceptive

14. See R. W. Funk, *Honest to Jesus: Jesus for a New Millennium* (San Francisco: HarperSanFrancisco, 1996), 306–14.

15. R. W. Funk, R. W. Hoover, and the Jesus Seminar, *The Five Gospels: The Search for the Authentic Words of Jesus* (New York: Macmillan, 1993), esp. 34–35.

16. See, e.g., L. T. Johnson, *The Real Jesus: The Misguided Quest for the Historical Jesus and the Truth of the Traditional Gospels* (San Francisco: HarperSanFrancisco, 1995); and M. J. Wilkins and J. P. Moreland, eds., *Jesus under Fire* (Grand Rapids, Mich.: Zondervan, 1995).

17. Funk, Hoover, and the Jesus Seminar, *Five Gospels*, 35.

plication of its "fifth pillar of contemporary scholarship," namely, "the liberation of the non-eschatological Jesus"[18] from the eschatological Jesus of New Testament scholarship since Schweitzer and Weiss, it created a twentieth-century "secular" Jesus who bears no relationship to his own place and time.

In the preceding paragraph, I first wrote "fraudulent" instead of "specious." I corrected myself because I do not doubt that most of the seminar fellows acted in good faith. (Many of them, in fact, are my friends, and a couple of them are former students of mine.) At the end of chapter 2, I referred to them as "secularized theologians." Trained in Christian theology, they seem to have become disaffected and alienated from religious convictions formerly held. Still doing "theology" of sorts, they have been unable to exercise *epoché,* to "bracket" their own religious or nonreligious convictions in studying the New Testament Gospels, especially those features in the Gospels' presentation of the figure of Jesus that seem to some twentieth-century people unbelievably strange and bizarre. The results of their work are almost comic: the creation of a secular Jesus who suits their taste but who could in no wise become an object of anyone's religious faith, not now and certainly not in the first century.

One of the problems with New Testament scholarship, as I see it, is traceable to the training its practitioners receive. Virtually all graduate programs in New Testament are organized as branches of Christian theology. Very few students in such programs ever receive any real training in the comparative history and phenomenology of religions. In my own case, my education in these things began years after I left graduate school, when I came to the Department of Religious Studies at Santa Barbara in 1969. I think it would be a salutary thing for critical biblical scholarship if all students in the various graduate programs were required to take courses in the comparative history and phenomenology of religions. Had the members of the Jesus Seminar been so educated, I dare say the results of their collaborative effort would look very different.

Chapters 3 and 4, the oldest parts of the book, represent standard historical-critical scholarship as applied to the New Testament. In chapter 3, historical criticism was wedded to a kind of literary criticism, "form criticism," as applied to a literary text. Thus, one of the arguments that I mounted against the Pauline authorship of 1 Thessalonians 2:13–16 was based on the formal

---

18. Ibid., 4.

analysis of Paul's letters (usually made up minimally of an opening salutation and a "thanksgiving" section, followed by "paraenesis" and closing greetings). 1 Thessalonians is anomalous in that a second "thanksgiving" section is introduced in 2:13 (the first one begins in 1:2). The other arguments against Pauline authorship of this passage were based on content (the use of an anti-Jewish topos in gentile propaganda) and history (the anachronistic reference to the destruction of Jerusalem in v. 16). Probably the strongest objection that can be mounted against an interpolation hypothesis such as the one that I proffered here is an *argumentum e silentio* ("an argument from silence"), that is, an argument based on the lack of manuscript evidence. There are, to be sure, no ancient manuscripts that contain 1 Thessalonians 2 wherein verse 12 is followed immediately by verse 17, as I argued was the case in Paul's original letter. I countered that objection with the observation that there are no known extant manuscripts earlier than the fourth century that contain 1 Thessalonians 2:13–16. It is precisely in the period from the first to the third centuries when we would expect the manuscript tradition to be in the greatest state of flux, and scribal "improvements" to become part of the normative text.[19]

Chapter 4 is an old-fashioned philological-exegetical study, in this case showing that a key text in 2 Peter reflects the direct influence of Greek mythology. The philological "legwork" of years past could now be aided by modern technology, specifically through a computer search of the database of the *Thesaurus Linguae Graecae,* which has virtually the entirety of Greek literature from Homer to the Byzantine period on a single CD-ROM disk. The results of this research shed light on the process of early Christian acculturation in the Greco-Roman culture of its time. Second Peter, the latest epistle in the New Testament, is an example of this acculturation.

Second Peter was taken up again in chapter 5, this time in the context of a comparison with another text falsely attributed to Peter, the *Apocalypse of Peter* found in the Nag Hammadi corpus of Coptic Gnostic texts. On the basis of a close textual analysis of the two writings, I concluded that the Gnostic author of the *Apocalypse* knew and used 2 Peter, which is usually construed as an orthodox anti-Gnostic writing. If I wanted to show how up-to-date I am, I could say that the relationship between the two writings is a case of "intertextuality," a term that is currently

---

19. See n. 12 in chapter 3.

"all the rage" in some sectors of biblical study[20] and is touted in literary-critical circles as "one of the most celebrated concepts of poststructuralism."[21] But I don't need to include in my professional jargon either "intertextuality" or "poststructuralism"; I was never a "structuralist" in any case.

Chapters 6–8 dealt with other aspects of ancient Gnosticism. "Gnosticism" had its allure among some educated people in the ancient world, and still does today,[22] even among certain intellectuals who have little or no knowledge or understanding of the ancient texts.[23] I hasten to say that my own extensive work on Gnosticism[24] has not been done because I find it "alluring" — I do find it interesting — but is, rather, the happy result of my work in editing and translating Coptic texts, especially ones from the Nag Hammadi corpus.[25] Thus, it was virtually inevitable that I should include some of that work in this book.

Chapters 6 and 7 belong together, in a sense, because they both deal with ancient Gnostic literature and hermeneutics (the science of "interpretation"). In chapter 6, I discussed the manifold ways in which Christian Gnostics (or Gnostic Christians) interpreted the Old Testament. At the end, I suggested that some of the earliest Gnostic literature can be taken as analogous to some ancient Jewish texts that, generically, can be seen as "rewritten scripture," that is, the creative paraphrasing of biblical texts. I suggested, too, that the earliest versions of Gnostic "rewritten scripture" were produced by Jews. In chapter 7, I discussed what is entailed in talking about "Jewish Gnostic" literature, and then analyzed two of the Nag Hammadi texts as examples of Jewish Gnostic literature: the *Apocryphon of John* and the *Apocalypse of Adam*. Whereas the latter is clearly a non-Christian writing (even if not pre-Christian), the former appears, in the shape that we now have it, as a Chris-

---

20. See, e.g., S. Draisma, ed., *Intertextuality in Biblical Writings: Essays in Honour of Bas van Iersel* (Kampen: Kok, 1989). Many other examples could be cited.

21. U. J. Hebel, *Intertextuality, Allusion, and Quotation: An International Bibliography of Critical Studies* (New York: Greenwood, 1989), 1.

22. See R. A. Segal, ed., *The Allure of Gnosticism: The Gnostic Experience in Jungian Psychology and Contemporary Culture* (Chicago: Open Court, 1995).

23. See, e.g., the Yale English professor H. Bloom, *The American Religion: The Emergence of the Post-Christian Nation* (New York: Simon and Schuster, 1992).

24. See, e.g., Pearson, *Gnosticism,* to which could be added numerous articles published over the years.

25. See Pearson, *Codex VII;* and Pearson, *Codices IX and X,* published as part of the Coptic Gnostic Library project of the Institute for Antiquity and Christianity in Claremont, California.

tian writing, a revelation given by Jesus Christ to his disciple John. In my analysis I argued that an originally Jewish Gnostic text has been "Christianized" by the introduction of a framework and a dialogue format. This kind of work on literary texts is a necessary component to the historical study of the interrelationships of Gnosticism, Judaism, and early Christianity.

Gnosticism is often regarded as a "heresy," and so it was regarded by many bishops and teachers in the ancient church. Some of those bishops, such as Irenaeus, Hippolytus, and Epiphanius, took the trouble to study the writings of their Gnostic opponents so as to be better equipped to refute them. Bishop Eusebius of Caesarea, however, represents an interesting and anomalous exception. I say "anomalous" because he was professedly a historian, and it is a historian's obligation to study the sources at his disposal. This is not only true in modern historiography, but was also true in antiquity. My study of Eusebius's treatment of Gnosticism, whose results constitute chapter 8 in this book, convinced me of something that I don't know has ever been noticed before: Eusebius, for all his fulmination against the Gnostic heretics, never bothered to read any of their literature! In that respect, Eusebius, for all the value of his work, is an example of how *not* to write church history.

There are many contexts in human experience in which "one" is more than "many"; in the history of religions, this is especially true of Judaism and Christianity (and later, Islam), wherein the oneness of God is correlative to the oneness of his people. But "unity" as such is never a fact when it comes to people, where more than one introduces "diversity." (The contemporary American celebration of "diversity" is really an innovation, a departure from the original ideal of *e pluribus unum,* expressed socially in terms of the "melting pot.") In chapter 9, I addressed the problem of the tension in early Christianity between "unity" and "diversity" of belief and practice, and the sociopolitical factors involved in this tension in the early history of the church. The results represent a not very sophisticated attempt to include social analysis in textual and historical research.

A somewhat similar attempt was made in chapter 10, wherein I did a textual and historical analysis of the use of the term *philanthropia* in pagan, Jewish, and Christian literature. I also discussed some of the social practices and institutions that embodied "philanthropy" in the respective cultures. Such a study could have benefited from more in-depth study of sociology and social theory than I have undertaken, and I must admit that many of my colleagues in New Testament studies are way ahead of me in that respect.[26] I did, however, make reference to the recent work of a real sociologist, Rodney Stark, one who has actually done the "number crunching" involved in survey research. His recent book *The Rise of Christianity* will no doubt drive many New Testament scholars "up the wall," in that it challenges long-held assumptions in New Testament studies (e.g., as to how Christian missions were conducted, and the demographic proportion of Jewish Christians to gentile Christians in the expansion of Christianity). But he has done his homework and has perused (if only in English) the main sources and historical studies. One of his conclusions was brought in at the end of chapter 10 of this book, namely, that the philanthropic practices of the early Christians were a real factor in the eventual success of the Christian religion in the Roman Empire. The "secularization" of the church that followed the Christian triumph was also taken into account in that chapter.

Contemporary study of the canonical part of early Christian literature, the New Testament, is undergoing fascinating new developments nowadays, with the introduction of many new methods being applied to the subject matter.[27] I have tended in my work to utilize such new theoretical approaches, especially social analysis, as will aid the historical-critical study that I see as my main task. Thus, recent developments in literary criticism (e.g., rhetorical criticism, narrative criticism, reader-response criticism, and structuralism) I have left to others to deal with. Since I don't do theology, "canonical criticism" is of no concern to me. As I learned from another of my revered teachers, Helmut Koester,[28] historians of ancient Christian literature do not recognize canonical boundaries. As for "poststructuralism," "postmodernism," and

---

26. A very sophisticated example of how literary criticism (especially "narrative criticism") and sociological method are integrated into the historical-critical method is provided in N. Petersen's prize-winning book *Rediscovering Paul: Philemon and the Sociology of Paul's Narrative World* (Philadelphia: Fortress Press, 1985). Another book on Paul that successfully utilizes social theory, and is on the way to becoming a classic in the field, is W. Meeks, *The First Urban Christians* (New Haven: Yale University Press, 1983). For a brilliant application of sociolinguistic theory to the Gospel of John, see N. Petersen, *The Gospel of John and the Sociology of Light: Language and Characterization in the Fourth Gospel* (Valley Forge, Pa.: Trinity Press International, 1993).

27. The new methods referred to here are discussed by W. Baird in his article "New Testament Criticism," in *ABD*, 1:730–36. Baird makes no reference to "poststructuralism," "postmodernism," or "deconstruction."

28. H. Koester has been a professor at Harvard for almost forty years. See, e.g., Koester, *Introduction*.

"deconstruction," according to which texts mean whatever anyone wants them to mean — that appears to me nothing more than intellectual auto-eroticism, symptomatic of the narcissistic culture in which we are currently living.

With this I bring these retrospective remarks to an end. I've probably offended too many of my colleagues as it is! I only hope that the vignettes on the emergence of the Christian religion provided in this book will help promote the emergence of its study out of the closet of theology and into the arena of comparative research, where the Christian religion can be studied as truly "one of the religions of the world."

Index of
Ancient Sources

2. OLD TESTAMENT PSEUDEPIGRAPHA

6. HELLENISTIC JEWISH WRITERS

10. PAPYRI

11. INSCRIPTIONS

Index of Modern Authors

6953
847-9917
646-9949
5